PHP 6
FAST & EASY WEB DEVELOPMENT

Julie Meloni | Matt Telles

Course Technology PTR

A part of Cengage Learning

COURSE TECHNOLOGY
CENGAGE Learning™

Australia, Brazil, Japan, Korea, Mexico, Singapore, Spain, United Kingdom, United States

COURSE TECHNOLOGY
CENGAGE Learning™

PHP 6 Fast & Easy Web Development
Julie Meloni, Matt Telles

Publisher and General Manager, Course Technology PTR: Stacy L. Hiquet

Associate Director of Marketing: Sarah Panella

Manager of Editorial Services: Heather Talbot

Marketing Manager: Mark Hughes

Acquisitions Editor: Mitzi Koontz

Project and Copy Editor: Marta Justak

Technical Reviewer: Jaelle Scheuerman

PTR Editorial Services Coordinator: Erin Johnson

Interior Layout Tech: Bill Hartman

Cover Designer: Mike Tanamachi

Indexer: Larry Sweazy

Proofreader: Gene Redding

For product information and technology assistance, contact us at
Cengage Learning Customer & Sales Support Center, 1-800-354-9706

For permission to use material from this text or product,
submit all requests online at **cengage.com/permissions**
Further permissions questions can be emailed to
permissionrequest@cengage.com

Library of Congress Control Number: 2007938248

ISBN-13: 978-1-59863-471-6

ISBN-10: 1-59863-471-2

Course Technology
25 Thomson Place
Boston, MA 02210
USA

Cengage Learning is a leading provider of customized learning solutions with office locations around the globe, including Singapore, the United Kingdom, Australia, Mexico, Brazil, and Japan. Locate your local office at: **international.cengage.com/region**

Cengage Learning products are represented in Canada by Nelson Education, Ltd.

For your lifelong learning solutions, visit **courseptr.com**

Visit our corporate website at **cengage.com**

Printed in the United States of America
1 2 3 4 5 6 7 11 10 09 08

Acknowledgments

Thanks as always to the PHP Group, Zend Technologies, the Apache Software Foundation, and MySQL AB for creating and maintaining such wonderful and accessible products for all users.

Thanks to every single PHP user and developer, because without you I wouldn't have anything to write about.

Great thanks to the all the editors who worked with me on all the editions of this book!

Enormous thanks to everyone at i2i Interactive, for their never-ending support and encouragement.

Matt would like to thank his wonderful editor, Marta, and phenomenal other half, Teresa, for getting him through this book.

About the Authors

Julie Meloni is the technical director for i2i Interactive, a multimedia company located in Los Altos, CA. She's been developing Web-based applications since the Web first saw the light of day and remembers the excitement surrounding the first GUI Web browser. She is the author of several books and articles on Web-based programming languages and database topics, and you can find translations of her work in several languages, including Chinese, Italian, Portuguese, Polish, and even Serbian.

Matt Telles is a senior consultant working in the software development world. He lives, breathes, and works with anything anyone pays him to while pining away for his beloved DEC-1091.

Contents

PART IV
GETTING TO KNOW YOUR MYSQL
DATABASE 175

PART V
USER AUTHENTICATION AND TRACKING 245

Introduction

If you would have told me four years ago that this little book would be so popular as to warrant another edition, I would have laughed at you. But the style of this book, and its contents, has proven to be quite suitable for the beginning PHP programmer. The *Fast & Easy Web Development* style is a step-by-step, learn-by-example path to learning a new programming language—with pictures included! Unlike the verbose text-only chapters found in most programming books, the *Fast & Easy Web Development* style appeals to users who are new to PHP, and especially to programming in general.

This edition takes into account feedback received from the other editions, but holds true to the original content structure and path to learning. In addition, all of the changes encompassed in the fifth and sixth releases of PHP are included. For example, the first three chapters are dedicated to getting Apache, MySQL, and PHP up and running on your Windows or Linux machine. You might be surprised at how simple it is, and how quickly you'll be up and running—which is good because you need all three technologies to be working in order to continue with the lessons.

In this edition, some chapters have been added to provide additional projects for practicing your new skills, and also to account for new elements present in version 6 of PHP. After completing this book, you will have a strong foundation in the basics of Web-based technologies and application design, and will be prepared to learn more advanced topics and programming methodologies. However, before jumping into all that, take a moment to familiarize yourself with PHP and why it is such a wonderful language to learn and use.

What Is PHP?

Its official name is PHP: Hypertext Preprocessor, and it is a server-side scripting language. When your Web browser accesses a URL, it is making a request to a Web server. When you request a PHP page, something like http://www.yourcompany.com/home.php, the Web server wakes up the PHP parsing engine and says, "Hey! You've got to do something before I send a result back to this person's Web browser." Then the PHP parsing engine runs through the PHP code found in home.php, and returns the resulting output. This output is passed back to the Web server as part of the HTML code in the document, which in turn is passed on to your browser, which displays it to you.

A Brief History of PHP

In 1994, an incredibly forward-thinking man named Rasmus Lerdorf developed a set of tools that used a parsing engine to interpret a few macros here and there. They were not extravagant: a guest book, a counter, and some other "home page" elements that were cool when the Web was in its infancy. He eventually combined these tools with a form interpretation (FI) package he had written, added some database support, and released what was known as PHP/FI.

Then, in the spirit of open source software development, developers all over the world began contributing to PHP/FI. By 1997, more than 50,000 Web sites were using PHP/FI to accomplish different tasks—connecting to a database, displaying dynamic content, and so on.

At that point, the development process really started becoming a team effort. With primary assistance from developers Zeev Suraski and Andi Gutmans, the version 3.0 parser was created. The final release of PHP 3.0 occurred in June of 1998, when it was upgraded to include support for multiple platforms (it's not just for Linux anymore!) and Web servers, numerous databases, and SNMP (Simple Network Management Protocol) and IMAP (Internet Message Access Protocol). Then the birth of PHP 4.0 occurred. No small version change, PHP 4.0 marked a complete rethinking of the PHP core and a rewrite of the internals of the scripting language itself. The PHP development team and Zend Technologies produced a remarkable product with nearly a fifty-fold performance improvement over version 3.0, with a long list of new and useful features. When PHP 5.0 was released, it marked a rather radical change for the language, including new concepts of object-oriented development and database work.

As if that weren't enough, PHP 6 has been in the works almost since PHP 5 was released, culminating in what we have today: an even faster, feature-rich programming language suitable for procedural or object-oriented scripts, which warrants a place in the enterprise.

What Does PHP Do?

PHP does anything you want, except sit on its head and spin. Actually, with a little on-the-fly image manipulation and dynamic HTML, it could probably do that, too.

According to the PHP manual, "The goal of the language is to allow Web developers to write dynamically generated pages quickly."

Here are some common uses of PHP, all of which are a part of what you'll learn in this book:

- Perform system functions: create, open, read from, write to, and close files on your system; execute system commands; create directories; and modify permissions.
- Gather data from forms: save the data to a file, send data via e-mail, and return manipulated data to the user.
- Access databases and generate content on the fly, or create a Web interface for adding, deleting, and modifying elements within your database.
- Set cookies and access cookie variables.
- Start sessions and use session variables and objects.
- Restrict access to sections of your Web site.
- Create images on the fly.
- Encrypt data.

These are just basic, everyday uses. PHP also includes support for integrating with Java servlets, XML, and myriad other higher-level functions. The possibilities literally are endless.

Why PHP 6?

It's natural that languages continue to develop, and PHP 6 has done just that—its changes represent the next step in the growth and development of the language. There was nothing fundamentally wrong with PHP 4 or 5, and, in fact, the vast majority of this book can be used on servers running PHP 4 or PHP 5. The changes in PHP 6 revolve around high-level aspects of the language, namely the object model, as well as cleaning up some long-neglected aspects of the language.

If you are coming to PHP from another programming language, especially a highly structured, specifically object-oriented language, the crossover to a flexible, procedural language that just happens to handle object-oriented programming can be frustrating. But the ease of use and robustness is one of the reasons new programmers are drawn to PHP in the first place—the learning curve isn't steep, *and* it gets the job done.

However, this also presents a marketing problem for PHP users working in an enterprise setting. Some "powers that be" might not think PHP is suitable for enterprise-level application development, because it is not a time-tested, structured, object-oriented programming language such as C or even Java. There might not be the time or opportunity for a developer to convince her managers otherwise by showing examples of PHP and C or Java performing the same tasks— if you even can, with the same level of structure, security, reusability, and exception-handling.

From these and other problems came the development path for PHP 6, the main purpose of which was to improve the object model, instill a sense of programming discipline, and specifically design a version of PHP that meets the needs of object-oriented developers and allows them to interface with Java, .NET, and other enterprise-level application frameworks. Finally, PHP 6.0 gives us a true Unicode-based language for the first time in the history of scripting languages for the Net.

But beginning users—likely the primary audience of this book—will not face objects, classes, .NET, or XML-integration their first day on the job. These users simply want a fast, flexible language they can use to create basic, dynamic Web sites, and PHP 6 still meets that need. Although PHP 6 contains an enhanced internal scripting engine and a vastly improved object-oriented framework, the PHP Group and Zend Technologies recognize and appreciate the roots of PHP and the core group of users who have made it so pervasive. As with PHP 5, PHP 6 does not force you to use the elements of the language you don't need.

Overview of Changes in PHP 6

PHP 6.0 is, in many ways, a "cleanup" release for the language. In addition to cleaning up the object model and fixing many bugs, PHP 6.0 adds full Unicode support from the ground up. It introduces large integers (64-bit) and better SQL Lite functionality, and includes all of the changes from PHP 5.1 through the final releases of the 5.0 line, as well as everything new in 6.0.

This book is not a be-all and end-all of the ins and outs of PHP, rather it is a way to learn the language and get up to speed quickly. For a complete discussion of the changes to the language in every detail, check the php.net site. While we will cover all of the new features in this book, you may need to see more detail than is presented here for your particular situation. As always, your mileage may vary.

Backward Compatibility with PHP 5

The changelog and PHP manual always indicate when a new implementation will cause problems in previous versions, so at least read the changelog thoroughly if not the manual entries for your favorite functions. However, the vast majority of PHP 6 focuses on additional functionality rather than completely replacing existing elements. If you have learned PHP using PHP 4 or PHP 5, you might find that none of your scripts *require* a rewrite.

Requiring a rewrite and rewriting scripts for the sake of utilizing new functionality are completely different—you might want to rewrite to take advantage of new object-oriented functionality, but you might not have to. If your code is primarily procedural (as with the scripts in this book), there's a better than 95 percent chance that no rewrites will be necessary.

Similarly, if you cannot install PHP on your own machine for development or product purposes, as outlined in Chapter 3, "Installing PHP," and must use PHP 5, do not fret. Anything taught in this book that doesn't work in PHP 5 is indicated as such.

Is PHP Right for You?

Only you can decide if PHP should be your language of choice, whether you're developing sites for personal or commercial use on a small or large scale. I can only tell you that in the commercial realm, I've worked with all the popular server-side scripting languages—Active Server Pages (ASP), ColdFusion, Java Server Pages (JSP), Perl, and PHP—on numerous platforms and various Web servers, with varying degrees of success. PHP is the right choice for me: It's flexible, fast, and simple in its requirements, yet powerful in its output.

Before deciding whether to use PHP in a large-scale or commercial environment, consider your answers to these questions:

- Can you say with absolute certainty that you will always use the same Web server hardware and software? If not, look for something cross-platform that is available for all types of Web servers—use PHP.

- Will you always have the exact same development team comprised entirely of ASP (or Java Server Pages or ColdFusion) developers? Or will you use whoever is available, thus necessitating a language that is easy to learn and syntactically similar to C and Perl? If you have reason to believe that your ASP or JSP or ColdFusion developers might drop off the face of the earth, don't use those tools—use PHP.

- Are memory and server loads an issue? If so, don't use bloated third-party software that leaks precious memory—use PHP.

Here's the bottom line: PHP is simple, so just try it! If you like it, continue using it.

It's open source, so help improve it. Join a mailing list and help others. If you don't like it, you're only out the money for this book, and the software can be uninstalled without rendering your machine completely inoperable.

Who Should Read This Book?

This book is designed for individuals who possess a general understanding of the concepts of working in a Web-based development environment, be it Linux/UNIX or Windows. Installation and configuration related chapters assume that you have familiarity with your operating system and the basic methods of building (on Linux/UNIX systems) or installing (on Windows systems) software.

Chapters discussing how to program with PHP, which make up the bulk of the book, assume no previous knowledge of the language. However, if you have experience with other programming languages such as C or Perl, you will find these lessons to be quite simple. Similarly, if you have worked with other databases, such as Oracle or Microsoft SQL Server, you will have a good foundation for working through the MySQL-related chapters.

The only real requirement before reading this book is that you understand static Web content creation with HTML. If you are just starting out in the world of Web development, you will still be able to use this book, but you should consider working through an HTML tutorial first. If you are comfortable creating basic documents and uploading them to your Web server, you will be fine.

How This Book Is Organized

This book is divided into eight parts, corresponding to particular topic groups. The chapters within each part build on the information found in those before it:

- **Part I, "Getting Started,"** walks you through the installation and configuration of MySQL, Apache, and PHP. You'll need to complete the lessons in Part I before moving on, unless you already have access to a working installation of these technologies.

- **Part II, "The Absolute Basics of Coding in PHP,"** teaches you the basics of the PHP language, starting with variables and the core structure of the language. The numerous hands-on examples will get you in the habit of writing code, uploading it, and testing the results.

- **Part III, "Start with the Simple Stuff,"** builds on the basics learned in the previous chapters, and helps you to create multi-part scripts and display dynamic content, among other things.

- **Part IV, "Getting to Know Your MySQL Database,"** introduces you to the concept of working with databases in general and MySQL in particular, and shows you how to create PHP scripts to communicate with MySQL and perform various tasks.

- **Part V, "User Authentication and Tracking,"** shows you how to use PHP to restrict access to your applications and how to set cookies and work with user sessions, including the storage of user preferences.

- **Part VI, "Creating Your Own Contact Management System,"** contains several chapters which walk you through the design and creation of a specific type of application, in this case a contact management system, also known as a Web-based address book.

- **Part VII, "Additional Project Examples,"** contains chapters devoted to other popular types of projects, such as managing a mailing list, creating custom reports, and working with XML.

- **Part VIII, "Appendixes,"** contains several handy references for the PHP and SQL languages, as well as other information including how to use SQLite and where to go to find help and additional tutorials.

Conventions Used in This Book

This book uses different typefaces to differentiate between code and plain English, and also to help you identify important concepts. Throughout the lessons, code, commands, and text you type or see on-screen appear in a `monospaced` typeface.

More Stuff

Any errata and additional information for this book can be found at courseptr.com/. At this site, you can download all the code samples in this book, and will be alerted to any printing errors.

PART I

Getting Started

1

Installing and Configuring MySQL

MySQL is the database of choice for a vast majority of Web developers who use PHP, because of its efficiency and ease of use. Plus, MySQL is free and runs on multiple platforms, and its documentation is superb. When using MySQL with PHP, it's easiest to install MySQL first, because during the PHP installation and configuration process, you must tell the PHP configuration script that you plan to use MySQL, in order to activate the MySQL-specific functions. As such, it's best to make sure that MySQL is at least present on your system, in case there are any library mismatch issues that would cause PHP to fail in its compilation. In this chapter, you learn how to:

- Install MySQL on Windows or Linux.
- Create a sample database.
- Create a sample table.

Various MySQL Distributions

The most popular distribution of MySQL is the open source version, from MySQL AB. However, there are also commercial versions of MySQL, as well as distributions of MySQL bundled with application server software. No matter which option you choose, a solution is available for you on all platforms—any operating system, as well as on Windows 95/98/NT/2000/XP/2003. This chapter assumes that you're using the MySQL installation files from the MySQL Web site (or the CD that accompanies this book).

If you are using MySQL as part of a Web-hosting package through an Internet service provider, you don't have to worry about downloading and installing the application in this chapter. Instead, you just need to work with your ISP to get your username and password. In almost all cases, your ISP will be running the MySQL distribution from MySQL AB. There's no harm in setting up MySQL on a development machine, if you have one available (your own workstation fits that bill), just to better understand the process. To that end, if you have a Linux workstation or server, MySQL was likely included on your OS distribution CDs as an installation option, and perhaps you even installed it already. In this case, you should check the MySQL Web site to compare the version numbers and download a newer version if one is available.

The installation instructions in this chapter are based on MySQL version 5.0.x, distributed by MySQL AB.

MYSQL 4.0.X

If you are using MySQL at your ISP and it is still using a 4.0.x version, don't worry—you will be able to use all of the database-related examples in this book.

Installing MySQL on Windows

The MySQL installation process on Windows 95/98/NT/2000/XP/2003 is based on an executable setup program provided by MySQL AB. Once you download the zip file, all you have to do is extract its contents into a temporary directory and run the `setup.exe` application. After the `setup.exe` application installs the MySQL server and client programs, you're ready to start the MySQL server.

1. Visit the MySQL 5.0.x download page at http://dev.mysql.com/downloads/ mysql/5.0.html and find the Windows section on the page. Click the button below the text that says MySQL Community Server. This will take you to a list of operating systems. Select Windows and then select the Windows Zip/Setup.exe link.

2. Clicking the "mirror" link will take you to a page of mirror sites. Select the mirror site closest to you and click either the HTTP or FTP link to download the file. Using the HTTP method is usually quicker. Note that you will be presented first with a login screen; you can bypass this via a link at the bottom of the page that says "No thanks, just take me to the downloads."

Figure 1.1 Installation Wizard Step 1.

3. After the zip file (`mysql-5.0.45-win32.zip`) is on your hard drive, extract its contents to a temporary directory.

4. From the temporary directory, find the `setup.exe` file and double-click it to start the installation. You will see the first screen of the Installation Wizard, as shown in the following figure. Click Next to continue (see Figure 1.1).

Figure 1.2 Installation Wizard Step 2.

Figure 1.3 Installation Wizard Custom option.

5. The second screen in the installation process, shown in Figure 1.2, asks you which type of installation you want to use. For our purposes, a Typical installation is fine. The other types of installation allow you to customize what will be installed and what features you will be using. For the majority of users, the Typical setup is fine. If you want to be sure you have everything you need, select the Complete install. The Custom install is really just for advanced users who are setting up production systems that are very specific. Note that if you want to change the installation location, you will need to customize it using the Custom option. If you select that option, you will see the screen shown in Figure 1.3.

Figure 1.4 MySQL installation summary.

6. The third screen in the installation process contains valuable information regarding the installation location. The information on this screen is also important for Windows NT users who want to start MySQL as a service. Read the information and note anything relevant to your situation; then click Next to continue (see Figure 1.4).

Figure 1.5 Installation screen for MySQL.

7. At this point, you are ready to do the installation process. Click the Install button on the screen to begin the installation process. You should see the display shown in Figure 1.5.

Figure 1.6 MySQL installer.

8. Once the installation process is complete, you will see an advertisement for the MySQL Enterprise edition. You can ignore this process. The series of screens begins with the one shown in Figure 1.6 and continues for two or three screens, depending on the version you installed.

Figure 1.7 MySQL installer confirmation.

9. The installation process now takes over and installs files in their proper locations. When the process is finished, you will see a confirmation of completion. Click Finish to complete the setup process (see Figure 1.7).

Figure 1.8 Configuration Wizard completion screen.

Figure 1.9 MySQL Server screen.

10. The final step in the process, once the installation is done, is to handle the configuration of the system. The final screen contains a check box that will allow you to do this configuration. Leave the check box checked and click the Finish button. You should now see the Configuration Wizard as shown in Figure 1.8. Clicking Next will bring you to the Server Instance screen, shown in Figure 1.9.

Figure 1.10 MySQL main options screen.

Figure 1.11 MySQL administration password screen.

11. Select the Standard configuration for your machine, since we are working with a system that has never been installed and doesn't need to be used by others for now. Clicking Next will bring up the main options screen for MySQL, as shown in Figure 1.10. Leave the Windows Service box checked, as this is the best way to run MySQL under Windows. We aren't going to be using the command line tools much, so we'll leave the Bin Directory box unchecked. Click Next when you are finished.

12. The screen shown in Figure 1.11 is extremely important. You will need to create a password for your root (administrator) user. The next button will not be enabled until the passwords in the New Root Password and Confirm boxes are entered and match.

Figure 1.12 MySQL final installation screen.

13. Finally, you will see the screen shown in Figure 1.12. This screen does all the setup of your MySQL system. Click the Execute button to finish the installation process.

MySQL is now installed on your system. Unlike previous versions of MySQL, the administration programs are a separate download. You can find them on the MySQL.com site at the URL http://dev.mysql.com/downloads/gui-tools/5.0.html. The installation process is quite simple and can be placed in the same location as the MySQL binaries (the default location is c:\Program Files\MySQL, with the database engine in MySQL Server 5.0.

USERNAMES AND PASSWORDS

You must use the same username (root) and password that you entered in the Configuration Wizard to enter the Administrator.

WinMySQLadmin will automatically interpret environment information, such as IP address, machine name, and so on. The tabs along the left side allow you to view system information and also edit MySQL configuration options. To shut down the MySQL server or the WinMySQLadmin tool, right-click again on the stoplight icon in your task bar and select the appropriate choice. As long as the MySQL server is running, you can run additional applications through a console window, such as the MySQL Monitor.

> ### MYSQL ADMINISTRATOR
>
> Current versions of MySQL use the Administrator application, which ships with MySQL. The screens are more or less the same, and the process to access them is the same, but you need to select MySQL, MySQL Administrator from the Windows Start button to access it instead.

In the next section, you will learn how to start MySQL manually and perform a few actions to familiarize yourself with the system.

Testing Your MySQL Installation

In this section, you work with the MySQL utilities via the command line in a console window. When using MySQL with PHP, you'll issue the same types of commands, only within the context of the PHP code. Use the information in this section to familiarize yourself with the types of commands and responses you'll be working with later in the book.

Starting MySQL

To start MySQL manually (without using the GUI described previously), go to the Windows Start menu, choose Run, type `c:\Program Files\MySQL\MySQL Server 5.0\bin\mysqld-nt.exe`, and press Enter.

> ### LOCATION OF MYSQL
>
> If you installed MySQL in a different directory, substitute that directory name in the previous command.

The MySQL process will now be running in the background. You can now connect to MySQL and create databases and tables.

Creating a Test Database

Before going any further, you should know the following:

- A database is a collection of tables.
- A table contains a set of records, also referred to as rows.
- All records have the same number of fields.
- Each field categorizes a piece of a data.

In this section, you'll conquer the first element and create a database. The utility to use is the `mysqladmin` program, which allows you to administer MySQL from the command line.

Go to the Windows Start menu, choose Run, and type `c:\Program Files\MySQL\ MySQL server 5.0\mysqladmin" -u root -p create testDB`; then press Enter. You will be prompted for a password; enter the one you created in the initial configuration setup.

The window will briefly flash and then close when the command has been processed. Next, you'll add a table to the `testDB` database.

Creating a Test Table

In this section, you create a table within the database you created in the preceding section. The utility to use is the `mysql` program, which allows you to work within the MySQL database system from the command line.

Figure 1.13 The MySQL command prompt.

```
Command Prompt - mysql -u root -p

C:\Program Files\MySQL\MySQL Server 5.0\bin>mysql -u root -p
Enter password: *******
Welcome to the MySQL monitor.  Commands end with ; or \g.
Your MySQL connection id is 14
Server version: 5.0.45-community-nt MySQL Community Edition (GPL)

Type 'help;' or '\h' for help. Type '\c' to clear the buffer.

mysql>
```

1. Go to the Windows Start menu, choose Run, type `mysql -u root -p`, and press Enter. The program will then prompt you for the password you used in the previous step. Enter it and you should see the MySQL prompt as shown in Figure 1.13.

When the MySQL Monitor starts, it provides its own prompt. At this prompt (mysql>), you type commands used to create tables, explain tables, insert data, select data, and so on. Get used to ending your commands with a semicolon (;) because it's a common instruction terminator that is used in PHP as well.

Now that you've connected to the MySQL Monitor, you need to tell it which database to use.

Figure 1.14 Using a database in MySQL.

2. At the prompt, type **use testDB;** and press Enter (see Figure 1.14).

The MySQL Monitor will respond with Database changed if the database exists and you have permission to access it.

It's time to create a test table. This table will have a column for an ID number and a column for some text.

DATABASE NORMALIZATION

For more information about the specifics of creating tables, see Appendix E, "Database Normalization and SQL Reference."

3. At the prompt, type **create table test_table (test_id int, test_note text);** and press Enter. This statement creates a table called test_table. Within the table, it creates a column called test_id of type int (integer). It also creates a column called test_note of type text.

The MySQL Monitor will respond with Query OK. It will also tell you how many rows were affected and how long it took to complete the task.

Figure 1.15 Viewing available tables in MySQL.

Figure 1.16 Looking at a table schema in MySQL.

Figure 1.17 Inserting data into a table in MySQL.

4. Verify the table creation by typing **show tables;** and pressing Enter (see Figure 1.15).

The MySQL Monitor will respond with a list of all the tables in the current database.

5. To verify the field names and types in a specific table, use the explain command. In this case, type **explain test_table;** and press Enter (see Figure 1.16).

The MySQL Monitor will respond with a list of all the fields and their types in the selected table. This is a very handy command to use to keep track of your table design.

It's time to insert a few rows of data in your table, because this is getting pretty boring. The first row will have an ID of 1, and the note will be "This is a note."

6. To insert this row, type **insert into test_table values('1', 'This is a note.');** and press Enter (see Figure 1.17).

The MySQL Monitor will respond with Query OK. It will also tell you how many rows were affected and how long it took to complete the task.

7. Insert another row by typing **insert into test_table values('99', 'Look! Another note.');** and pressing Enter.

> **INSERTION REFERENCE**
>
> For more information about the specifics of inserting data into tables, see Appendix E.

Now that you have some data in your table, even if it is only two rows, it's time to get familiar with selecting data. Keep the MySQL Monitor open, because you'll be using it in the next section as well.

Selecting Data from Your Test Table

The SELECT command is very powerful and will likely be the command you use most often when working with PHP and MySQL. You can find more information about the SELECT command in Appendix E, but for now, let's do some simple data selections.

Figure 1.18 Viewing data in a table in MySQL.

1. At the prompt, type **select * from test_table;** and press Enter (see Figure 1.18).

This command simply selects all fields from all rows (that's what the * does) in the table called test_table and returns the data to the screen in a nicely formatted table. The MySQL Monitor tells you how many rows were returned and how long it took the query to run.

Figure 1.19 Ordering data in a select statement.

```
Command Prompt - mysql -u root -p                    _ □ x
mysql> insert into test_table values('1', 'This is a note');
Query OK, 1 row affected (0.05 sec)

mysql> insert into test_table values('99', 'Look! Another note.');
Query OK, 1 row affected (0.03 sec)

mysql> select * from test_table;
+---------+---------------------+
| test_id | test_note           |
+---------+---------------------+
|       1 | This is a note      |
|      99 | Look! Another note. |
+---------+---------------------+
2 rows in set (0.00 sec)

mysql> select * from test_table order by test_id desc;
+---------+---------------------+
| test_id | test_note           |
+---------+---------------------+
|      99 | Look! Another note. |
|       1 | This is a note      |
+---------+---------------------+
2 rows in set (0.00 sec)

mysql>
```

Add a little order to the results. Try to get the results ordered by ID number—largest number first.

2. At the prompt, type `select * from test_table order by test_id desc;` and press Enter (see Figure 1.19).

The result now shows the row with a `test_id` of 99 as the first row in the table. The `desc` in the command stands for descending. There is another option, `asc`, which stands for ascending. Ascending order is the default order.

The next section is for the installation of MySQL on Linux, so assuming you don't have two machines, skip ahead to Chapter 2, "Installing Apache," to install the Apache Web server.

Installing MySQL for Linux

This section takes you through the installation process of MySQL 5.0.x (community) on Linux, using the distribution from MySQL AB. If you're using another flavor of UNIX, download the appropriate files and follow the instructions included with the distribution.

The recommended installation method for MySQL is with RPMs. There are several RPMs that make up a full distribution, but for a minimal installation you need the following:

- MySQL-server-VERSION.i386.rpm—The MySQL server.
- MySQL-client-VERSION.i386.rpm—The standard MySQL client programs.

To download these files, visit the MySQL 5.0.x download page at http://dev.mysql.com/downloads/mysql/5.0.html and find the "Linux x86 RPM downloads" section on the page (or IA64 or AMD64, depending on your architecture). When you click the download link for one of the packages, you will be taken to a page of mirror sites. Select the mirror site closest to you and download the files.

When the files are downloaded to your system, perform the minimal installation by typing the following at your prompt, replacing VERSION with the appropriate version number of your downloaded files:

```
#prompt> rpm -i MySQL-server-VERSION.i386.rpm MySQL-client-VERSION.i386.rpm
```

If the RPM method doesn't work for you, you can also install MySQL from a binary distribution, which requires gunzip and tar to uncompress and unpack the distribution and also requires the capability to create groups and users on the system.

In the first series of commands, you will add a group and a user and then unpack the distribution, as follows:

1. At the prompt, type `groupadd mysql`.

2. At the prompt, type `useradd -g mysql mysql`.

3. At the prompt, type `cd /usr/local`.

INSTALLING MYSQL

You can install MySQL in any directory. If you do not use /usr/local/ as in this example, be sure to modify subsequent commands appropriately.

---

4. At the prompt, type `gunzip < /path/to/mysql-standard-VERSION-OS.tar.gz | tar xvf -`.

5. To create a link with a shorter name, type `ln -s mysql-VERSION-OS mysql`.

6. Change directories by typing `cd mysql`.

Once the distribution is unpacked, the `README` and `INSTALL` files will walk you through the remainder of the installation process for the version of MySQL you've chosen. In general, the next series of commands will be used:

1. Type `scripts/mysql_install_db` to run the MySQL install script.

2. Type `chown -R root /usr/local/mysql` to change ownership of the `mysql` directory.

3. Type `chown -R mysql /usr/local/mysql/data` to change ownership of the `mysql/data` directory.

4. Type `chgrp -R mysql /usr/local/mysql` to change the group of the `mysql` directory.

5. Type `chown -R root /usr/local/mysql/bin` to change ownership of the `mysql/bin` directory.

If you have any problems during the installation of MySQL, the first place you should look is the "Problems and Common Errors" chapter of the MySQL manual, which is located at http://www.mysql.com/doc/P/r/Problems.html. Some common problems include:

- Incorrect permissions do not allow you to start the MySQL daemon. If this is the case, be sure you have changed owners and groups to match those indicated in the installation instructions.

- If you see the message `Access denied` when connecting to MySQL, be sure you are using the correct username and password.

- If you see the message `Can't connect to server`, make sure the MySQL daemon is running.

In the next section, you will learn how to start MySQL and perform a few actions to familiarize yourself with the system.

Testing Your MySQL Installation

In this section, you work with the MySQL utilities via the command line, in a console window. When using MySQL with PHP, you'll issue the same types of commands, only within the context of the PHP code. Use the information in this section to familiarize yourself with the types of commands and responses you'll be working with later in the book.

Starting MySQL

The MySQL distribution comes with a start-up script, called `safe_mysqld`, found in the `bin` subdirectory of the MySQL installation directory. Follow these steps to start this script:

1. If you're not already there, enter the MySQL parent directory by typing `cd /usr/local/mysql` at the prompt and pressing Enter.

2. Start the MySQL process by typing `./bin/safe_mysqld &` and pressing Enter.

The MySQL process will now be running in the background, and you can connect to MySQL and create databases and tables.

Creating a Test Database

Before going any further, you should know the following:

- A database is a collection of tables.
- A table contains a set of records, also referred to as rows.
- All records have the same number of fields.
- Each field categorizes a piece of a data.

In this section, you'll conquer the first element and create a database. The utility to use is the `mysqladmin` program, which allows you to administer MySQL from the command line.

At the prompt, type **./bin/mysqladmin create testDB** and press Enter. You will be returned to the prompt if the database called testDB has been successfully created. Next, you'll add a table to that database.

Creating a Test Table

In this section, you'll create a table within the database you created in the preceding section. The utility to use is the mysql program, which allows you to work within the MySQL database system from the command line.

Figure 1.20 MySQL installation on UNIX.

1. At the prompt, type **./bin/mysql** and press Enter (see Figure 1.20).

   The MySQL monitor will start. The MySQL Monitor provides its own prompt. At this prompt (mysql>) you will type commands used to create tables, explain tables, insert data, select data, and so on. Get used to ending your commands with a semicolon (;) because it's a common instruction terminator that is used in PHP as well.

Now that you've connected to the MySQL Monitor, you need to tell it which database to use.

2. At the prompt, type **use testDB;** and press Enter.

   The MySQL Monitor will respond with Database changed if the database exists and you have permission to access it.

   It's time to create a test table. This table will have a column for an ID number and a column for some text.

CREATING TABLES

For more information about the specifics of creating tables, see Appendix E.

3. At the prompt, type `create table test_table (test_id int, test_note text);` and press Enter. This statement creates a table called `test_table`. Within the table, it creates a column called `test_id` of type `int` (integer). It also creates a column called `test_note` of type `text`.

The MySQL Monitor will respond with `Query OK`. It will also tell you how many rows were affected and how long it took to complete the task.

4. Verify the table creation by typing `show tables;` and pressing Enter.

The MySQL Monitor will respond with a list of all tables in the current database.

Figure 1.21 Viewing the schema of a table in MySQL.

5. To verify the field names and types in a specific table, use the `explain` command. In this case, type `explain test_table;` and press Enter (see Figure 1.21).

The MySQL Monitor will respond with a list of all the fields and their types in the selected table. This is a very handy command to use to keep track of your table design.

It's time to insert a few rows of data in your table because this is getting pretty boring. The first row will have an ID of 1, and the note will be "This is a note."

Figure 1.22 Inserting data into a table.

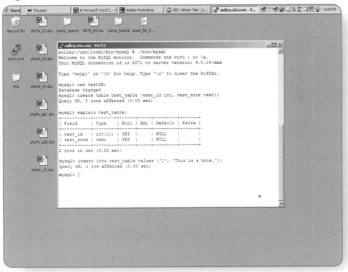

6. To insert this row, type `insert into test_table values('1', 'This is a note.');` and press Enter (see Figure 1.22).

The MySQL Monitor will respond with `Query OK`. It will also tell you how many rows were affected and how long it took to complete the task.

7. Insert another row by typing `insert into test_table values('99', 'Look! Another note.');` and pressing Enter.

DATABASE NORMALIZATION

For more information about the specifics of inserting data into tables, see Appendix E.

Now that you have some data in your table, even if it is only two rows, it's time to get familiar with selecting data. Keep the MySQL Monitor open, because you'll be using it in the next section as well.

Selecting Data from Your Test Table

The SELECT command is very powerful and will likely be the command you use most often when working with PHP and MySQL. You can find more information about SELECT in Appendix E, but for now, let's do some simple data selections.

Figure 1.23 Selecting data from a table.

Figure 1.24 Controlling the order of data in a selection.

1. At the prompt, type `select * from test_table;` and press Enter (see Figure 1.23).

This command simply selects all fields from all rows in the table called `test_table` and returns the data to the screen in a nicely formatted table. The MySQL Monitor tells you how many rows were returned and how long it took the query to run.

Add a little order to the results. Try to get the results ordered by ID number—largest number first.

2. At the prompt, type `select * from test_table order by test_id desc;` and press Enter (see Figure 1.24).

The result now shows the row with a `test_id` of 99 as the first row in the table. The `desc` in the command stands for descending. There is another option, `asc`, which stands for ascending. Ascending order is the default order.

In the next chapter, you'll install the Apache Web server and be one step closer to developing dynamic, database-driven Web sites!

2

Installing Apache

Because it's the most popular Web server in use, you might think that Apache is a complicated piece of software, but it's not difficult at all. In this chapter, you learn how to:

- Install Apache on Windows or Linux.
- Connect to your new Web server.

Installing Apache for Windows

Installing Apache for Windows is a simple task, due in great part to the Installation Wizard distributed by the Apache Group. Whether you're using Windows 95, 98, Me, 2000, XP, or NT, the installation process of the precompiled binaries is definitely the way to go, and the same installation file is used for all flavors of Windows.

Being able to use Apache on consumer-oriented operating systems such as Windows 95/98/Me/XP doesn't mean that you should use it, at least not in a production environment. Simply put, running any Web server on a Windows operating system is not as fast, stable, or secure as running a Web server on a Linux/UNIX machine. However, installing and configuring a development Web server on a Windows-based operating system is perfectly acceptable and is how most users get their start.

APACHE GROUP

The Apache Group also distributes the source code for Apache on Windows, should you have a need to compile the code yourself. However, that process is well beyond the scope of this book!

To download the Apache distribution for Windows, start at the Apache Server Web site, http://httpd.apache.org/, and follow the link to Download. Before going any further, be sure to follow the link in the sentence, "If you are downloading the Win32 distribution, please read these important notes." (The actual link depends on the mirror you are using.)

When you've determined your system is stable enough to continue, look for the bulleted item on the page for Win32 Binary (MSI Installer), followed by a link to the software.

Distribution files follow a naming convention, with `apache` followed by the version number and then `-win32-x86-no_ssl.msi`. As of this writing, the current version is 2.2.4, so the file used as an example throughout this section is `apache_2.2.4-win32-x86-no_ssl.msi`.

Once you have downloaded the installation file to your hard drive, the following steps will take you through the Installation Wizard:

Figure 2.1 Apache Installation Wizard.

1. Double-click the file called `apache_2.2.4-win32-x86-no_ssl.msi`. The installer will start, and the Installation Wizard will begin. Click Next to continue (see Figure 2.1).

2. Read the licensing information on the screen, choose the I Accept radio button, and then click Next.

Figure 2.2 Apache information screen.

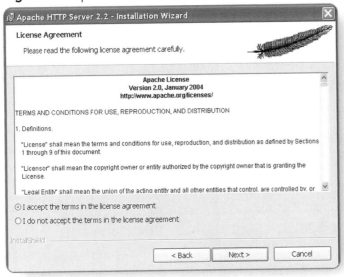

3. Read the general Apache information on the screen and then click Next.

4. The next screen requires you to fill in some details about your server: the network domain, server name, and the administrator's e-mail address (see Figure 2.2).

NETWORK DOMAIN INFORMATION

If you do not know the network domain or server name at this point, enter some dummy information so that the installation moves forward. You will learn how to edit this information post-installation, so no matter what you enter in this step, you will soon be able to fix it. If you do know your domain and server name, go ahead and enter it.

5. Choose the Run as Service for All Users radio button and click Next.

6. Choose the Typical setup type and click Next.

7. Accept the default destination folder and then click Next.

DESTINATION FOLDERS

If you elect to change the destination folder for the Apache installation files, please adjust the instructions and paths accordingly throughout this book.

Figure 2.3 Apache installation confirmation screen.

8. Choose Install on the next screen, and the final installation sequence will begin. When the sequence is finished, you will see the confirmation screen. Click Finish to complete the installation and close the installer (see Figure 2.3).

Figure 2.4 Apache console window.

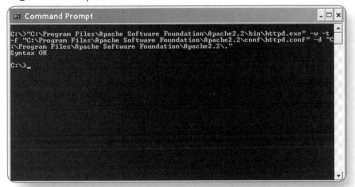

At this point, all of the necessary Apache files are installed, as well as a group of handy shortcuts in your Windows Start menu, called Apache HTTP Server 2.2.4. To run a basic test before moving forward into configuring your server, choose Program Files, Apache HTTP Server 2.2.4, Configure Apache Server, Test Configuration from the Windows Start menu. This will launch a console window showing a successful installation (see Figure 2.4).

If you have any errors at this point, rerun the installation program. In the next section, you'll make some minor changes to the Apache configuration file before you start Apache for the first time.

Configuring Apache on Windows

To run a basic installation of Apache, the only changes you need to make are to the server name, which you might already have done during the Installation Wizard. However, if you entered dummy information for the server name or want to modify any other part of the basic configuration, now is the time to do so.

The master configuration file for Apache is called `httpd.conf`, and it lives in the `conf` directory, within the Apache installation directory. So if your installation directory is `C:\Program Files\Apache Group\Apache2\`, the `httpd.conf` file will be in `C:\Program Files\Apache Group\Apache2\conf\`.

Again with the handy shortcut, you can quickly access this file by selecting Program Files, Apache HTTP Server 2.2.4, Configure Apache Server, Edit the Apache `httpd.conf` Configuration File from the Windows Start menu. This shortcut is the same as opening a text editor and navigating to the file location. To modify the basic configuration, primarily the server name, look for a heading called Main Server Configuration. You will find two important sections of text (see Figure 2.5). We are going to change these values so that Apache knows where to direct traffic from and to.

Figure 2.5 Apache configuration file.

1. Change the value of `ServerAdmin` to your e-mail address, if it isn't already accurate.

2. Change the value of `ServerName` to something accurate, if it's isn't already.

3. Save the file.

The `ServerName` modification is the most important change you'll make to your Apache configuration file because if the `ServerName` isn't correct, you won't be able to connect to Apache. As it states in the configuration file itself, "You cannot just invent host names and hope they work." If you do not know your full machine name, you can use an IP number. If you have a static IP number (that is, one that does not change), use it as your `ServerName`. If you have a dial-up connection that does not assign a static IP (that is, your IP number changes each time you connect to your Internet service provider), you will have to change the IP number in `httpd.conf` each time you dial up.

SERVER NAME

The `ServerName` changes described here are relevant only if you want people from the outside world to be able to connect to your new Web server. If you are the only person who will be accessing the server, you can use the IP number 127.0.0.1, which is recognized by machines as the local loop-back address, also known as `localhost`. You can use either the word `localhost` or the IP number 127.0.0.1 as `ServerName` in `httpd.conf`. The IP number will probably work out better because some Windows machines do not automatically know that `localhost` equals 127.0.0.1.

Once the appropriate modifications are made to the `httpd.conf` file, Apache is ready to run on your machine. In the next section, you start and connect to Apache.

Starting and Connecting to Apache

To first start the Apache server, select Program Files, Apache HTTP Server 2.2.4, Control Apache Server, Start from the Windows Start menu. This will launch a console window, which will then close. Apache will be running in the background.

With your Web server running, you can connect to the server via your Web browser of choice. The URL will be whatever you used as `ServerName`—an actual name or IP, `localhost`, or 127.0.0.1.

A NOTE ABOUT `localhost`

Remember, you can only connect to your Web server using 127.0.0.1 or the name `localhost`. This book assumes that you'll be using 127.0.0.1 as the `ServerName`, so if you are not, just substitute your machine name for 127.0.0.1 in the examples.

Figure 2.6 Default Apache Web page.

To test your installation, open your Web browser, type `http://127.0.0.1/` in the Location bar, and press Enter. You should see a default Web page (see Figure 2.6).

This default Start page comes from the `htdocs` directory within your Apache installation directory. You can go into that directory and delete all the default files if you want to, or you can leave them. They're not hurting anything, but you'll eventually be filling the `htdocs` directory with your own files and subdirectories, so you might want to delete them now for the sake of good housekeeping.

Move ahead to the next chapter, where you install PHP and make a few more minor changes to your Apache configuration files before you're ready for some action.

Installing Apache for Linux/UNIX

To download the Apache distribution for Linux, start at the Apache Server Web site, http://httpd.apache.org/, and follow the link to Download. This is the proper place for Linux/UNIX distribution files and announcements.

Distribution files follow a naming convention, with `httpd` followed by the version number, and then the compression type (`.tar.gz`, `.tar.Z`, and `.zip`). As of this writing, the current version is 2.2.4, and I prefer `*.tar.gz` files, so the file used as an example throughout this section is `httpd_2.2.4.tar.gz`.

CHECKING FOR PROPER DISTRIBUTIONS

The source code distribution should work for most flavors of UNIX, but if you have any concerns, read through the Apache documentation at the Apache Web site to find a better set of files for your specific operating system.

After you have downloaded the file of choice to your hard drive, the following steps help you build a basic version of Apache.

1. Type `cp httpd_2.2.4.tar.gz /usr/local/` and press Enter to copy the Apache installation file to the `/usr/local/src/` directory.

APACHE LOCATION

You can put Apache anywhere you want on your file system, such as `/usr/local/bin/` or `/opt/`. Just be sure to substitute your path for the path indicated in these directions.

---

2. Go to `/usr/local/src/` by typing `cd /usr/local/src/` and pressing Enter.

3. Unzip the Apache installation file by typing `gunzip httpd_2.2.4.tar.gz` and pressing Enter.

4. Extract the files by typing `tar -xvf httpd_2.2.4.tar` and pressing Enter. A directory structure will be created, and you'll be back at the prompt. The parent directory will be `/usr/local/src/httpd_2.0.49/`.

5. Enter the parent directory by typing `cd httpd_2.2.4` and pressing Enter.

6. Type the following and press Enter to prepare to build Apache:

```
./configure --prefix=/usr/local/apache2 --enable-module=so
```

The configuration script will run through its process of checking your configuration and creating makefiles, and then it will put you back at the prompt.

MAKEFILES

A *makefile* lists the files, dependencies, and rules required to build an executable application.

Figure 2.7 Apache build example.

7. Type **make** and press Enter. This second step of the installation process will produce many lines of output on your screen. When it is finished, you will be back at the prompt.

8. Type **make install** and press Enter. This final step of the installation process will again produce many lines of output on your screen. When it is finished, you will be back at the prompt (see Figure 2.7).

If your installation process produces any errors up to this point, go through the process again or check the Apache Web site for any system-specific notes. In the next section, you'll make some minor changes to the Apache configuration file before you start Apache for the first time.

Configuring Apache on Linux/UNIX

To run a basic installation of Apache, the only changes you need to make are to the server name, which resides in the master configuration file called `httpd.conf`. This file lives in the `conf` directory, within the Apache installation directory. So if your installation directory is `/usr/local/apache2/`, the configuration files will be in `/usr/local/apache2/conf/`.

Figure 2.8 Apache configuration file.

To modify the basic configuration, most importantly the server name, open the httpd.conf file with a text editor and look for a heading called Main server configuration. You will find two important sections of text (see Figure 2.8).

We are going to change the values in the configuration file so that Apache knows where to find things and who to send complaints to. The ServerAdmin, which is you, is simply the e-mail address that people can send mail to in reference to your site. The ServerName is what Apache uses to route incoming requests properly.

1. Change the value of ServerAdmin to your e-mail address.

2. Change the value of ServerName to something accurate and remove the preceding # so that the entry looks like this:

```
ServerName somehost.somedomain.com
```

You do not want it to look like this:

```
#ServerName somehost.somedomain.com
```

3. Save the file.

The ServerName modification is the most important change you'll make to your Apache configuration file because, if the ServerName isn't accurate, you won't be able to connect to Apache on your machine. As it states in the configuration file itself, "You cannot just invent host names and hope they work." If you do not know your full machine name, you can use an IP number. If you have a static IP number (that is, one that does not change), use it as your `ServerName`. If you have a dial-up connection that does not assign a static IP (that is, your IP number changes each time you connect to your Internet service provider), you will have to change the IP number in `httpd.conf` each time you dial up.

SERVER NAME

The `ServerName` changes described here are relevant only if you want people from the outside world to be able to connect to your new Web server. If you are the only person who will be accessing the server, you can use the IP number 127.0.0.1, which is recognized by machines as the local loop-back address, also known as `localhost`. You can use either the word `localhost` or the IP number 127.0.0.1 as `ServerName` in `httpd.conf`.

Once the appropriate modifications are made to the `httpd.conf` file, Apache is ready to run on your machine. In the next section, you'll start and connect to Apache.

Starting and Connecting to Apache

There's a handy utility in the `bin` directory within your Apache installation directory called `apachectl`. It allows you to issue `start`, `stop`, and `restart` commands. Use this utility to start Apache for the first time.

1. To get to the Apache installation directory, type `cd /usr/local/apache2` and press Enter.

2. Type `./bin/apachectl start` and press Enter.

You should see a message: `httpd started`. If you do not see this message, you have an error somewhere in your configuration file, and the error message will tell you where to look.

To stop Apache, you can type `./bin/apachectl stop` and press Enter. For now, keep it running, as the next step is to connect to the server via a Web browser, and this would not be a good time to shut it down.

With Apache running, you can connect to the server via your Web browser of choice. The URL will be whatever you used as `ServerName`—an actual name or IP, or the `localhost` name or IP.

A NOTE ON `localhost`

Remember, only you can connect to your Web server using 127.0.0.1 or the name `localhost`. This book assumes that you'll be using 127.0.0.1 as the `ServerName`, so if you are not, just substitute your machine name for 127.0.0.1 in the examples.

Figure 2.9 Default Apache Web page under Linux/UNIX.

To finally test your installation, open your Web browser, type `http://127.0.0.1/` in the Location bar, and press Enter. You should see a default Web page (see Figure 2.9).

This default Start page comes from the `htdocs` directory within your Apache installation directory. You can go into that directory and delete all the default files if you want to, or you can leave them. They're not hurting anything, but you'll eventually be filling the `htdocs` directory with your own files and subdirectories, so you might want to delete them for the sake of good housekeeping.

Move ahead to the next chapter, where you'll install PHP and make a few more minor changes to your Apache configuration files before you're ready for some action.

3

Installing PHP

This is it—the final piece of the puzzle that will get you started in the world of creating dynamic, database-driven Web sites. In this chapter, you learn how to:

- Install PHP on Windows or Linux.
- Make final modifications to Apache.
- Use the `phpinfo()` function to retrieve system information.

Installing PHP for Windows

Installing PHP for Windows doesn't occur through a wizard interface. Basically, you just unzip some files and move them around. No big deal. Just follow along very closely because this is the area where most people miss an instruction, and if you do that, it won't work.

USING DIFFERENT WEB SERVERS

Okay, so there is a Windows installer for PHP, if you're going to use PHP with Microsoft IIS, Microsoft PWS, or the Xitami Web server. This book is based on a recommendation of using Apache as the Web server and performing the manual installation of PHP. If you choose to install PHP with a different Web server or are using a different method, please read the installation instructions contained within the software you choose.

To download the PHP binary distribution for Windows, visit the Downloads page at the PHP Web site: http://www.php.net/downloads.php.

PRE-PRODUCTION BINARIES

As of the writing of this book, the PHP 6.0 binaries had not yet been released as a general product. Instead, the binaries and source were available on the snapshot page (http://snaps.php.net/) for PHP. This may or may not be true at the time of the book's release, but the binaries should be available shortly.

---

1. From the Windows Binaries section, follow the link for `PHP6.0-win32-dev.zip package`, where `x.x` refers to the version. Currently, the version for Windows is 6.0, and all subsequent installation instructions will be based on this version. Future versions will follow the same installation procedure; just substitute the new version name as appropriate.

2. Once downloaded to your system, double-click the file called `ph6.0-win32-dev.zip`. Your zipping program of choice, such as WinZip or PKZip, will open this file.

3. Extract the files to the top level of your hard drive, into a directory called `php`.

You now have all the basic PHP distribution files; you just need to move a few of them around.

CHANGING INSTALLATION LOCATION

If you change the installation directory name, be sure to substitute your new directory name in the remaining instructions in this chapter.

---

1. Using Windows Explorer (or whatever method you prefer for moving through your file system), go to the `C:\php` directory.

2. Rename the `php.ini-dist` file to `php.ini` and move this file to `C:\WINDOWS\`, `C:\WINNT\`, or wherever you usually put your `*.ini` files.

3. Move `php6ts.dll` to `C:\WINDOWS\SYSTEM\`, `C:\WINDOWS\SYSTEM32\`, or wherever you usually put your `*.dll` files.

To get a basic version of PHP working with Apache, you'll need to make a few minor modifications to the Apache configuration file.

Configuring Apache to Use PHP

You can install PHP as a CGI binary or as an Apache module. The current recommendation by the PHP Group (and me) is to use the module version, because it offers greater performance and some additional functionality. However, you might encounter some conflicts with advanced functionality when using the module, depending on your particular operating system. Additionally, using the CGI version instead of the module version will allow you to create virtual hosts, each with its own PHP CGI executable, therefore allowing PHP to run as a named user instead of the default Apache process owner.

If you would like to install the CGI version, please read the installation information in the PHP manual at www.php.net/manual/. In the next section, you'll learn to install the module version of PHP for the Apache 2 server.

The Apache Module Version of PHP

To configure Apache to use the module version, you have to move one piece of PHP and also make a few modifications to the Apache configuration file, the `httpd.conf` file located in the `conf` directory within the Apache installation directory.

Figure 3.1 Apache configuration file.

Figure 3.2 Type handlers in configuration files.

1. Choose Program Files, Apache HTTP Server 2.2.4, Configure Apache Server, Edit the Apache `httpd.conf` Configuration File from the Windows Start menu.

2. Look for a section of text like the one shown in Figure 3.1.

3. Add the following code to the end of that section:

```
LoadModule php6_module
c:/php//php6apache2.dll
```

Next, you have to add a directive to the `httpd.conf` file to define the file extensions used by PHP files. Common extensions are `.php` and `.phtml`, but you can use whatever you want.

4. Look for a section of text like the one shown in Figure 3.2.

5. Add the following line:

```
AddType application/x-httpd-php .phtml .php
```

6. Save and close the `httpd.conf` file.

This final modification tells Apache that any time a file with an extension of `.php` or `.phtml` is requested, Apache should utilize the module version of the PHP parser before sending any output to the Web browser.

Testing the PHP Installation

Now that all of your modifications have been made to the `httpd.conf` file—no matter the configuration method—you can restart Apache using the method you learned in Chapter 2. To test that Apache and PHP are playing nice together, you'll create a simple PHP script to test your installation. PHP scripts and other files (HTML, images, and so on) should be placed in the document root of your Web server. For Apache, the document root is the `htdocs` directory within your Apache installation directory.

1. Open a new file in your text editor and type the following:

```
<? phpinfo(); ?>
```

2. Save the file with the name `phpinfo.php` and place this file in the document root of your Web server.

FILE EXTENSIONS

Be absolutely sure that your file extension is `.php` or `.phtml` (or another extension you configured for PHP). It is very common for Windows-based text editors to add a hidden file extension of `.txt` to the end of the filename. If that happens to you, your script will not parse as PHP, only text. So keep an eye on your extension!

Figure 3.3 The `phpinfo` script.

3. Open your Web browser and type `http://127.0.0.1/phpinfo.php`. See Figure 3.3.

The output of the `phpinfo.php` script should be a long page full of system and environment information. This information is very helpful when you're trying to figure out what's available to you. If you browse through the results, you'll see that the following extensions are preinstalled (along with many others):

- Perl-compatible regular expression support
- ODBC support
- Session support
- XML support
- MySQL support

Having these items preinstalled means that no additional `.dll` files are necessary for these functions to be available to you. For more information on obtaining `.dll` files for additional PHP functionality, see Appendix A, "Additional Configuration Options."

You're now ready to move on to Part II, "The Absolute Basics of Coding in PHP," and learn the fundamentals of the PHP language.

Installing PHP for Linux/UNIX

This section shows you how to install PHP on Linux/UNIX as a dynamic module for Apache. By building a dynamic rather than a static module, you can upgrade or recompile PHP without having to recompile Apache as well. For example, all you'll be doing in this section is configuring PHP for MySQL support. If you decide that you want additional options later in the game, such as image-creation functions or additional encryption functions, you'll only have to change the configuration command for PHP, recompile the module, and restart Apache. No additional changes will be needed for the Apache installation, because one PHP module file just replaces another.

To download the PHP source distribution, visit the Downloads page at the PHP Web site: www.php.net/downloads.php. If you want to use the very latest builds rather than the released stable versions, you can find them at snaps.php.net. These builds, done nightly or more often, are not considered to be of production quality.

1. From the "Complete Source Code" section, follow the link for PHP 6.x.x where x.x refers to the version. The current source code version is 6.0.0, and that version number will be used in the following steps. Although your version number (and therefore filename) might vary in the future, the procedure will remain the same, substituting the new name as appropriate.

2. Once downloaded to your system, type `cp php-6.0-dev.tar.gz /usr/local/src/` and press Enter to copy the PHP source distribution to the `/usr/local/src/` directory.

INSTALLATION LOCATION

You can put PHP anywhere you want on your file system, such as `/usr/local/bin/` or `/opt/` or wherever you want to put the file. Just be sure to substitute your path for the path indicated in these directions.

---

3. Go to `/usr/local/src/` by typing `cd /usr/local/src/` and pressing Enter.

4. Unzip the source file by typing `gunzip php-6.0-dev.tar.gz` and pressing Enter.

5. Extract the files by typing `tar -xvf php-6.0-dev.tar` and pressing Enter. This will create a directory structure and then put you back at the prompt. The parent directory will be `/usr/local/src/php-6.0.0/`.

6. Enter the parent directory by typing `cd php-6.0-dev` and pressing Enter.

7. Type the following and press Enter to prepare to build PHP:

```
./configure --prefix=/usr/local/php5 --with-mysql=/usr/local/mysql/
--with-apxs2=/usr/local/apache2/bin/apxs
```

PHP AND APACHE PATHS

In configuration directives, use your own paths to the MySQL and Apache directories, should they reside elsewhere on your file system.

The configuration script will run through its process of checking your configuration and creating makefiles and then will put you back at the prompt.

8. Type `make` and press Enter. This second step of the installation process will produce many lines of output on your screen. When it is finished, you will be back at the prompt.

9. Type `make install` and press Enter. This final step of the installation process will produce many lines of output on your screen. When it is finished, you will be back at the prompt.

Now, to get a basic version of PHP working with Apache, all you need to do is to make a few modifications to the `httpd.conf` file.

Configuring Apache to Use PHP

The installation process will have placed a module in the proper place within the Apache directory structure. Now you must make some modifications to the `httpd.conf` file before starting up Apache with PHP enabled.

1. Open the `httpd.conf` file in your text editor of choice.

2. Look for the following line, which will have been inserted into the file by the installation process:

```
LoadModule php6_module      modules/libphp6.so
```

You want this line to be uncommented, so ensure that it is (as shown).

3. Look for the following lines:

```
# AddType allows you to add to or override the MIME configuration
# file mime.types for specific file types.
#AddType application/x-tar .tgz
```

4. Add to these lines the following:

```
AddType application/x-httpd-php .phtml .php
```

5. Save and close the `httpd.conf` file.

This modification tells Apache that anytime a file with an extension of `.php` or `.phtml` is requested, Apache should first run that file through the PHP parser before sending any output to the Web browser.

After these changes have been made to `httpd.conf`, you're ready to start Apache and test your PHP installation.

Testing the PHP Installation

Now that all of your modifications have been made to the `httpd.conf` file, you can restart Apache using the method you learned in Chapter 2. To test that Apache and PHP are playing nice together, you'll create a simple PHP script to test your installation. PHP scripts and other files (HTML, images, and so on) should be located in the document root of your Web server. For Apache, the document root is the `htdocs` directory within your Apache installation directory.

1. Open a new file in your text editor and type the following:

```
<? phpinfo(); ?>
```

2. Save the file with the name `phpinfo.php`.

Figure 3.4 The phpinfo script.

3. Place this file in the document root of your Web server.

4. Open your Web browser, type **http://127.0.0.1/ phpinfo.php**, and then press Enter (see Figure 3.4).

The output of the phpinfo.php script should be a long page full of system and environment information. This information is very helpful when you're trying to figure out what's available to you.

For more information on configuring and building additional functionality into your PHP installation, see Appendix A.

You're now ready to move on to Part II and learn the fundamentals of the PHP language.

PART II

The Absolute Basics of Coding in PHP

4

Mixing PHP and HTML

Now that you have a working development environment with PHP, Apache, and MySQL happily running on your machine, it's time to delve into the PHP language. In this chapter, you'll learn how to do the following:

- Recognize and use the different kinds of PHP start and end tags.
- Mingle PHP and HTML within your source code.
- Escape special characters in your scripts to produce valid output.

How PHP Is Parsed

So you have a file, and in that file you have some HTML and some PHP code. This is how it all works, assuming a PHP document with an extension of .php.

FILE EXTENSIONS

The file extension does not have to be .php, but it does have to be an extension that Apache understands should be parsed as PHP, which you learned in Chapter 2, "Installing Apache."

---

1. The Web browser requests a document with a .php extension.

2. The Web server says, "Hey! Someone wants a PHP file, which means this is a file that needs to be parsed," and sends the request on to the PHP parser.

3. The PHP parser finds the requested file and scans it for PHP code.

4. When the PHP parser finds PHP code, it executes that code and places the resulting output (if any) into the place in the file formerly occupied by the code.

5. This new output file is sent back to the Web server.

6. The Web server sends it along to the Web browser.

7. The Web browser displays the output.

Because the PHP code is parsed on the server, this method of code execution is called *server-side code*. When code is executed in a browser, such as JavaScript, it is called *client-side code*.

To combine PHP code with HTML, the PHP code must be set apart from the HTML. In the next section, you'll learn how this is done, using PHP start and end tags.

PHP Start and End Tags

The PHP parser recognizes a few types of PHP start and end tags. It will attempt to execute anything between these tags, so it had better be valid code!

Study Table 4.1 to learn the three main sets of start and end tags recognized by the PHP parser.

Table 4.1 Basic PHP Start and End Tags

Opening Tag	Closing Tag
`<?php`	`?>`
`<?`	`?>`
`<script language="php">`	`</script>`

Next, you'll use all three sets of tags in a script, which I promise will execute without errors.

TEXT EDITORS

For PHP files, you may use any text editor that produces plain text. In the Windows™ world, for example, we will use Notepad (an application that ships with Windows) to produce the files. Using something like Microsoft Word can be problematic because of the special characters it embeds in your text files.

1. Open a new file in your text editor.

2. Type the following code, which uses the first tag type:

```
<?php
echo "<P>This is a test using the first tag type.</P>";
?>
```

3. Type the following code, which uses the second tag type:

```
<?
echo "<P>This is a test using the second tag type.</P>";
?>
```

Figure 4.1 Your first PHP script.

4. Type the following code, which uses the third tag type:

```
<script language="php">
echo "<P>This is a test using
the third tag type.</P>";
</script>
```

You should see a listing like the one shown in Figure 4.1.

5. Save the file with the name `phptags.php`.

6. Place this file in the document root of your Web server.

7. Open your Web browser and type `http://127.0.0.1/phptags.php`.

DOMAIN NAMES

While executing the examples in this book, if you are using PHP on an external Web server, substitute that server's domain name for the 127.0.0.1 address in the URL.

Figure 4.2 The `phptags` script running.

In your Web browser, you should see the results of your script (see Figure 4.2).

In the next section, you'll learn that putting PHP blocks inside HTML is not a scary thing.

Code Cohabitation

In the previous section, your file consisted of three chunks of PHP code, each of which printed some HTML text. In this section, you'll create a script that has PHP code stuck in the middle of your HTML, and you'll learn how these two types of code can peacefully coexist.

1. Open a new file in your text editor.

2. Type the following HTML:

```
<HTML>
<HEAD>
<TITLE>My First PHP Script</TITLE>
</HEAD>
<BODY>
```

3. Type the following PHP code:

```
<?
echo "<P><em>Hello World! I'm using PHP!</em></P>";
?>
```

4. Add some more HTML so that the document is valid:

```
</BODY>
</HTML>
```

Figure 4.3 The `firstscript.php` script running.

5. Save the file with the name `firstscript.php`.

6. Place this file in the document root of your Web server.

7. Open your Web browser and type **http://127.0.0.1/ firstscript.php**. In your Web browser, you should see the results of your script (see Figure 4.3).

Figure 4.4 The HTML source for `firstscript.php`.

8. In your Web browser, view the source of this document (see Figure 4.4).

Notice that the HTML source contains only HTML code, which is correct because this block of PHP was executed:

```
<?
echo "<P><em>Hello World! I'm
using PHP!</em></P>";
?>
```

This block contains three elements: the command (echo), the string (`<P><em>Hello World! I'm using PHP!</em></P>`), and the instruction terminator (;).

Familiarize yourself now with echo, because it will likely be your most often-used command. The echo statement is used to output information—in this case, to print this HTML output:

```
<P><em>Hello World! I'm using PHP!</em></P>
```

The next section discusses a common error, with the hope that you'll be able to avoid it.

The Importance of the Instruction Terminator

The instruction terminator, also known as the semicolon (;), is absolutely required at the end of commands. The instruction terminator tells the PHP parser, "I'm done with this command, try the next one."

If you do not end commands with a semicolon, the PHP parser will become confused, and your code will display errors. These next steps show you how these errors come about and, more importantly, how to fix them.

1. Open a new file in your text editor.

2. Type the following HTML:

```
<HTML>
<HEAD>
<TITLE>Making an Error</TITLE>
</HEAD>
<BODY>
```

3. Type the following PHP code:

```
<?
echo "<P>I am trying to produce an error</P>"
echo "<P>Was I successful?</P>";
?>
```

4. Add some more HTML so that the document is valid:

```
</BODY>
</HTML>
```

Figure 4.5 The errorscript.

5. Save the file with the name `errorscript.php`.

6. Place this file in the document root of your Web server.

7. Open your Web browser and type `http://127.0.0.1/errorscript.php`. See Figure 4.5.

What a nasty error! The error message says that the error is on line 8. Take a look at lines 7 and 8 of the script:

```
echo "<P>I am trying to produce an error</P>"
echo "<P>Was I successful?</P>";
```

Line 7 does not have an instruction terminator, and line 8 starts a new command. The PHP parser doesn't like this, and it tells you so by producing the parse error.

This error is easy enough to fix:

1. Open the `errorscript.php` file.

Figure 4.6 The updated `errorscript.php` file.

2. On line 7, add the instruction terminator (;) to the end of the line (see Figure 4.6):

```
echo "<P>I am trying to produce
an error</P>";
```

3. Save the file.

4. Place this file in the document root of your Web server.

Figure 4.7 The updated `errorscript` running.

5. Open your Web browser and type **http://127.0.0.1// errorscript.php**. See Figure 4.7.

After you fix line 7, the PHP parser can deal with the file, and the rest of the output is successful. Avoid this and other errors by paying close attention to things such as semicolons and, as you'll learn in the next section, quotation marks!

Escaping Your Code

Right up there with remembering to terminate your commands with semicolons is remembering to escape characters such as quotation marks. When you use quotation marks inside other quotation marks, the inner pairs must be delineated from the outside pair using the escape (\) character (also known as a backslash).

The following steps show you what happens when your code isn't escaped and how to fix it.

1. Open a new file in your text editor.

2. Type the following HTML:

```
<HTML>
<HEAD>
<TITLE>Trying For Another Error</TITLE>
</HEAD>
<BODY>
```

3. Type the following PHP code:

```
<?
echo "<P>I think this is really "cool"!</P>";
?>
```

4. Add some more HTML so that the document is valid:

```
</BODY>
</HTML>
```

5. Save the file with the name errorscript2.php.

6. Place this file in the document root of your Web server.

Figure 4.8 The `errorscript2` script running.

7. Open your Web browser and type **http://127.0.0.1/ errorscript2.php**. See Figure 4.8.

Another parse error! Take a look at the PHP code:

```
echo "<P>I think this is really "cool"!</P>";
```

Because you have a set of quotation marks within another set of quotation marks, that inner set has to be escaped.

This error also has a simple fix:

1. Open the `errorscript2.php` file.

2. On line 9, escape the inner quotation marks by placing a backslash before each one:

   ```
   echo "<P>I think this is really \"cool\"!</P>";
   ```

3. Save the file.

4. Place this file in the document root of your Web server.

Figure 4.9 Fixed `errorscript2` script running.

5. Open your Web browser and type **http://127.0.0.1/ errorscript2.php**. See Figure 4.9.

Now that the inner quotation marks are escaped, the PHP parser will skip right over them, knowing that these characters should just be printed and have no other meaning. In the next section, you'll learn a good programming practice: commenting your code so other people know what the heck is going on in it, should they have to edit it.

Commenting Your Code

Commenting your code is a good habit to have. Entering comments in HTML documents helps you (and others who might have to edit your document later) keep track of what's going on in large documents. Comments also allow you to write notes to yourself during the development process or comment out parts of code when you are testing your scripts, so the code is not executed.

HTML comments are ignored by the browser and are contained within `<!--` and `-->` tags. For example, the following comment reminds you that the next bit of HTML code contains a logo graphic:

```
<!-- logo graphic goes here -->
```

PHP uses comments, too, which are ignored by the PHP parser. PHP comments are usually preceded by double slashes, like this:

```
// this is a comment in PHP code
```

But you can use other types of comments, such as

```
# This is shell-style style comment
```

and

```
/* This begins a C-style comment that runs
onto two lines */
```

Create a script full of comments so that you can see how they're ignored. Yes, I'm telling you to write a script that does absolutely nothing!

1. Open a new file in your text editor.

2. Type the following HTML:

```
<HTML>
<HEAD>
<TITLE>Code Comments</TITLE>
</HEAD>
<BODY>
<!-- This is an HTML comment. -->
```

3. Type the following PHP code:

```
<?
// This is a simple PHP comment.
/* This is a C-style, multiline comment. You can make this as
long as you'd like. */
# Used to shells? Use this kind of comment.
?>
```

4. Add some more HTML so that the document is valid:

```
</BODY>
</HTML>
```

5. Save the file with the name comments.php.

6. Place this file in the document root of your Web server.

Figure 4.10 The comments script.

7. Open your Web browser and type `http://127.0.0.1/comments.php`. See Figure 4.10.

You should see absolutely nothing in your Web browser, because all you did was print an HTML comment (which is ignored by the browser). Because the PHP parser ignores comments and the PHP block didn't contain any actual commands, there was no other output to display. If you view the source of this document in your Web browser, you will notice that only the HTML comment is visible. Although the PHP code was all comments, it was still parsed and therefore is not visible to the users.

HTML and PHP comments are used extensively throughout this book to explain blocks of code. Get used to reading comments, and try to pick up the habit of using them. Writing clean, bug-free code that also contains comments and plenty of white space for easy reading will make you popular among your developer peers because they won't have to work extra hard to figure out what your code is trying to do. In the next chapter, you'll learn all about variables, or as I like to call them, "those things with the dollar signs."

5

Introducing Variables and Operators

In the last chapter, you were introduced to the process of parsing PHP code and how the code output is displayed in your Web browser. In the next few chapters, you'll learn a bit about the inner workings of the PHP language—all the bits and pieces that, when you put them together, actually produce a working script! In this chapter, you'll learn how to do the following:

- Recognize and use variables.
- Recognize and use operators.

What's a Variable?

A variable is a representation of a particular value, such as `blue` or `19349377`. By assigning a value to a variable, you can reference the variable in other places in your script, and that value will always remain the same (unless you change it, which you'll learn about later).

To create a variable, do the following (in your head):

1. Think of a good name! For instance, if I want to create a variable to hold a username, I name my variable:

`username`

2. Put a dollar sign ($) in front of that name:

`$username`

3. Use the equals sign after the name (=) to assign a literal value to that variable. Put the value in quotation marks:

`$username = "joe"`

4. Assigning a value to a variable is an instruction and as such should be terminated with a semicolon:

`$username = "joe";`

There you have it—a variable called `username` with a value of `joe`. Later in this chapter, you'll do some exciting things (such as math) with your variables.

Naming Your Variables

As you've seen, variables begin with a dollar sign ($) and are followed by a meaningful name. The variable name cannot begin with a numeric character, but it can contain numbers and the underscore character (_). Additionally, variable names are case sensitive, meaning that `$YOURVAR` and `$yourvar` are two different variables.

Creating meaningful variable names is another way to lessen headaches while coding. For example, if your script deals with name and password values, don't create a variable called $n for the name and $p for the password—those are not meaningful names. If you pick up that script weeks later, you might think that $n is the variable for "number" rather than "name" and that $p stands for "page" rather than "password."

PHP Variable and Value Types

You will create two main types of variables in your PHP code: *scalar* and *array*. Scalar variables contain only one value at a time, and arrays contain a list of values or even another array.

The example at the beginning of this chapter created a scalar variable, and the code in this book deals primarily with scalar variables. You can find information on arrays in Appendix B, "Basic PHP Language Reference."

When you assign a value to a variable, you usually assign a value of one of the following types:

- **Integers.** Whole numbers (numbers without decimals). Examples are 1, 345, and 9922786. You can also use octal and hexadecimal notation: The octal 0123 is decimal 83 and the hexadecimal 0x12 is decimal 18.

NEW! 64-BIT INTEGERS
Note that PHP 6.0 introduces the idea of a 64-bit integer, for those of you who are using really, really big numbers.

- **Floating-point numbers ("floats" or "doubles").** Numbers with decimals. Examples are 1.5, 87.3446, and 0.88889992.

- **Strings.** Text or numeric information, specified within double quotes (" ") or single quotes (' ').

NEW! UNICODE STRINGS

A change from previous versions of PHP is that starting with version 6.0, all strings are now in Unicode format by default. You can change this in the `php.ini` file by finding the `unicode.semantics` variable and setting it to `false`.

As you begin your PHP script, plan your variables and variable names carefully, and use comments in your code to remind yourself of the assignments you have made.

Figure 5.1 A simple variable script.

Create a simple script that assigns values to different variables and then simply prints the values to the screen (see Figure 5.1).

1. Open a new file in your text editor and type the following HTML:

```
<HTML>
<HEAD>
<TITLE>Printing
Variables</TITLE>
</HEAD>
<BODY>
```

2. Add a PHP block and create a variable that holds an integer:

```
<?
$intVar = "955421";
```

3. Create a variable that holds a floating-point number:

```
$floatVar = "1542.2232235";
```

4. Create a variable that holds a string:

```
$stringVar = "This is a string.";
```

5. Add an `echo` statement for each variable:

```
echo "<P>integer: $intVar</P>";
echo "<P>float: $floatVar</P>";
echo "<P>string: $stringVar</P>";
```

6. Close your PHP block and add some more HTML so that the document is valid:

```
?>
</BODY>
</HTML>
```

Figure 5.2 The `printvarscript` running.

7. Save the file with the name `printvarscript.php` and place this file in the document root of your Web server.

8. Open your Web browser and type **http://127.0.0.1/ printvarscript.php**. See Figure 5.2.

You can see by this output that the values you assigned to the variables $intVar, $floatVar, $bigintVar, and $stringVar were the values printed to the screen. In the next section, you'll learn how to use operators to change the values of your variables.

Local and Global Variables

Variables can be *local* or *global*, the difference having to do with their definition and use by the programmer and where they appear in the context of the scripts you are creating. The variables described in the previous section, and for the majority of this book, are local variables.

When you write PHP scripts that use variables, those variables can be used only by the script in which they live. Scripts cannot magically reach inside other scripts and use the variables created and defined there—unless you say they can and you purposefully link them together. When you do just that, such as when you create your own functions (blocks of reusable code that perform a particular task), you will define the shared variables as global. That is, you will define them as able to be accessed by other scripts and functions, as needed.

You can learn about creating your own functions, and using global as well as local variables, in Appendix C, "Writing Your Own Functions." For now, just understand that there are two variable scopes—local and global—that come into play as you write more advanced scripts.

Predefined Variables

In all PHP scripts, a set of predefined variables is available to you. You might have seen some of these variables in the output of the `phpinfo()` function, if you scrolled and read through the entire results page. Some of these predefined variables are called *superglobals*, meaning that they are always present and available to all of your scripts, without any intervention by you, the programmer.

Please study the following list of superglobals, because they will be used extensively throughout this book. Each of these superglobals is actually an array of other variables. Don't worry about fully understanding this concept now, because it will be explained as you move along through the book.

- `$_GET` contains any variables provided to a script through the GET method.
- `$_POST` contains any variables provided to a script through the POST method.
- `$_COOKIE` contains any variables provided to a script through a cookie.
- `$_FILES` contains any variables provided to a script through file uploads.
- `$_ENV` contains any variables provided to a script as part of the server environment.
- `$_SESSION` contains any variables that are registered in a session.

Using Constants

A *constant* is an identifier for a value that cannot change during the course of a script. Once a constant has a value, it remains through its execution lifetime. Constants can be user defined, or you can use some of the predefined constants that PHP always has available. Unlike simple variables, constants do not have a dollar sign before their name, and they are usually uppercase to show their difference from a scalar variable. Next, you'll test the user-defined type.

1. Open a new file in your text editor and open a PHP block:

```
<?
```

2. The function used to define a constant is called `define()`, and it requires the name of the constant and the value you want to give it. Here you define a constant called `MYCONSTANT` with a value of `"This is a test of defining constants."`.

```
define("MYCONSTANT", "This is a test of defining constants.");
```

3. Print the value of the constant and then close the PHP block:

```
echo MYCONSTANT;
?>
```

Figure 5.3 The constants script running.

4. Save the file with the name `constants.php` and place this file in the document root of your Web server.

5. Open your Web browser and type `http://127.0.0.1/constants.php`. See Figure 5.3.

Some predefined constants include:

- **__FILE__** The name of the script file being parsed.
- **__LINE__** The number of the line in the script being parsed.
- **PHP_VERSION** The version of PHP in use.
- **PHP_OS** The operating system using PHP.

Let's test these constants:

1. Open a new file in your text editor and open a PHP block:

```
<?
```

2. Use the echo statement to display an introductory string, and concatenate the __FILE__ constant to the end of it:

```
echo "<br>This file is ".__FILE__;
```

CONCATENATION

Concatenate means to add one string to the end of another, making a new string.

---

3. Use the echo statement to display an introductory string and concatenate the __LINE__ constant to the end of it:

```
echo "<br>This is line number ".__LINE__;
```

4. Use the echo statement to display an introductory string and concatenate the PHP_VERSION constant to the end of it:

```
echo "<br>I am using ".PHP_VERSION;
```

5. Use the echo statement to display an introductory string and concatenate the PHP_OS constant to the end of it. Also, close up the PHP block:

```
echo "<br>This test is being run on ".PHP_OS;
?>
```

Figure 5.4 The constants2 script running.

6. Save the file with the name `constants2.php` and place this file in the document root of your Web server.

7. Open your Web browser and type `http://127.0.0.1/ constants2.php`. See Figure 5.4.

You should see the strings you typed, plus the values of the constants. Your values will likely differ from those you see here.

What's an Operator?

In the previous section, you used an assignment operator (=) to assign values to your variables. There are other types of assignment operators, as well as other types of operators in general. The basic function of an operator is to do something with the value of a variable. That "something" can be to assign a value, change a value, or compare two or more values.

Here are the main types of PHP operators:

- **Assignment operators.** Assign values to variables. Can also add to or subtract from a variable's current value.

- **Arithmetic operators.** Addition, subtraction, division, and multiplication occur when these operators are used.

- **Comparison operators.** Compare two values and return either `true` or `false`. You can then perform actions based on the returned value.

- **Logical operators.** Determine the status of conditions.

The rest of this chapter is devoted to discussing some of the main operators used in PHP. You'll be writing example scripts for each, so hang on to your hat!

Assignment Operators

You've already seen an assignment operator at work: The equals sign is the basic assignment operator. Burn this into your brain: = does *not* mean "equal to"! Instead, == (two equals signs) means "equal to," and the single = means "is assigned to." In fact, you've also seen the concatenation operator in this chapter, as it is used to put strings together.

Take a look at the assignment operators in Table 5.1 and prepare to write a new script.

Table 5.1 Assignment Operators

Operator	Example	Action
+=	`$a += 3;`	Changes the value of a variable to the current value plus the value on the right side.
-=	`$a -= 3;`	Changes the value of a variable to the current value minus the value on the right side.
.=	`$a .= "string";`	Concatenates (adds on to) the value on the right side with the current value.

Create a simple script to show how all of these assignment operators work. This script will assign an original value to one variable and then change that value as the script executes, all the while printing the result to the screen.

1. Open a new file in your text editor and type the following HTML:

```
<HTML>
<HEAD>
<TITLE>Using Assignment Operators</TITLE>
</HEAD>
<BODY>
```

2. Start a PHP block. Create a variable with a value of 100 and then print it:

```
<?
$origVar = 100;
echo "<P>Original value is $origVar</P>";
```

3. Add to that value and then print it:

```
$origVar += 25;
echo "<P>Added a value, now it's $origVar</P>";
```

4. Subtract from that value and then print it:

```
$origVar -= 12;
echo "<P>Subtracted a value, now it's $origVar</P>";
```

5. Concatenate a string and then print it:

```
$origVar .= " chickens";
echo "<P>Final answer: $origVar</P>";
```

Figure 5.5 The assignment script source code.

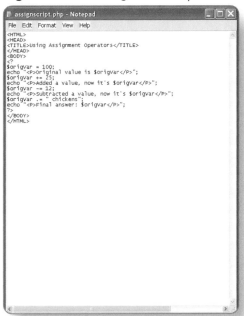

6. Close your PHP block and add some more HTML so that the document is valid:

```
?>
</BODY>
</HTML>
```

It should now look something like the script shown in Figure 5.5.

7. Save the file with the name assignscript.php and place this file in the document root of your Web server.

Figure 5.6 The assignment script running.

8. Open your Web browser and type **http://127.0.0.1/ assignscript.php**. See Figure 5.6.

The results of your calculations will be printed to the screen. The next section moves to arithmetic operators, none of which should be strange to you as long as you made it through your first few years of school.

Arithmetic Operators

Arithmetic operators simply perform basic mathematical tasks. Take a look at Table 5.2, be sure you remember your basic math, and start creating the test script for this section.

Table 5.2 Arithmetic Operators

Operator	Example	Action
+	$b = $a + 3;	Adds values
-	$b = $a - 3;	Subtracts values
*	$b = $a * 3;	Multiplies values
/	$b = $a / 3;	Divides values
%	$b = $a % 3;	Returns the modulus, or remainder

Figure 5.7 An example of operators in a script.

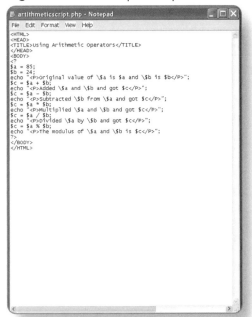

Create a simple script to show how all of these arithmetic operators work. This script assigns original values to two variables, performs mathematical operations, and prints the results to the screen (see Figure 5.7).

1. Open a new file in your text editor and type the following HTML:

```
<HTML>
<HEAD>
<TITLE>Using Arithmetic
Operators</TITLE>
</HEAD>
<BODY>
```

2. Start a PHP block, create two variables with values, and print the values:

```
<?
$a = 85;
$b = 24;
echo "<P>Original value of \$a is $a and \$b is $b</P>";
```

ESCAPING THE DOLLAR SIGN

If you escape the dollar sign (\$), it will print literally instead of being interpreted as a variable.

3. Add the two values and print the result:

```
$c = $a + $b;
echo "<P>Added \$a and \$b and got $c</P>";
```

4. Subtract the two values and print the result:

```
$c = $a - $b;
echo "<P>Subtracted \$b from \$a and got $c</P>";
```

5. Multiply the two values and print the result:

```
$c = $a * $b;
echo "<P>Multiplied \$a and \$b and got $c</P>";
```

6. Divide the two values and print the result:

```
$c = $a / $b;
echo "<P>Divided \$a by \$b and got $c</P>";
```

7. Check the modulus of the two values and print the result:

```
$c = $a % $b;
echo "<P>The modulus of \$a and \$b is $c</P>";
```

8. Close your PHP block and add some more HTML so that the document is valid:

```
?>
</BODY>
</HTML>
```

9. Save the file with the name `arithmeticscript.php` and place this file in the document root of your Web server.

Figure 5.8 The arithmetic script running.

10. Open your Web browser and type **http:// 127.0.0.1/ arithmeticscript.php**. See Figure 5.8.

Your original values, as well as the results of the various calculations, are printed to the screen.

Next, you move to comparison operators, which are crucial in coding but not nearly as much fun as arithmetic operators.

Comparison Operators

It should come as no surprise to you that comparison operators compare two values. As with the arithmetic operators, you have probably already seen most of the comparison operators, but you might not know what they are called. Take a look at Table 5.3, and then you can start creating the test script for this section.

Table 5.3 Comparison Operators

Operator	Definition
==	Equal to
!=	Not equal to
>	Greater than
<	Less than
>=	Greater than or equal to
<=	Less than or equal to

The result of any of these comparisons is either true or false. This isn't much fun, but you can act on the result using control statements, such as `if...else` and `while` to perform a specific task.

Create a simple script to show the result of some comparisons, using the `if...else` control statements to print a result to the screen.

1. Open a new file in your text editor and type the following HTML:

```
<HTML>
<HEAD>
<TITLE>Using Comparison Operators</TITLE>
</HEAD>
<BODY>
```

2. Start a PHP block, create two variables with values, and print the values:

```
<?
$a = 21;
$b = 15;
echo "<P>Original value of \$a is $a and \$b is $b</P>";
```

3. Within an `if...else` statement, test whether `$a` is equal to `$b`. Depending on the answer (true or false), one of the `echo` statements will print:

```
if ($a == $b) {
echo "<P>TEST 1: \$a equals \$b</P>";
} else {
echo "<P>TEST 1: \$a is not equal to \$b</P>";
}
```

A NOTE ON CONDITIONAL EXPRESSIONS

Conditional expressions are enclosed in parentheses, such as:

```
if ($a == $b)
```

and not:

```
if $a == $b
```

4. Within an `if...else` statement, test whether `$a` is not equal to `$b`. Depending on the answer (true or false), one of the `echo` statements will print:

```
if ($a != $b) {
echo "<P>TEST 2: \$a is not equal to \$b</P>";
} else {
echo "<P>TEST 2: \$a is equal to \$b</P>";
}
```

CURLY BRACES AND BLOCKS

The curly braces { and } separate the blocks of statements within a control structure.

5. Within an `if...else` statement, test whether $a is greater than $b. Depending on the answer (true or false), one of the `echo` statements will print:

```
if ($a > $b) {
echo "<P>TEST 3: \$a is greater than \$b</P>";
} else {
echo "<P>TEST 3: \$a is not greater than \$b</P>";
}
```

6. Within an `if...else` statement, test whether $a is less than $b. Depending on the answer (true or false), one of the `echo` statements will print:

```
if ($a < $b) {
echo "<P>TEST 4: \$a is less than \$b</P>";
} else {
echo "<P>TEST 4: \$a is not less than \$b</P>";
}
```

7. Within an `if...else` statement, test whether $a is greater than or equal to $b. Depending on the answer (true or false), one of the `echo` statements will print:

```
if ($a >= $b) {
echo "<P>TEST 5: \$a is greater than or equal to \$b</P>";
} else {
echo "<P>TEST 5: \$a is not greater than or equal to \$b</P>";
}
```

8. Within an `if...else` statement, test whether $a is less than or equal to $b. Depending on the answer (true or false), one of the `echo` statements will print:

```
if ($a <= $b) {
echo "<P>TEST 6: \$a is less than or equal to \$b</P>";
} else {
echo "<P>TEST 6: \$a is not less than or equal to \$b</P>";
}
```

9. Close your PHP block and add some more HTML so that the document is valid:

```
?>
</BODY>
</HTML>
```

Figure 5.9 The comparison script running.

10. Save the file with the name `comparisonscript.php` and place this file in the document root of your Web server.

11. Open your Web browser and type `http://127.0.0.1/comparisonscript.php`. See Figure 5.9.

The original values, as well as the results of the various comparisons, are printed to the screen. The last group of operators you'll tackle are logical operators, which are also used frequently inside blocks of code.

Logical Operators

Logical operators allow your script to determine the status of conditions (such as the comparisons in the preceding section). In the context of `if...else` or `while` statements, logical operators execute certain code based on which conditions are true and which are false.

For now, focus on the `&&` (and) and `||` (or) operators to determine the validity of a few comparisons.

1. Open a new file in your text editor and type the following HTML:

```
<HTML>
<HEAD>
<TITLE>Using Logical Operators</TITLE>
</HEAD>
<BODY>
```

2. Start a PHP block and create two variables with values. The comparisons in this script are based on these two variables:

```
<?
$degrees = "95";
$hot = "yes";
```

3. Within an `if...else` statement, test whether `$degrees` is greater than 100 or if the value of `$hot` is yes. Depending on the result of the two comparisons, one of the `echo` statements will print:

```
if (($degrees > 100) || ($hot == "yes")) {
    echo "<P>TEST 1: It's <strong>really</strong> hot!</P>";
} else {
    echo "<P>TEST 1: It's bearable.</P>";
}
```

A NOTE ON PARENTHESES

Because this conditional expression is actually made up of two smaller conditional expressions, an extra set of parentheses surrounds it.

4. Repeat the same `if...else` statement as in Step 3, but change the operator from the || operator to the && operator:

```
if (($degrees > 100) && ($hot == "yes")) {
echo "<P>TEST 2: It's <strong>really</strong> hot!</P>";
} else {
echo "<P> TEST 2: It's bearable.</P>";
}
```

5. Close your PHP block and add some more HTML so that the document is valid:

```
?>
</BODY>
</HTML>
```

Figure 5.10 The logical script running.

6. Save the file with the name `logicalscript.php` and place this file in the document root of your Web server.

7. Open your Web browser and type `http://127.0.0.1/logicalscript.php`. See Figure 5.10.

The text message associated with each comparison result is printed to the screen. In the first test, only one expression has to be true, and that is satisfied by `$hot` having a value of `yes`. In the second test, both expressions have to be true, and they are not; `$degrees` has a value of 95, which is not greater than 100, even though `$hot` has a value of `yes`. In this case, the second message is displayed.

Numerous other types of operators are used in PHP. They are explained as they appear throughout the book. The operators listed in this chapter give you a solid foundation in the basics of using variables and operators. In the next chapter, you'll use your newly acquired knowledge of variables and operators to build scripts that perform more intriguing actions than those explained so far.

6

Using PHP Variables

Now that you know a little bit about variables in general, it's time to take that knowledge one step further and do more interesting things with variables. In this chapter, you'll learn how to do the following:

- Use HTML forms to send variables to your scripts.
- Use environment variables.

Getting Variables from Forms

HTML forms contain at least the following elements:

- A method
- An action
- A submit button

In your HTML code, the first line of a form looks something like this:

```
<FORM METHOD="post" ACTION="yourscript.php">
```

When you click a submission button in an HTML form, variables are sent to the script specified by the action via the specified method. The method can be either POST or GET. Variables passed from a form to a PHP script are placed in the superglobal called $_POST or $_GET, depending on the form method. In the next section, you'll see how this works by creating an HTML form and accompanying PHP script that performs calculations, depending on the form input.

Creating a Calculation Form

In this section, you'll create the front end to a calculation script. This form will contain two input fields and a radio button to select the calculation type. We are going to create a new form in HTML and use the POST method to send data to the back-end processing script. Let's look at how easy it is to do:

1. Open a new file in your text editor.

2. Type the following HTML:

```
<HTML>
<HEAD>
<TITLE>Calculation Form</TITLE>
</HEAD>
<BODY>
```

3. Begin your form. Assume that the method is POST and the action is a script called calculate.php:

```
<FORM METHOD="post" ACTION="calculate.php">
```

4. Create an input field for the first value with a text label:

```
<P>Value 1: <INPUT TYPE="text" NAME="val1" SIZE=10></P>
```

5. Create an input field for the second value with a text label:

```
<P>Value 2: <INPUT TYPE="text" NAME="val2" SIZE=10></P>
```

6. Add a submit button:

```
<P><INPUT TYPE="submit" NAME="submit" VALUE="Calculate"></P>
```

7. Close your form and add more HTML so that the document is valid:

```
</FORM>
</BODY>
</HTML>
```

8. Save the file with the name calculate_form.html and place this file in the document root of your Web server.

Figure 6.1 Calculate form.

9. Open your Web browser and type http://127.0.0.1/calculate_form.html. See Figure 6.1.

You will see a form containing the Value 1 and Value 2 fields, along with a Calculate button. Take a moment to examine the HTML form, to understand just how variables will get their names.

When submitted, this form will send two variables to your script, $_POST[val1] and $_POST[val2], because those are the NAMEs used in each text field. The values for those variables are the values typed in the form fields by the user.

There's one more item to add: a series of radio buttons to determine the type of calculation to perform on the two values.

1. Open calculate_form.html in your text editor.

2. Add this block before the submit button:

```
<P>Calculation:<br>
<INPUT TYPE="radio" NAME="calc" VALUE="add"> add<br>
<INPUT TYPE="radio" NAME="calc" VALUE="subtract"> subtract<br>
<INPUT TYPE="radio" NAME="calc" VALUE="multiply"> multiply<br>
<INPUT TYPE="radio" NAME="calc" VALUE="divide"> divide</P>
```

3. Save the file and place it in the document root of your Web server.

Figure 6.2 Updated calculate form.

4. Open your Web browser and type http://127.0.0.1/ calculate_form.html. See Figure 6.2.

Your form will now contain the Value 1 and Value 2 fields, a set of radio buttons, and a Calculate button. Now, in addition to the two values ($_POST[val1] and $_POST[val2]), a variable called $_POST[calc] will be sent to your script. Move on to the next section and create the calculation script.

Creating the Calculation Script

According to the form action in `calculate_form.html`, you need a script called `calculate.php`. The goal of this script is to accept the two values (`$_POST[val1]` and `$_POST[val2]`) and perform a calculation according to the value of `$_POST[calc]`.

1. Open a new file in your text editor.

2. Start a PHP block and prepare an `if` statement that checks for the presence of the three values:

```
<?
if (($_POST[val1] == "") || ($_POST[val2] == "") || ($_POST[calc] =="")) {
    // more code goes here
}
```

This statement says "If any of these three variables do not have a value, do something else."

Figure 6.3 The initial calculation script.

3. Replace "more code goes here" with the following two lines:

```
header("Location:
calculate_form.html");
exit;
```

The entire list of changes is shown in Figure 6.3.

The first of these two lines outputs a header statement—in this case, one that sends the browser back to the calculation form. The second line causes the script to exit. So if any of the three required variables do not have a value, this action will occur.

> ## WARNING: WHITE SPACE!
>
> Be sure that there are no line breaks, spaces, or any other text before your PHP block starts. You cannot use the `header()` function if output has already been sent to the browser.

4. Begin an `if...else` statement to perform the correct calculation, based on the value of `$_POST[calc]`, starting with a value of `add`:

```
if ($_POST[calc] == "add") {
    $result = $_POST[val1] + $_POST[val2];
```

5. Continue the statement for the remaining three calculation types and then close your PHP block:

```
} else if ($_POST[calc] == "subtract") {
    $result = $_POST[val1] - $_POST[val2];
} else if ($_POST[calc] == "multiply") {
    $result = $_POST[val1] * $_POST[val2];
} else if ($_POST[calc] == "divide") {
    $result = $_POST[val1] / $_POST[val2];
}
?>
```

6. Start the HTML output:

```
<HTML>
<HEAD>
<TITLE>Calculation Result</TITLE>
</HEAD>
<BODY>
```

7. Using HTML mingled with PHP code, display the value of `$result`:

```
<P>The result of the calculation is: <? echo "$result"; ?></P>
```

8. Add some more HTML so that the document is valid:

```
</BODY>
</HTML>
```

9. Save the file with the name `calculate.php`, and place this file in the document root of your Web server.

In the next section, you'll submit the form and even try to break it, which is just a bit of good, healthy debugging.

Submitting Your Form and Getting Results

Now that you've created both the front end (form) and the back end (script), it's time to hold your breath and test it.

1. To access the calculation form, open your Web browser and type `http://127.0.0.1/calculate_form.html`.

2. Click the Calculate button without typing anything in the form fields. Your Web browser will reload the page because you didn't enter any values for the three required fields.

3. Enter a value for Value 1, but not for Value 2, and do not select a calculation option. After you click Calculate, the page should reload.

4. Enter a value for Value 2, but not for Value 1, and do not select a calculation option. After you click Calculate, the page should reload.

5. Enter a value for Value 1 and for Value 2, but do not select a calculation option. After you click Calculate, the page should reload.

6. Select a calculation option, but do not enter any values for Value 1 or Value 2. After you click Calculate, the page should reload.

Now that you've debugged the script by attempting to bypass your validation routine, try some calculations, such as:

Figure 6.4 The addition result for the calculation script.

1. Enter 9732 for Value 1 and 27 for Value 2.

2. Select add and click the Calculate button (see Figure 6.4).

   The result of the addition calculation is printed on the screen.

   Knock yourself out by trying all sorts of number calculations to prove that it works.

HTTP Environment Variables

When a Web browser makes a request of a Web server, it sends along with the request a list of extra variables. These are called *environment variables*, and they can be very useful for displaying dynamic content or authorizing users.

The `phpinfo()` function displays a wealth of information about your Web server software and the version of PHP you are running, in addition to the basic HTTP environment. Let's see what you have.

1. Open a new file in your text editor.

2. Type the following line of PHP code:

   ```
   <? phpinfo(); ?>
   ```

3. Save the file with the name `phpinfo.php` and place this file in the document root of your Web server.

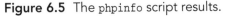

Figure 6.5 The `phpinfo` script results.

4. Open your Web browser and type `http://127.0.0.1/phpinfo.php`. See Figure 6.5.

You should see a very long page full of interesting information.

DIFFERENT LOOK ON YOUR BROWSER?

This information will differ, not only from machine to machine, but also from platform to platform and version to version. Your results will vary, but the overall template is the same.

As you scroll down, look for a section titled Apache Environment. In the next sections, you'll learn how to use two environment variables found here: `REMOTE_ADDR` and `HTTP_USER_AGENT`. For an explanation of some of the other HTTP environment variables shown in the `phpinfo()` output, visit `http://hoohoo.ncsa.uiuc.edu/cgi/env.html`.

Retrieving and Using REMOTE_ADDR

By default, environment variables are available to PHP scripts as `$VAR_NAME`. For example, the `REMOTE_ADDR` environment variable is already contained as `$REMOTE_ADDR`. However, to be absolutely sure that you're reading the correct value, you can use the `getenv()` function to assign a value to a variable of your choice.

The REMOTE_ADDR environment variable contains the IP address of the machine making the request. Let's get the value of your REMOTE_ADDR.

1. Open a new file in your text editor.

2. Open a PHP block, and then use getenv() to place the value of REMOTE_ADDR in a variable called $address:

```
<?
$address = getenv("REMOTE_ADDR");
```

3. Print the value of $address to the screen and close your PHP block:

```
echo "Your IP address is $address.";
?>
```

Figure 6.6 The remote address script.

4. Save the file with the name remoteaddress.php, and then place this file in the document root of your Web server.

5. Open your Web browser and type **http://127.0.0.1/ remoteaddress.php**. See Figure 6.6.

Your current IP address is printed to the screen.

IP ADDRESS DIFFERENT?

Your IP address will differ from that shown here, which is my own IP at the moment I ran this script.

In the next section, you'll get the value of another handy environment variable, HTTP_USER_AGENT, which is the environment variable that holds the identifying string of the Web browser being used.

Retrieving and Using HTTP_USER_AGENT

The HTTP_USER_AGENT variable contains the browser type, browser version, language encoding, and platform. For example, the following value string refers to the Netscape browser, version 7.1, in English, on the Windows platform:

```
Mozilla/5.0 (Windows; U; Windows NT 5.1; en-US; rv:1.4)
Gecko/20030624 Netscape/7.1 (ax).
```

Here is another common HTTP_USER_AGENT value:

```
Mozilla/4.0 (compatible; MSIE 6.0; Windows NT 5.1)
```

This value refers to Microsoft Internet Explorer (MSIE) version 6.0 on Windows. Sometimes, you will see MSIE return an HTTP_USER_AGENT value that looks like a Netscape value, such as this one, which begins with Mozilla, until you notice that the value says it's compatible and is actually MSIE 6.0.

Finally, don't count out the text-only browsers! A Lynx HTTP_USER_AGENT value looks something like this:

```
Lynx/2.8rel.3 libwww-FM/2.14
```

Let's find your HTTP_USER_AGENT.

1. Open a new file in your text editor.

2. Open a PHP block, and then use getenv() to place the value of HTTP_USER_AGENT in a variable called $agent:

```
<?
$agent = getenv("HTTP_USER_AGENT");
```

3. Print the value of $agent to the screen and then close your PHP block:

```
echo " You are using $agent.";
?>
```

Figure 6.7 The useragent script.

4. Save the file with the name useragent.php and place this file in the document root of your Web server.

5. Open your Web browser and type **http://127.0.0.1/ useragent.php**. See Figure 6.7.

Your current HTTP_USER_AGENT value is printed to the screen.

USER AGENT DIFFERENT?

Your user agent string might be different than the one shown, because each browser, version, and platform creates its own identification string.

In this chapter, you've used several types of variables, including variables from forms. Variables are absolutely essential bits of your scripts, so becoming intimately familiar with them is a good thing. In the next chapter, you'll learn many of the basic tasks for Web developers, including displaying dynamic content, sending e-mail, and working with your file system—all of which build on the use of variables.

NEW VERSION ALERT!

One final note for those of you that have used PHP 5.0 and previous versions: The HTTP_*_VARS variables, such as HTTP_SERVER_VARS or HTTP_POST_VARS, are no longer supported as of release 6.0.

PART III

Start with the Simple Stuff

7

Displaying Dynamic Content

The Web is a dynamic environment, so why not use your programming skills to display dynamic content? Dynamic content can be as simple or as complex as you want it to be. In this chapter, you'll learn how to do the following:

- Display browser-specific HTML.
- Display platform-specific HTML.
- Use PHP string functions on HTML form input.
- Create a redirection menu using an HTML form and the header() function.

Displaying Browser-Specific HTML

In the previous chapter, you learned to retrieve and print the HTTP_USER_AGENT environment variable to the screen. In this chapter, you'll do something a bit more interesting with the value of HTTP_USER_AGENT, and that's to print browser-specific HTML.

However, having seen some of the possible values of HTTP_USER_AGENT in the last chapter, you can imagine that there are hundreds of slightly different values. So it's time to learn some basic pattern matching.

You'll use the preg_match() function to perform this task. This function needs two arguments: what you're looking for, and where you're looking:

```
preg_match("/[what you're looking for]/", "[where you're looking]");
```

This function returns a value of true or false, which you can use in an if...else block to do whatever you want. The goal of the first script is to determine whether a Web browser is Microsoft Internet Explorer, Netscape, or something else.

Within the value of HTTP_USER_AGENT, Netscape always uses the string Mozilla to identify itself. Unfortunately, the value of HTTP_USER_AGENT for Microsoft Internet Explorer also uses Mozilla to show that it's compatible. Luckily, it also uses the string MSIE, so you can search for that. If the value of HTTP_USER_AGENT doesn't contain either Firefox or MSIE, chances are very good that it's not one of those Web browsers.

1. Open a new file in your text editor and start a PHP block, and then use getenv() to place the value of HTTP_USER_AGENT in a variable called $agent:

```
<?
$agent = getenv("HTTP_USER_AGENT");
```

2. Start an if...else statement to find which of the preg_match() functions is true, starting with the search for MSIE:

```
if (preg_match("/MSIE/i", "$agent")) {
    $result = "You are using Microsoft Internet Explorer.";
}
```

3. Continue the statement, testing for `Mozilla`:

```
else if (preg_match("/Mozilla/i", "$agent")) {
    $result = "You are using Firefox.";
}
```

CASE SENSITIVITY

The `i` in the `preg_match()` function performs a case-insensitive search.

4. Finish the statement by defining a default:

```
else {
    $result = "You are using $agent";
}
```

5. Close your PHP block and add some HTML to begin the display:

```
?>
<HTML>
<HEAD>
<TITLE>Browser Match Results</TITLE>
</HEAD>
<BODY>
```

6. Type the following PHP code to print the result of the `if...else` statement:

```
<? echo "<P>$result</P>"; ?>
```

7. Add some more HTML so that the document is valid:

```
</BODY>
</HTML>
```

8. Save the file with the name `browsermatch.php` and place this file in the document root of your Web server.

9. Open your Web browser and type `http://127.0.0.1/browsermatch.php`.

Figure 7.1 The Browser Match script for Netscape.

Depending on the Web browser you use, you might see a result such as Figure 7.1…

Figure 7.2 The Browser Match script for Internet Explorer.

…or Figure 7.2.

If you're using neither Mozilla nor Microsoft Internet Explorer, the actual value of HTTP_USER_AGENT will be printed.

Various flavors of Microsoft Internet Explorer (MSIE) account for approximately 78% of Web browsers in use, whereas versions of Mozilla (NS) take up about 15%. Throw in the die-hard Lynx, Opera, Konquerer, and other users to reach 100%.

Although an 80/20 split might seem like a majority, if 500 million people have access to the Internet, 100 million non-MSIE users is a huge number of users to consider when developing a good Web site. HotWired maintains a browser reference at http://hotwired.lycos.com/webmonkey/reference/browser_chart/, which shows you some of the differences between the major browsers. In the next section, you'll take into consideration how not all platforms are created equal and, in fact, might not display HTML similarly either.

Displaying Platform-Specific HTML

There are differences not only between browsers, but also between platforms. This difference is most clear with regard to fonts and font sizes. In the Windows world, you have fonts such as Times New Roman and Courier New. Slight variations of these fonts appear on the Macintosh and Linux/UNIX platforms; they are called Times and Courier. It doesn't end there—the font sizes all display differently. A 10-point font on Macintosh or Linux is sometimes barely legible, but if you bump it up to 11 or 12 point, you're in business. If that same 12-point font is viewed on Windows, however, it might look like your text is trying to take over the world.

So what to do? Use your new pattern-matching skills to extract the platform from the HTTP_USER_AGENT string, and then display platform-specific HTML. As with matching on a keyword—which you did in the previous section—to nail down the platform, you also need to know what you're looking for. In the next script, you'll check for the keywords Win and Linux and print an appropriate style sheet block in your HTML result page.

1. Open a new file in your text editor, start a PHP block, and use getenv() to place the value of HTTP_USER_AGENT in a variable called $agent:

```
<?
$agent = getenv("HTTP_USER_AGENT");
```

2. Start an if...else statement to find which of the preg_match() functions is true, starting with the search for Win:

```
if (preg_match("/Win/i", "$agent")) {
    $style = "win";
}
```

3. Continue the statement, testing for `Linux`:

```
else if (preg_match("/Linux/i", "$agent")) {
    $style = "linux";
}
```

4. Create a basic style sheet block for Windows users:

```
$win_style = "<style type=\"text/css\">p, ul, ol, li
        {font-family:Arial;font-size:10pt;font-weight:normal;}
h1       {font-family:Arial;font-size:16pt;font-weight:bold;}
h2       {font-family:Arial;font-size:14pt;font-weight:bold;}
strong   {font-family:Arial;font-size:10pt;font-weight:bold;}
em       {font-family:Arial;font-size:10pt;font-style:italic;}
</style>";
```

USING QUOTATION MARKS IN PHP

When you use quotation marks inside other quotation marks, the inner pair must be delineated from the outside pair using the escape (\) character (also known as a backslash).

5. Create a basic style sheet block for Linux users:

```
$linux_style = "<style type=\"text/css\">
p, ul, ol, li {font-family:Times;font-size:12pt;font-weight:normal;}
h1       {font-family:Times;font-size:18pt;font-weight:bold;}
h2       {font-family:Times;font-size:16pt;font-weight:bold;}
strong   {font-family:Times;font-size:12pt;font-weight:bold;}
em       {font-family:Times;font-size:12pt;font-style:italic;}
</style>";
```

6. Close your PHP block and add the following HTML:

```
?>
<HTML>
<HEAD>
<TITLE>Platform Matching</TITLE>
```

7. Type the following PHP code, creating an `if...else` statement used to print the correct style sheet block:

```
<?
if ($style == "win") {
    echo "$win_style";
} else if ($style == "linux") {
    echo "$linux_style";
}
?>
```

8. Close the top section of your HTML and start the body:

```
</HEAD>
<BODY>
```

9. Type the following HTML to show the use of your style sheet:

```
<h1 align=center>This is a level 1 heading</h1>
<h2 align=center>Look! A level 2 heading</h2>
<P align=center>This is a simple paragraph with some
<strong>bold</strong> and <em>emphasized</em> text.</P>
```

10. Add some more HTML so that the document is valid:

```
</BODY>
</HTML>
```

11. Save the file with the name `platformmatch.php` and place it in the document root of your Web server.

12. Open your Web browser and type `http://127.0.0.1/` `platformmatch.php`.

Figure 7.3 The Platform Match Style using Netscape.

Depending on the Web browser you use, you might see a result such as this shown in Figure 7.3...

Figure 7.4 The Platform Match Style using Internet Explorer.

...or Figure 7.4.

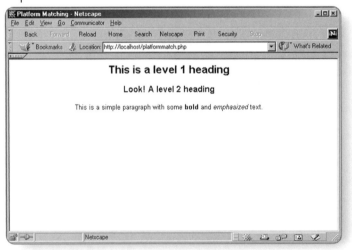

You can see that the proper style sheet block was printed, based on the result of the platform match. In the next section, you'll move away from pattern matching and work with some of the string functions in PHP to modify form input before displaying it back to the browser.

Working with String Functions

Numerous string functions are built into PHP, all of which are designed to make your life easier. Suppose that you have to normalize strings for news headlines or product ID numbers, or calculate the length of a string before trying to stuff it into a database field. Those are just a few of the string functions you'll learn about in the next section. For more string functions, take a look at the PHP manual at http://www.php.net/strings. The function list grows daily as more people contribute to the language.

Creating an Input Form

In this section, you'll create the front end to a string modification script. This form will contain one text area and several radio buttons. The radio buttons will determine the string function to use.

1. Open a new file in your text editor and type the following HTML:

```
<HTML>
<HEAD>
<TITLE>Generic Input Form</TITLE>
</HEAD>
<BODY>
```

2. Begin your form. Assume that the method is POST, and the action is a script called display_input.php:

```
<FORM METHOD="post" ACTION="display_input.php">
```

3. Create a text area with a text label:

```
<P><strong>Text Field:</strong><br>
<TEXTAREA NAME="text1" COLS=45 ROWS=5 WRAP=virtual></TEXTAREA></P>
```

4. Add this block of radio buttons:

```
<P><strong>String Function:</strong><br>
<INPUT TYPE="radio" NAME="func" VALUE="md5"> get md5<br>
<INPUT TYPE="radio" NAME="func" VALUE="strlen"> get length of string<br>
<INPUT TYPE="radio" NAME="func" VALUE="strrev"> reverse the string<br>
```

```
<INPUT TYPE="radio" NAME="func" VALUE="strtoupper"> make string
uppercase<br>
<INPUT TYPE="radio" NAME="func" VALUE="strtolower"> make string
lowercase<br>
<INPUT TYPE="radio" NAME="func" VALUE="ucwords"> make first letter of all
words uppercase</P>
```

PHP RADIO BUTTON NAMING

The value for each radio button is its exact PHP function name. This will make the back-end script very simple to create, as you'll see in the next section.

---

5. Add a submit button:

```
<P><INPUT TYPE="submit" NAME="submit" VALUE="Do Something With the
String"></P>
```

6. Close your form and add some more HTML so that the document is valid:

```
</FORM>
</BODY>
</HTML>
```

Figure 7.5 A generic form in PHP.

7. Save the file with the name `generic_form.html` and place this file in the document root of your Web server (see Figure 7.5).

8. Open your Web browser and type `http://127.0.0.1/generic_form.html`.

You'll see a form with a text area and several radio buttons, along with a Do Something with the String form submission button. In the next section, you'll create the back-end script. That script will expect two variables: `$_POST[text1]` and `$_POST[func]`.

Creating a Script to Display Form Values

According to the form action in `generic_form.html`, you need a script called `display_input.php`. The goal of this script is to accept the text in `$_POST[text1]` and use a particular string function (the value of `$_POST[func]`) to get a new result (`$result`).

1. Open a new file in your text editor and type the following PHP code. This will ensure that the user is sent back to the form if no value is entered in the text area and no function is selected from the list of radio buttons:

```
<?
if (($_POST[text1] == "") || ($_POST[func] == "")) {
    header("Location: generic_form.html");
    exit;
}
```

2. Type the next bit of PHP, which assigns the value of the function output to a variable called `$result`, and then close the PHP block:

```
$result = $_POST[func]($_POST[text1]);
?>
```

3. Start the HTML output:

```
<HTML>
<HEAD>
<TITLE>Generic Input Results</TITLE>
</HEAD>
<BODY>
```

4. Display the value of `$result`:

```
<? echo "$result"; ?>
```

5. Add a link back to the form:

```
<P><a href="generic_form.html">Go again!</a></P>
```

6. Add some more HTML so that the document is valid:

```
</BODY>
</HTML>
```

7. Save the file with the name `display_input.php` and place this file in the document root of your Web server.

Your code should look something like this:

```
<?
if (($_POST[func] == "") || ($_POST[text1] == "")) {

        header("Location: generic_form.html");
        exit;
}
$result = $_POST[func]($_POST[text1]);
?>
<HTML>
<HEAD>
<TITLE>Generic Input Results</TITLE>
</HEAD>
<BODY>
<? echo "$result"; ?>
<p><a href="generic_form.html">Go again!</a></p>
</BODY>
</HTML>
```

In the next section, you'll submit the form and see all these different types of string functions at work.

Submitting Your Form and Getting Results

Now that you've created both a front-end form and a back-end script, it's time to try them out.

1. Open your Web browser and type `http://127.0.0.1/generic_form.html`.

2. Type the following text in the text area:

```
I think PHP is just the coolest server-side scripting language around!
Who knew it would be this simple?
```

A NOTE ON TEXT ENTRY

You might want to copy that chunk of text to the clipboard, because it will be used in all of the following examples.

Figure 7.6 The generic form filled out.

3. Select the get md5 radio button and click the Do Something with the String button, as shown in Figure 7.6.

Figure 7.7 The MD5 checksum calculation script display.

MD5 HASHES

The md5() function gets a *hash* of the string. A hash is like a digital summary of the string. It can be used to compare versions of strings (or files) to determine whether the versions differ (see Figure 7.7).

You should see a hash of the string, along with a link back to the form. Return to the form and enter the same text, only this time select the button that will use the strlen() function to find the length of the string, including white space and all characters.

Figure 7.8 The ucwords script display.

Continue testing each of the remaining functions. When you select the button to use the strrev() function, you will see your original string has been completely reversed. The strtoupper() function returns the string with all letters in uppercase, whereas the strtolower() function returns the string with all letters in lowercase. Finally, use the ucwords() function to return the string with the first letter of each word in uppercase (see Figure 7.8).

Redirecting to a New Location

Redirecting a user to a new location means that your script has sent an HTTP header to the browser, indicating a new location. HTTP headers of any kind (authentication, redirection, cookies, and so on) must be sent to the browser before anything else, including white space, line breaks, and any characters.

Although you've already used the `header()` function to redirect the user in the case of an incomplete form, in the next section, you'll create a specific redirection menu; the goal is to have the users select a new location from a drop-down menu and then have the script automatically send them there.

Creating a Redirection Form

In this section, you'll create the front end to a redirection script. This form will contain a drop-down list of the names of various Web sites. The value for each option is the Web site's URL.

1. Open a new file in your text editor and type the following HTML:

```
<HTML>
<HEAD>
<TITLE> Redirection Menu</TITLE>
</HEAD>
<BODY>
```

2. Begin your form. Assume that the method is POST and the action is a script called `do_redirect.php`:

```
<FORM METHOD="post" ACTION="do_redirect.php">
```

3. Add this drop-down list:

```
<P>Send me to:
<SELECT name="location">
    <OPTION value="">-- Select One --</OPTION>
    <OPTION value="http://www.thickbook.com/">thickbook.com</OPTION>
    <OPTION value="http://www.i2ii.com/">i2i Interactive</OPTION>
```

```
<OPTION value="http://www.php.net/">PHP.net</OPTION>
<OPTION value="http://www.zend.com/">Zend Technologies</OPTION>
</SELECT>
```

LIST BOXES AND PHP

Note that the "value" of a list box item is the string you will get back when the user makes a selection in that list box.

---

4. Add a submit button:

```
<P><INPUT TYPE="submit" NAME="submit" VALUE="Go!"></P>
```

5. Close your form and add some more HTML so that the document is valid:

```
</FORM>
</BODY>
</HTML>
```

Figure 7.9 Redirection with PHP.

6. Save the file with the name `redirect_form.html` and place this file in the document root of your Web server (see Figure 7.9).

7. Open your Web browser and type **http://127.0.0.1/ redirect_form.html**.

In the next section, you'll create the back-end script. That script will expect one variable: `$_POST[location]`.

Creating the Redirection Script and Testing It

According to the form action in `redirect_form.html`, you need a script called `do_redirect.php`. The goal of this script is to accept the value of `$_POST[location]` and print that value within the `header()` function so that the user is redirected to the chosen location.

1. Open a new file in your text editor and type the following PHP to create the proper redirection header, including a check to ensure that something was selected:

```php
<?
if ($_POST[location] == ""){
    header("Location: redirect_form.html");
    exit;
} else {
    header("Location: $_POST[location]");
    exit;
}
?>
```

2. Save the file with the name `do_redirect.php` and place this file in the document root of your Web server.

3. Open your Web browser and type **http://127.0.0.1/redirect_form.html**.

Figure 7.10 The result of the redirection script.

4. Select PHP.net from the drop-down list and click the Go! button (see Figure 7.10).

Users are now redirected to the PHP Web site. Try some of the other selections, or add your own, for practice.

In this chapter, you learned some of the different types of dynamic content that can be used in a Web site and some other things you can do, such as redirect users based on a drop-down menu. In the next chapter, you'll learn how to utilize one of the more popular Web tools—sending e-mail.

8

Sending E-Mail

Using PHP to send the contents of a form to a specified e-mail address is so easy that you'll wonder why more people don't do it every day. In this chapter, you'll learn how to do the following:

- Modify the PHP configuration file so you can send mail.
- Create and send a simple feedback form.
- Use the $PHP_SELF variable to create a feedback form with custom error messages.

Using an SMTP Server

SMTP is an acronym for Simple Mail Transfer Protocol, and an SMTP server is a machine that transports mail, just like a Web server is a machine that displays Web pages when requested. An SMTP server is sometimes referred to as an outgoing mail server, which brings me to the point—you need one in order to complete the exercises in this chapter. On Linux/UNIX, Sendmail and Qmail are popular packages. On Windows, the SMTP service in the Windows NT Service Pack, or the service built into the Windows 2000 operating system, is often used.

However, if you have installed Apache, PHP, and MySQL as part of a development environment on your personal machine, you probably do not have SMTP running locally. If that's the case, you can access an outgoing mail server that might already be available to you.

EXPECTED INSTALLS

If you skipped the first three chapters of this book and are using PHP as part of an Internet service provider's virtual hosting package, the SMTP server should already be installed on that machine, and PHP should be properly configured to access it.

If your machine is connected to the Internet via a dial-up connection, DSL, cable, or other type of access, you can use your Internet service provider's outgoing mail server. For example, if your development machine is a Windows box with a DSL connection to the Internet, you can use something like `mail.yourprovider.com` as your outgoing mail server. The rule of thumb is that whatever you have configured within your e-mail client (Eudora, Outlook, Netscape Mail, and so on) as your outgoing mail server will also function within your PHP code as your SMTP server. The trick is making PHP aware of this little fact, which you'll learn about next.

SMTP-Related Changes in `php.ini`

In the `php.ini` master configuration file, there are a few directives that need to be set up so that the `mail()` function works properly. Open `php.ini` with a text editor and look for these lines:

```
[mail function]
; For Win32 only.
SMTP = localhost
; For Win32 only.
sendmail_from = me@localhost.com
; For Unix only. You may supply arguments as well (default: 'sendmail -t -i').
;sendmail_path =
```

If you are using Windows, you'll need to modify the first two directives, `SMTP` and `sendmail_from`. If you plan to use the outgoing mail server of your ISP (in this example, suppose it's called DSLProvider.net), the entry in `php.ini` would look like this:

```
SMTP = mail.dslprovider.net
```

The second configuration directive is `sendmail_from`, and this is the e-mail address used in the From header of the outgoing e-mail. It can be overwritten in the mail script itself but normally operates as the default value. For example:

```
sendmail_from = youraddress@yourdomain.com
```

Of course, replace `youraddress@yourdomain.com` with your own address.

If you're on Linux or a UNIX variant, `sendmail_path` is all you need to worry about, and it should look something like this:

```
sendmail_path = /usr/sbin/sendmail
```

Or, if you're using Qmail:

```
sendmail_path = /var/qmail/bin/sendmail
```

In the `sendmail_path` directive, you can also set configuration flags to specify queuing options or to explicitly set the `Return-Path` header, such as:

```
sendmail_path = /usr/sbin/sendmail -t -fyou@yourdomain.com
```

After making changes to the `php.ini` file, restart the Web server and use the `phpinfo()` function to verify that the changes have been made. When that's done, you're ready to send some e-mail using PHP.

A Simple Feedback Form

A simple feedback form usually contains fields for the respondent's name and e-mail address and a text area for some sort of message. In this section, you'll create two files: one for the feedback form, and one for the PHP script to process the form, send the mail, and return a response to the browser.

Creating the Feedback Form

In this section, you'll create the first half of the form/script combo—the feedback form itself, often referred to as the front-end form.

1. Open a new file in your text editor.

2. Type the following HTML:

```
<HTML>
<HEAD>
<TITLE>Simple Feedback Form</TITLE>
</HEAD>
<BODY>
```

3. Begin your form. Assume that the method is POST and the action is a script called `send_simpleform.php`:

```
<FORM METHOD="POST" ACTION="send_simpleform.php">
```

4. Create an input field for the user's name with a text label:

```
<P><strong>Your Name:</strong><br>
<INPUT type="text" NAME="sender_name" SIZE=30></P>
```

5. Create an input field for the user's e-mail address with a text label:

```
<P><strong>Your E-Mail Address:</strong><br>
<INPUT type="text" NAME="sender_email" SIZE=30></P>
```

6. Create a text area to hold the message with a text label:

```
<P><strong>Message:</strong><br>
<TEXTAREA NAME="message" COLS=30 ROWS=5 WRAP=virtual></TEXTAREA></P>
```

7. Add a submit button:

```
<P><INPUT TYPE="submit" NAME="submit" VALUE="Send This Form"></P>
```

8. Close your form and add some more HTML so that the document is valid:

```
</FORM>
</BODY>
</HTML>
```

9. Save the file with the name `simple_form.html`, and place this file in the document root of your Web server.

Figure 8.1 A simple form for mailing.

10. Open your Web browser and type **http://127.0.0.1/ simple_form.html**. See Figure 8.1.

You should see a form containing a text field for the person's name, a text field for the person's e-mail address, a text area for the message, and a button that says Send This Form.

In the next section, you'll create the back-end script. That script will expect three variables: $_POST[sender_name], $_POST[sender_email], and $_POST[message].

Creating a Script to Mail Your Form

According to the form action in simple_form.html, you need a script called send_simpleform.php. The goal of this script is to accept the text in $_POST[sender_name], $_POST[sender_email], and $_POST[message] format, send an e-mail, and display a confirmation to the Web browser.

1. Open a new file in your text editor.

2. Begin a PHP block and then add some error-checking code into the mix:

```
<?
if (($_POST[sender_name] == "") ||
    ($_POST[sender_email] == "") ||
    ($_POST[message] == "")) {
    header("Location: simple_form.html");
    exit;
}
```

3. Start building a message string, which will contain the content for the e-mail itself:

```
$msg = "E-MAIL SENT FROM WWW SITE\n";
```

4. Continue building the message string by adding an entry for the sender's name:

```
$msg .= "Sender's Name:\t$_POST[sender_name]\n";
```

NEWLINES

The use of the newline (\n) character ensures that your code will print on multiple lines. This is helpful when you are viewing your HTML source.

BUILDING A MESSAGE STRING

The next few steps will continue building the message string by concatenating smaller strings to form one long message string.

---

5. Continue building the message string by adding an entry for the sender's e-mail address:

```
$msg .= "Sender's E-Mail:\t$_POST[sender_email]\n";
```

6. Continue building the message string by adding an entry for the message:

```
$msg .= "Message:\t$_POST[message]\n";
```

7. Create a variable to hold the recipient's e-mail address (substitute your own):

```
$to = "you@youremail.com";
```

8. Create a variable to hold the subject of the e-mail:

```
$subject = "Web Site Feedback";
```

9. Create a variable to hold additional mail headers:

```
$mailheaders = "From: My Web Site <genericaddress@yourdomain.com>\n";
```

MAIL HEADERS

Mail headers are the strings at the beginning of mail messages that formulate their structure and essentially make them valid mail messages.

---

10. Add the following to the $mailheaders variable:

```
$mailheaders .= "Reply-To: $_POST[sender_email]\n";
```

11. Add the mail() function:

```
mail($to, $subject, $msg, $mailheaders);
```

Figure 8.2 The mail script.

12. Close your PHP block (see Figure 8.2):

```
?>
```

Although this code will send the mail, you should return something to the user's screen so that he knows the form has been sent. Otherwise, he might sit there and continually click the Send This Form button.

13. Start the HTML output:

```
<HTML>
<HEAD>
<TITLE>Simple Feedback Form Sent</TITLE>
</HEAD>
<BODY>
```

14. Add some information to tell the user what has happened:

```
<H1>The following e-mail has been sent:</H1>
```

15. Add the text label for the Your Name field and display the user's input, and do the same for the other fields:

```
<P><strong>Your Name:</strong><br>
<? echo "$_POST[sender_name]"; ?>
<P><strong>Your E-Mail Address:</strong><br>
<? echo "$_POST[sender_email]"; ?>
<P><strong>Message:</strong><br>
<? echo "$_POST[message]"; ?>
```

Figure 8.3 A simple mail sending script.

16. Add some more HTML so that the document is valid:

```
</BODY>
</HTML>
```

17. Save the file with the name send_simpleform.php and place this file in the document root of your Web server. Your code should look something like Figure 8.3.

A NOTE ON ERRORS

Don't worry if you get the error displayed here, indicating that the e-mail address is invalid. This will occur if you are working behind a firewall and use an internal e-mail account. Your own server should not display this error.

In the next section, you'll submit the form and see all these different types of string functions at work.

Submitting Your Form and Getting Results

Now that you've created both a front-end form and a back-end script, it's time to try them out.

1. Open your Web browser and type `http://127.0.0.1/simple_form.html`.

2. Type your name in the Your Name field.

Figure 8.4 The mail form in action.

3. Type your e-mail address in the Your E-Mail Address field.

4. Type the following message in the Message field:

```
PHP is so cool!
```

5. Click the Send This Form button (see Figure 8.4).

Figure 8.5 Mail alert.

The information you entered, along with a confirmation that your e-mail has been sent, will appear.

Now check your e-mail and see if a message is waiting for you (see Figure 8.5).

An e-mail sent through this form will look something like this. If it drives you crazy that the tabbed text doesn't line up properly, you can insert as much white space as you'd like in the message string.

1. Open `send_simpleform.php` in your text editor.

2. Modify the string containing `Sender's Name` by replacing the tab character (`\t`) with two spaces:

```
$msg .= "Sender's Name:  $_POST[sender_name}\n";
```

3. Modify the string containing `Sender's E-Mail` by replacing the tab character (`\t`) with four spaces:

```
$msg .= "Sender's E-Mail:    $_POST[sender_email]\n";
```

4. Modify the string containing `Message` by replacing the tab character (`\t`) with 10 spaces:

```
$msg .= "Message:          $_POST[message]\n";
```

5. Save the file and upload it to your server.

Submit the form again. When you receive the e-mail, this time it should all line up.

In the next section, you'll create custom error messages for when fields are blank, and you'll streamline the two-step process of sending mail into one cohesive script.

A Feedback Form with Custom Error Messages

In the previous section, you created two separate files. One file contained the front end (form), and the other contained the back end (script). In this section, you'll learn how to use the `$_SERVER[PHP_SELF]` variable in a form action to create a single file that holds both form and script, and how to create custom error messages when required fields are not completed.

Creating the Initial Script

As you did earlier in this chapter, the first step in creating a form/script pair is to create the front-end form. However, in this all-in-one form, the front-end form is simply the first half of the script and not a separate file.

1. Open a new file in your text editor.

2. Type the following HTML:

```
<HTML>
<HEAD>
```

```
<TITLE>All-In-One Feedback Form</TITLE>
</HEAD>
<BODY>
```

3. Start a PHP block and then create a variable called `$form_block`, which will hold the entire form. Start with the form action and assume that the method is POST and the action is `$_SERVER[PHP_SELF]`:

```
<?
$form_block = "
<FORM METHOD=\"POST\" ACTION=\"$_SERVER[PHP_SELF]\">
```

REMEMBER TO ESCAPE!

Because you're putting a long string inside a variable, chances are good that you'll have a quotation mark or two. Remember to escape all your quotation marks with a backslash!

---

4. Create an input field for the user's name with a text label:

```
<P><strong>Your Name:</strong><br>
<INPUT type=\"text\" NAME=\"sender_name\" SIZE=30></P>
```

5. Create an input field for the user's e-mail address with a text label:

```
<P><strong>Your E-Mail Address:</strong><br>
<INPUT type=\"text\" NAME=\"sender_email\" SIZE=30></P>
```

6. Create a text area to hold the message with a text label:

```
<P><strong>Message:</strong><br>
<TEXTAREA NAME=\"message\" COLS=30 ROWS=5 WRAP=virtual></TEXTAREA></P>
```

7. Add a submit button:

```
<P><INPUT TYPE=\"submit\" NAME=\"submit\" VALUE=\"Send This Form\"></P>
```

8. Close the form and then add the ending quotation marks and instruction terminator (semicolon):

```
</FORM>";
```

Figure 8.6 The all-in-one form.

9. Close the PHP block and then add some more HTML so that the document is valid:

```
?>
</BODY>
</HTML>
```

10. Save the file with the name `allinone_form.php`. See Figure 8.6.

If you looked at this code in your Web browser, you'd only see a title in the title bar. The burning question should be, "Why do we need all that HTML in a variable called $form_block?" In the next section, you'll add to the script so that it displays particular chunks of code based on certain actions. The string in $form_block is one of those chunks.

Adding Error Checking to the Script

The plan is to use the global variable $_SERVER[PHP_SELF], which has a value of the script's current name. So really, $_SERVER[PHP_SELF] will have a value of allinone_form.php in this instance. When you use $_SERVER[PHP_SELF] as a form action, you're saying, "When the submit button is clicked, reload this script and do something," instead of "When the submit button is clicked, go find another script and do something."

Now that you have a shell of a script, think about what this all-in-one script must do:

- Display the form.
- Submit the form.
- Check for errors.
- Print error messages without sending the form.
- Send the form if no errors are found.

Make a few modifications to the script to help it determine which actions it should take. Inside the `$form_block` variable, before the HTML code for the submit button, add this line:

```
<INPUT type=\"hidden\" name=\"op\" value=\"ds\">
```

This line creates a hidden variable called `$_POST[op]`, which has a value of `ds`. The `op` stands for "operation," and `ds` stands for "do something." I made these names up; they have nothing to do with any programming language. You can call them whatever you want, as long as you understand what they do (which you'll soon see).

Figure 8.7 The all-in-one script.

The `$_POST[op]` variable is present only if the form has been submitted. So if the value of `$_POST[op]` is not `ds`, the user hasn't seen the form. If the user hasn't seen the form, you need to show it, so add the following `if...else` statement before the end of the PHP block:

```
if ($_POST[op] != "ds") {
    // they need to see the form
    echo "$form_block";
}
```

You're not done yet, but your code should now look something like Figure 8.7.

You'll make a few more modifications in the next step to add your error messages. If the form is submitted, the value of $_POST[op] will be ds, and now you must account for that. Assume that all the form fields are required; after checking for the value of $_POST[op], you'll check for a value in all the fields.

1. Continue the if...else statement:

```
else if ($_POST[op] == "ds") {
```

2. Add an if statement within the parent statement to check for values. Start with $_POST[sender_name]:

```
if ($_POST[sender_name] == "") {
```

3. Create an error message for $_POST[sender_name] called $name_err:

```
$name_err = "<font color=red>Please enter your name!</font><br>";
```

4. Set the value of $send to "no":

```
$send = "no";
```

5. Create a similar if statement for $_POST[sender_email]:

```
if ($_POST[sender_email] == "") {
$email_err = "<font color=red>Please enter your e-mail
address!</font><br>";
$send = "no";
}
```

6. Create a similar if statement for $_POST[message]:

```
if ($_POST[message] == "") {
    $message_err = "<font color=red>Please enter a message!</font><br>";
    $send = "no";
}
```

7. Start an if...else statement to handle the value of $send:

```
if ($send != "no") {
    // it's ok to send!
```

8. Create a variable to hold the recipient's e-mail address (substitute your own):

```
$to = "you@youremail.com";
```

9. Create a variable to hold the subject of the e-mail:

```
$subject = "All-in-One Web Site Feedback";
```

10. Create a variable to hold additional mail headers:

```
$mailheaders = "From: My Web Site <genericaddress@yourdomain.com> \n";
```

11. Add to the `$mailheaders` variable:

```
$mailheaders .= "Reply-To: $_POST[sender_email]\n";
```

12. Build the message string:

```
$msg = "E-MAIL SENT FROM WWW SITE\n";
$msg .= "Sender's Name:    $_POST[sender_name]\n";
$msg .= "Sender's E-Mail:  $_POST[sender_email]\n";
$msg .= "Message:          $_POST[message]\n\n";
```

13. Add the `mail()` function:

```
mail($to, $subject, $msg, $mailheaders);
```

14. Add a simple statement to let the user know the mail has been sent and close the `if` statement:

```
echo "<P>Mail has been sent!</p>";
}
```

15. Continue the `if...else` statement to deal with a value of `no` for `$send`:

```
else if ($send == "no") {
```

16. Print the error messages:

```
echo "$name_err";
echo "$email_err";
echo "$message_err";
```

17. Print the form again:

```
echo "$form_block";
```

18. Close the current if...else block and the parent if...else block:

```
        }
    }
```

19. Save the file.

The entire code should look something like this:

```
<HTML>
<HEAD>
<TITLE>All-In-One Feedback Form</TITLE>
</HEAD>
<BODY>
<?
$form_block = "
<FORM METHOD=\"POST\" ACTION=\"$PHP_SELF\">
<P><strong>Your Name:</strong><br>
<INPUT type=\"text\" NAME=\"sender_name\"  SIZE=30></P>
<P><strong>Your E-Mail Address:</strong><br>
<INPUT type=\"text\" NAME=\"sender_email\"  SIZE=30></P>
<P><strong>Message:</strong><br>
<TEXTAREA NAME=\"message\" COLS=30 ROWS=5 WRAP=virtual></TEXTAREA></P>
<INPUT type=\"hidden\" name=\"op\" value=\"ds\">
<P><INPUT TYPE=\"submit\" NAME=\"submit\" VALUE=\"Send This Form\"></p>
</FORM>";

if ($_POST[op] != "ds") {
    // they need to see the form
    echo "$form_block";
} else if ($_POST[op] == "ds") {
    // check value of $_POST[sender_name]
    if ($_POST[sender_name] == "") {
        $name_err = "<font color=red>Please enter your name!</font><br>";
        $send = "no";
    }
    // check value of $_POST[sender_email]
    if ($_POST[sender_email] == "") {
        $email_err = "<font color=red>Please enter your
        e-mail address!</font><br>";
        $send = "no";
    }
    // check value of $_POST[message]
    if ($_POST[message]== "") {
        $message_err = "<font color=red>Please enter a message!</font><br>";
        $send = "no";
```

```
    }
    if ($send != "no") {
        // it's ok to send, so build the mail
        $msg = "E-MAIL SENT FROM WWW SITE\n";
        $msg .= "Sender's Name:     $_POST[sender_name]\n";
        $msg .= "Sender's E-Mail:   $_POST[sender_email]\n";
        $msg .= "Message:           $_POST[message]\n\n";

        $to = "you@yourdomain.com";
        $subject = "All-in-One Web Site Feedback";
        $mailheaders = "From: My Web Site
        <genericaddress@yourdomain.com>\n";
        $mailheaders .= "Reply-To: $_POST[sender_email]\n";
        //send the mail
        mail($to, $subject, $msg, $mailheaders);
        //display confirmation to user
        echo "<P>Mail has been sent!</p>";
    } else if ($send == "no") {
        //print error messages
        echo "$name_err";
        echo "$email_err";
        echo "$message_err";
        echo "$form_block";
    }
}
?>
```

Submitting Your Form and Getting Results

Now that you've created both a front-end form and a back-end script, it's time to try them out.

Figure 8.8 The all-in-one form displayed.

1. Open your Web browser and type **http://127.0.0.1/allinone_form.php**. See Figure 8.8.

You will see a form containing a text field for the person's name, a text field for the person's e-mail address, a text area for the message, and a button that says Send This Form.

Figure 8.9 A blank entry.

2. Submit the form without typing anything in any of the fields (see Figure 8.9).

The form, with all three error messages at the top, will appear in your browser window.

Figure 8.10 An unfinished entry.

3. Type your name in the Your Name field and then submit the form (see Figure 8.10).

The form will reappear, this time without the Name error message.

Figure 8.11 An almost finished entry.

4. Type your name in the Your Name field, your e-mail address in the Your E-Mail Address field, and then submit the form (see Figure 8.11).

The form will reappear again, this time with only the Message error.

5. Type your name in the Your Name field, your e-mail address in the Your E-Mail Address field, and the following message:

```
This all-in-one thing is pretty cool!
```

6. Submit the form.

Check your e-mail and see if a message is waiting for you.

Saving the Values if You Make an Error

One thing you probably noticed in the original script is that if you made an error, the form was reset, and you lost the values you had entered. A simple modification to the original $form_block will take care of that problem. Just add a VALUE attribute to the form field to hold any previous value for the given variable.

1. Open allinone_form.php in your text editor.

2. Inside the $form_block variable and modify the input field for Your Name:

```
<INPUT type=\"text\" NAME=\"sender_name\"
VALUE=\"$_POST[sender_name]\" SIZE=30></P>
```

3. Modify the input field for Your E-Mail Address:

```
<INPUT type=\"text\" NAME=\"sender_email\"
VALUE=\"$_POST[sender_email]\" SIZE=30></P>
```

4. Modify the text area for Message:

```
<TEXTAREA NAME=\"message\" COLS=30 ROWS=5
WRAP=virtual>$_POST[message]</TEXTAREA></P>
```

TEXTAREA TYPES

There's no VALUE attribute for TEXTAREA. Instead, the value goes between the start and end tags.

Figure 8.12 Saving values after errors.

5. Save the file and then open your Web browser and type **http://127.0.0.1/ allinone_form.php**.

6. Type your name in the Your Name field and then submit the form (see Figure 8.12).

The form, complete with error messages, will appear. This time, though, your name has been saved!

Repeat the process for the other fields in the form to verify that the values were saved. You've just mastered another aspect of dynamic content, this time in relation to displaying error messages when users don't perform the proper tasks, such as completing all of the fields in a form. This chapter was all about forms and sending mail, and the next chapter is all about working with elements of your file system, such as files and directories.

9

Using Your File System

Using simple PHP scripts, you can do anything with your file system—it's yours, after all! In this chapter, you'll learn how to do the following:

- Display the contents of a directory.
- Create a new file.
- Open an existing file and append data to it.
- Copy, rename, and delete files.

File Paths and Permissions

The scripts used in these chapters can be executed on both Windows and Linux/UNIX operating systems. If you are using Windows, you can use both the forward slash (/) and the backslash (\) in file paths, whereas other operating systems use only the forward slash. The scripts in this chapter use the forward slash method in all instances. This method works even if you don't specify a drive letter. For example:

```
$path = "/Program Files/Apache Group/Apache/htdocs";
```

This path, on Windows, is assumed to be on the current drive (in my case, C:/). If you need to specific a drive letter, go for it:

```
$path = "K:/Program Files/Apache Group/Apache/htdocs/";
```

You'll have to modify file paths to fit your own directory structure, but you shouldn't have to do anything more than that.

PERMISSIONS

For each directory specified in this chapter, you must have the proper permissions to create, modify, and delete files within it. This is an especially important note for non-Windows users, whose operating system is multi-user by nature. If you are unsure how to assign or modify permissions on your system, please contact your system administrator.

Displaying Directory Contents

Believe it or not, this script will be the most complicated in this chapter, and it has only 32 lines! The goal is to open a directory, find the names of all the files in the directory, and print the results in a bulleted list.

1. Open a new file in your text editor and start a PHP block:

```
<?
```

2. Create a variable to hold the full path name of a directory:

```
$dir_name = "c:/";
```

DIRECTORY PATHS

We are using the root of the C drive for simplicity. Substitute your own directory name so that this works for you.

---

3. Create a handle and use the `opendir()` function to open the directory specified in Step 2.

```
$dir = opendir($dir_name);
```

HANDLES

The term *handle* is used to refer to the just-opened directory.

---

4. You'll eventually place the results in a bulleted list inside a string called `$file_list`. Start that bulleted list now:

```
$file_list = "<ul>";
```

5. Start a `while` loop that uses the `readdir()` function to determine when to stop and start the loop. The `readdir()` function returns the name of the next file in the directory and, in this case, assigns the value to a variable called `$file_name`:

```
while ($file_name = readdir($dir)) {
```

6. Get rid of those . and .. filenames using an `if` statement:

```
if (($file_name != ".") && ($file_name != "..")) {
```

7. If `$file_name` is neither of the "dot" filenames, add it to `$file_list` using the concatenation assignment operator:

```
$file_list .= "<li>$file_name";
```

8. Close the `if` statement and the `while` loop:

```
}
}
```

9. Add the closing tag to the bulleted list:

```
$file_list .= "</ul>";
```

10. Close the open directory:

```
closedir($dir);
```

11. Close your PHP block and then add some HTML to begin the display:

```
?>
<HTML>
<HEAD>
<TITLE>Directory Listing</TITLE>
</HEAD>
<BODY>
```

12. Mingle some HTML and PHP to print the name of the directory you just read:

```
<P>Files in: <? echo "$dir_name"; ?></P>
```

Figure 9.1 The `listfiles` script.

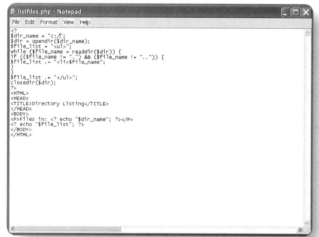

13. Print the file list and then close your HTML tags so the document is valid:

```
<? echo "$file_list"; ?>
</BODY>
</HTML>
```

14. Save the file with the name `listfiles.php`.

Your code should look something like Figure 9.1:

Figure 9.2 The listfiles script output.

To test it, place the file in the document root of your Web server and then open your Web browser and type `http://127.0.0.1/` `listfiles.php`. See Figure 9.2.

Assuming that this worked, try it for other directories on your system. If a directory doesn't exist, the script won't return an error—it just won't have any results. One thing you should know is that if you do not have warnings turned off in the php configuration file, you will see a list of warnings displayed on the screen. You can avoid this by turning them off in the configuration file or by using the @ symbol in front of the function call, as we shall see in just a bit.

In the next section, you'll work with the fopen() and fclose() functions to open and close specific files.

Working with fopen() and fclose()

Before you jump headfirst into working with files, you need to learn a bit about the fopen() function, which is used to open files. This function requires a filename and mode, and it returns a file pointer. A file pointer provides information about the file and is used as a reference.

The filename is the full path to the file you want to create or open, and the mode can be any of the modes listed in Table 9.1.

Table 9.1 Modes Used with `fopen()`

Mode	Usage
r	Opens an existing file and reads data from it. The file pointer is placed at the beginning of the file.
r+	Opens an existing file for reading or writing. The file pointer is placed at the beginning of the file.
w	Opens a file for writing. If a file with that name does not exist, the function creates a new file. If the file exists, the function deletes all existing content and places the file pointer at the beginning of the file.
w+	Opens a file for reading and writing. If a file with that name does not exist, the function creates a new file. If the file exists, the function deletes all existing content and places the file pointer at the beginning of the file.
a	Opens a file for writing. If a file with that name does not exist, the function creates a new file. If the file exists, the function places the file pointer at the end of the file.
a+	Opens a file for reading and writing. If a file with that name does not exist, the function attempts to create a new file. If the file exists, the function places the file pointer at the end of the file.

Creating a New File

Compared to the first section of this chapter, this next task is a piece of cake. The goal is simply to create a new, empty file in a specified location.

1. Open a new file in your text editor and start a PHP block:

```
<?
```

2. Create a variable to hold the full path name to a file:

```
$filename = "c:/newfile.txt";
```

> ## FILE NAMING
> This file is one that exists on my own machine. Substitute your own directory name so that this works for you!

3. Create a file pointer and use the `fopen()` function to open the file specified in Step 3 for reading and writing. The `die()` function will cause the script to end and a message to display if the file doesn't open properly.

```
$newfile = fopen($filename, "w+") or die("Couldn't create file.");
```

> ## FILE POINTERS
> The term *file pointer* is used to refer to the just-opened file.

4. Close the file pointer:

```
fclose($newfile);
```

5. Create a message to print upon success and then close your PHP block:

```
$msg = "<P>File created!</P>";
?>
```

6. Add this HTML:

```
<HTML>
<HEAD>
<TITLE>Creating a New File</TITLE>
</HEAD>
<BODY>
```

7. Print the message:

```
<? echo "$msg"; ?>
```

8. Add some more HTML so that the document is valid:

```
</BODY>
</HTML>
```

9. Save the file with the name `newfile.php` and place this file in the document root of your Web server.

10. Open your Web browser and type `http://127.0.0.1/newfile.php`.

Figure 9.3 Creating a new file successfully.

If the file creation was successful, you should see the success message in Figure 9.3.

However, if your file creation failed, you will see a nasty parse error. You can force an error by using an invalid value for `$filename`, such as this:

```
$filename =
"/bozo/mydata.txt";
```

DIRECTORY NAMING

Of course, this assumes that you have no directory called `bozo` on your current drive. If you happen to have such a thing, just change the name to a directory name that doesn't exist.

Figure 9.4 The Bozo script.

When you run your script, you'll see something like Figure 9.4.

Although the die() function will do its job by printing the specified error message, PHP will issue its own warnings based on the failure of the function to do its job. You can suppress errors and warnings from PHP by using the @ sign in front of functions.

In your script, change this line:

```
$newfile = fopen($filename, "w+") or die("Couldn't create file.");
```

to this:

```
$newfile = @fopen($filename, "w+") or die("Couldn't create file.");
```

Figure 9.5 The Bozo script without warnings.

Save the file and access the script via your Web browser. You'll now see just the message from the die() function and no other warnings (see Figure 9.5).

Checking if a File Already Exists

To avoid any possible housekeeping errors when running around your file system, you can use the `file_exists()` function to check if a file already exists before you create it. This next script will do just that and will print a message one way or the other.

1. Open a new file in your text editor and start a PHP block:

```
<?
```

2. Create a variable to hold the full path name to a file (use your own file path):

```
$filename = "c:/mydata.txt";
```

PREVIOUS FILE WARNING

Yes, this is the same file you probably created in the previous section. That's fine because it can trip the error checking!

---

3. Start an `if...else` statement that checks for a true/false result to the `file_exists()` function:

```
if (file_exists($filename)) {
```

4. Create a variable to hold a message regarding the file's existence:

```
$msg = "<P>File already exists.</P>";
```

5. Continue the `else` statement to do something if the file doesn't exist:

```
} else {
```

6. Create a file pointer and use the `fopen()` function to open the file specified in Step 2 for reading and writing. The `die()` function will cause the script to end and a message to display if the file doesn't open properly.

```
$newfile = @fopen($filename, "w+") or die("Couldn't create file.");
```

7. Create a variable to hold a success message:

```
$msg = "<P>File created!</P>";
```

8. Close the file pointer, the if...else statement, and your PHP block:

```
fclose($newfile);
}
?>
```

9. Add this HTML:

```
<HTML>
<HEAD>
<TITLE>Creating a New File</TITLE>
</HEAD>
<BODY>
```

10. Print the message:

```
<? echo "$msg"; ?>
```

11. Add some more HTML so that the document is valid:

```
</BODY>
</HTML>
```

12. Save the file with the name newfile-checkfirst.php and place this file in the document root of your Web server.

Figure 9.6 Failure message for creating a new file.

13. Open your Web browser and type http://127.0.0.1/ newfile-checkfirst.php.

Assuming that you used the filename of a previously created file, you should see the failure message, as shown in Figure 9.6.

If you change the value of `$filename` to a file that doesn't exist and then access the script again, you'll see the success message. Because just creating a file is boring, in the next section you'll learn to write data to the file.

Appending Data to a File

The goal of the next script is to append data to a file. If the file exists, the script will just write data into it. If the file doesn't exist, it will be created before data is written to it.

1. Open a new file in your text editor and start a PHP block:

```
<?
```

2. Create a variable to hold the full path name to a file (use your own file path):

```
$filename = "c:/textfile.txt";
```

3. Create a variable called `$newstring` to hold the string you want to write to the file. Populate that string with this very exciting message:

```
$newstring = "
Check it out!\n
I've created a new file and stuck all this text into it!";
```

NEW LINES AND FILES

The use of the newline character causes a line break to occur at that point in the text.

4. Create a file pointer and use the `fopen()` function to open the file specified in Step 2 for reading and writing. The `die()` function will cause the script to end and a message to display if the file doesn't open properly.

```
$myfile = @fopen($filename, "w+") or die("Couldn't open file.");
```

5. Use the `fwrite()` function to place the text (`$newstring`) inside the file (`$myfile`). The `die()` function will cause the script to end and a message to display if the `fwrite()` function fails.

```
@fwrite($myfile, $newstring) or die("Couldn't write to file.");
```

6. Create a variable to hold a success message:

```
$msg = "<P>File has data in it now...</p>";
```

7. Close the file pointer and the PHP block:

```
fclose($myfile);
?>
```

8. Add this HTML:

```
<HTML>
<HEAD>
<TITLE>Adding Data to a File</TITLE>
</HEAD>
<BODY>
```

9. Print the message:

```
<? echo "$msg"; ?>
```

10. Add some more HTML so that the document is valid:

```
</BODY>
</HTML>
```

11. Save the file with the name `writedata.php` and place this file in the document root of your Web server.

Figure 9.7 The file writing script in action.

12. Open your Web browser and type `http://127.0.0.1/writedata.php`. See Figure 9.7.

In the next section, you'll read the data from the text file created by this script.

Reading Data from a File

You'll now create a script to read the data from the file you created in the previous section. You could just open that file in a text editor, but where's the fun in that? PHP has a handy function called `fread()` that does the job for you.

1. Open a new file in your text editor and start a PHP block:

```
<?
```

2. Create a variable to hold the full path name to the file you created in the previous section (use your own path):

```
$filename = "c:/textfile.txt";
```

3. Create a file pointer and use the `fopen()` function to open the file specified in Step 2 for reading only. The `die()` function will cause the script to end and a message to display if the file doesn't open properly.

```
$whattoread = @fopen($filename, "r") or die("Couldn't open file");
```

4. Create a variable called `$file_contents`, and use the `fread()` function to read all the lines from the open file pointer (`$whattoread`) for as long as there are lines in the file:

```
$file_contents = fread($whattoread, filesize($filename));
```

FILE SIZES

Using the `filesize()` function on an existing file lets PHP do the work for you. The second argument of the `fread()` function is for the length of the file. If you don't know the length, but you know you want all of it, you can use `filesize($filename)` to get that length.

5. Create a variable to print a message, including the contents of the file:

```
$msg = "The file contains:<br>$file_contents";
```

6. Close the file pointer and your PHP block:

```
fclose($whattoread);
?>
```

7. Add this HTML:

```
<HTML>
<HEAD>
<TITLE>Reading Data From a File</TITLE>
</HEAD>
<BODY>
```

8. Print the message:

```
<? echo "$msg"; ?>
```

9. Add some more HTML so that the document is valid:

```
</BODY>
</HTML>
```

Figure 9.8 The file reading script in action.

10. Save the file with the name `readdata.php` and place this file in the document root of your Web server.

11. Open your Web browser and type **http://127.0.0.1/ readdata.php**. See Figure 9.8.

That's definitely the string written to the file, but what happened to that line break? The newline character means nothing to a Web browser, which renders only HTML. Luckily, the PHP development team had great forethought and created the `nl2br()` function (newline-to-break; get it?). Make some slight adjustments to the `readdata.php` script:

1. Add this line after the line containing the `fread()` function:

```
$new_file_contents = nl2br($file_contents);
```

Figure 9.9 The amended file reading script in action.

2. Modify the `$msg` string so that it looks like this:

```
$msg = "The file
contains:<br>
$new_file_contents";
```

3. Save the file.

Now open this file in your Web browser and notice the line break (see Figure 9.9).

In the next section, you'll read the same message, but instead of printing it on the screen, you'll send it via e-mail.

Sending File Contents via E-Mail

If you're saving the results of HTML forms to a plain text file that you want to read only at specific times, you can write a little script that mails the contents of the file to you on demand.

1. Open a new file in your text editor and start a PHP block:

```
<?
```

2. Create a variable to hold the full path name to the file containing the data (use your own path):

```
$filename = "c:/textfile.txt";
```

3. Create a file pointer and use the `fopen()` function to open the file specified in Step 2 for reading only. The `die()` function will cause the script to end and a message to display if the file doesn't open properly.

```
$whattoread = @fopen($filename, "r") or die("Couldn't open file");
```

4. Create a variable called `$file_contents`, and use the `fread()` function to read all the lines from the open file pointer (`$whattoread`) for as long as there are lines in the file:

```
$file_contents = fread($whattoread, filesize($filename));
```

5. Create a variable to hold your e-mail address:

```
$to = "you@yourdomain.com";
```

6. Create a variable for the subject of the e-mail:

```
$subject = "File Contents";
```

7. Create a variable for additional mail headers:

```
$mailheaders = "From: <genericaddress@yourdomain.com> \n";
```

8. Populate the `mail()` function using the `$file_contents` string as the third argument (the message):

```
mail($to, $subject, $file_contents, $mailheaders);
```

9. Create a variable to print a message to the screen:

```
$msg = "<P>Check your mail!</P>";
```

10. Close the file pointer and your PHP block:

```
fclose($whattoread);
?>
```

11. Add this HTML:

```
<HTML>
<HEAD>
<TITLE>Mailing Data From a File</TITLE>
</HEAD>
<BODY>
```

12. Print the message:

```
<? echo "$msg"; ?>
```

13. Add some more HTML so that the document is valid:

```
</BODY>
</HTML>
```

14. Save the file with the name `mailcontents.php` and place this file in the document root of your Web server.

15. Open your Web browser and type `http://127.0.0.1/mailcontents.php`.

Figure 9.10 E-mail with file attachment.

Like the message says, go check your mail! You should have an e-mail waiting for you, with the contents of the file printed in it (see Figure 9.10).

Unlike the previous script, you didn't need to use the nl2br() function, because you weren't displaying text in a Web browser window. The plain-text e-mail will keep the original line break.

File System Housekeeping

The next series of scripts will help you perform very basic file system tasks, such as copying, renaming, and deleting files. Remember that you can perform file system functions only if the proper permissions are in place for the PHP user.

Copying Files

The copy() function is very simple: It needs to know the original filename and a new filename, and that's all there is to it.

1. Open a new file in your text editor and start a PHP block:

```
<?
```

2. Create a variable to hold the full path name to the original file (use your own path):

```
$orig_filename = "c:/textfile.txt";
```

3. Create a variable to hold the full path name to the new file (use your own path):

```
$new_filename = "c:/textfile.bak";
```

4. Create a variable to hold the true/false result of the function. Suppress warnings by using the @ in front of the function and use `die()` to print a message if the function fails:

```
$success = @copy($orig_filename, $new_filename) or die("Couldn't copy
file.");
```

5. Start an `if...else` statement to print the proper message based on the outcome of the function:

```
if ($success) {
```

6. The message string, if successful, should print a confirmation of the copy:

```
$msg = "Copied $orig_filename to $new_filename";
```

7. Continue the statement for a failure and then close the PHP block:

```
} else {
    $msg = "Could not copy file.";
}
?>
```

ERROR HANDLING

Using the `else` statement in this case is actually unnecessary, but it's good practice for providing a default result. If the `copy()` function fails, the `die()` function will exit the script and print the error before even getting to the `if...else` part of the script.

---

8. Add this HTML:

```
<HTML>
<HEAD>
<TITLE>Copy a File</TITLE>
</HEAD>
<BODY>
```

9. Print the message:

```
<? echo "$msg"; ?>
```

10. Add some more HTML so that the document is valid:

```
</BODY>
</HTML>
```

Figure 9.11 The copy file script in action.

11. Save the file with the name `copyfile.php` and place this file in the document root of your Web server.

12. Open your Web browser and type `http://127.0.0.1/copyfile.php`. See Figure 9.11.

See if your error handling works by changing the value of `$new_filename` to something that doesn't exist:

```
$new_filename = "/bozo/textfile.bak";
```

Access the script via your Web browser, and you should see the appropriate message.

Next, let's move on to renaming files. The script is remarkably similar!

Renaming Files

Like the `copy()` function, the `rename()` function just needs to know the original filename and a new filename. In this case, you're just renaming the original, not copying it.

1. Open a new file in your text editor and start a PHP block:

```
<?
```

2. Create a variable to hold the full path name to the original file (use your own path):

```
$orig_filename = "c:/textfile.bak";
```

3. Create a variable to hold the full path name to the new file (use your own path):

```
$new_filename = "c:/textfile.old";
```

4. Create a variable to hold the true/false result of the function. Suppress warnings by using the @ in front of the function and use `die()` to print a message if the function fails:

```
$success = @rename($orig_filename, $new_filename)
    or die("Couldn't rename file.");
```

5. Start an `if...else` statement to print the proper message based on the outcome of the function:

```
if ($success) {
```

6. The message string, if successful, should print a confirmation of the renaming function:

```
$msg = "Renamed $orig_filename to $new_filename";
```

7. Continue the statement for a failure and then close your PHP block:

```
} else {
    $msg = "Could not rename file.";
}
?>
```

ERROR HANDLING REDUX

As in the previous script, the `else` statement in this case is unnecessary, but good practice for providing a default result.

---

8. Add this HTML:

```
<HTML>
<HEAD>
<TITLE>Rename a File</TITLE>
</HEAD>
<BODY>
```

9. Print the message:

```
<? echo "$msg"; ?>
```

10. Add some more HTML so that the document is valid:

```
</BODY>
</HTML>
```

11. Save the file with the name `renamefile.php` and place this file in the document root of your Web server.

Figure 9.12 The `rename` script in action.

12. Open your Web browser and type `http://127.0.0.1/renamefile.php`. See Figure 9.12.

See if your error handling works by changing the value of `$new_filename` to something that doesn't exist:

```
$new_filename =
"/bozo/textfile.bak";
```

There's one more housekeeping function in the next section: deleting files.

Deleting Files

Be very careful when using the `unlink()` function because once you've deleted a file, it's gone for good.

1. Open a new file in your text editor and start a PHP block:

```
<?
```

2. Create a variable to hold the full path name to the file you want to delete (use your own path):

```
$filename = "c:/ textfile.old";
```

3. Create a variable to hold the true/false result of the function. Suppress warnings by using the @ in front of the function and use `die()` to print a message if the function fails:

```
$success = @unlink($filename) or die("Couldn't delete file.");
```

4. Start an `if...else` statement to print the proper message based on the outcome of the function:

```
if ($success) {
```

5. The message string, if successful, should print a confirmation of the deletion:

```
$msg = "Deleted $filename";
```

6. Continue the statement for a failure and then close your PHP block:

```
} else {
    $msg = "Could not delete file.";
}
?>
```

ERROR HANDLING AGAIN

As in the previous scripts, using the `else` statement in this case is unnecessary, but good practice for providing a default result.

---

7. Add this HTML:

```
<HTML>
<HEAD>
<TITLE>Delete a File</TITLE>
</HEAD>
<BODY>
```

8. Print the message:

```
<? echo "$msg"; ?>
```

9. Add some more HTML so that the document is valid:

```
</BODY>
</HTML>
```

Figure 9.13 The delete file script in action.

10. Save the file with the name deletefile.php and place this file in the document root of your Web server.

11. Open your Web browser and type http://127.0.0.1/ deletefile.php. See Figure 9.13.

See if your error handling works by changing the value of $filename to something that doesn't exist:

```
$filename = "/bozo/textfile.old";
```

Figure 9.14 The delete file script with an error displayed.

Access the script via your Web browser, and you should see an example like Figure 9.14.

In the next chapter, you'll create a two-step process (front-end form and back-end script) to initiate file uploads from a Web browser to your file system.

10

Uploading Files to Your Web Site

If you need a quick interface for uploading files to your Web site from a remote location, you can create a two-step form and script interface with PHP. In this chapter, you learn how to:

- Create an HTML form for file uploads.
- Create a PHP script to handle file uploads.

Checking Your `php.ini` File

Before you start uploading files, check a few values in your `php.ini` file. Look for this section of text:

```
;;;;;;;;;;;;;;;;
; File Uploads ;
;;;;;;;;;;;;;;;;
; Whether to allow HTTP file uploads.
File_uploads = On

; Temporary directory for HTTP uploaded files (will use system default if not
; specified).
;upload_tmp_dir =

; Maximum allowed size for uploaded files.
Upload_max_filesize = 2M
```

To ensure the file upload process will work smoothly, make the following modifications:

1. Uncomment the `upload_tmp_dir` line by deleting the initial semicolon.

2. Enter a directory name after the `=` for `upload_tmp_dir`.

3. If you want to allow larger uploads, change the number of bytes for `upload_max_filesize`.

For example, on a Windows system, this section of the `php.ini` file might look like this:

```
;;;;;;;;;;;;;;;;
; File Uploads ;
;;;;;;;;;;;;;;;;
; Whether to allow HTTP file uploads.
file_uploads = On

; Temporary directory for HTTP uploaded files (will use system default if not
; specified).
upload_tmp_dir = /temp

; Maximum allowed size for uploaded files.
ipload_max_filesize = 2M
```

If you are not using Windows, you don't have to modify the value for `upload_tmp_dir`, as long as you want files to be placed in `/tmp` (the default).

Understanding the Process

The process of uploading a file to a Web server through an HTML form interface puzzles a lot of people. Take a moment to understand the process you'll create in the following sections.

To start and finish this process, you need the following:

- An HTML form
- A file to upload
- A place to put the file
- A script to put it there

The process itself goes something like this:

1. The user accesses the HTML form and sees a text field and the Browse button in his Web browser.

2. The user browses his hard drive for the file to upload and then selects a file.

3. The full file path and filename appear in the text field.

4. The user clicks the submit button.

5. The selected file goes out and lands at the Web server and sits around in a temporary directory.

6. The PHP script used in the form action checks that a file was sent and executes a copy command on the temporary file to move it to a real directory on the Web server.

7. The PHP script confirms the action for the user.

PERMISSIONS

The PHP user (the user under which PHP runs, such as `nobody` or `www` or `joe`) must have write permissions in the temporary directory as well as the target directory for the file. If you have difficulty with permissions, contact your system administrator.

Start with simply creating the HTML form interface in the next section.

Creating the Form

Start out by creating a one-field form. You can create a form to upload as many files as you like after you get this sequence to work with one file.

1. Open a new file in your text editor and type the following HTML:

```
<HTML>
<HEAD>
<TITLE>Upload a File</TITLE>
</HEAD>
<BODY>
<H1>Upload a File</H1>
```

2. Begin your form. Assume that the method is `POST` and the action is a script called `do_upload.php`. Because you'll be sending more than just text, use the `ENCTYPE` attribute.

```
<FORM METHOD="POST" ACTION=" do_upload.php" ENCTYPE="multipart/form-data">
```

3. Create an input field for the file with a text label. Assume that you'll be uploading an image file, and name the input field `img1`:

```
<p><strong>File to Upload:</strong><br>
<INPUT TYPE="file" NAME="img1" SIZE="30"></P>
```

INPUT FIELDS AND HTML

The TYPE="file" attribute in the form field will display an input field with a Browse button. The Browse button launches a file manager through which you select the file to upload.

4. Add a submit button and then close your form and add some more HTML so that the document is valid:

```
<P><INPUT TYPE="submit" NAME="submit" VALUE="Upload File"></P>
</FORM>
</BODY>
</HTML>
```

Figure 10.1 The upload form.

5. Save the file with the name upload_form.html and place this file in the document root of your Web server.

6. Open your Web browser and type http://127.0.0.1/ upload_form.html. See Figure 10.1.

In the next section, you'll create the script that handles the file upload.

Creating the Upload Script

Take a moment to commit the following list to memory—it contains the variables that are automatically placed in the `$_FILES` superglobal after a successful file upload. The base of `img1` comes from the name of the input field in the original form.

- `$_FILES[img1][tmp_name]`. The value refers to the temporary file on the Web server.

- `$_FILES[img1][name]`. The value is the actual name of the file that was uploaded. For example, if the name of the file was `me.jpg`, the value of `$_FILES[img1][name]` is `me.jpg`.

- `$_FILES[img1][size]`. The size of the uploaded file in bytes.

- `$_FILES[img1][type]`. The MIME type of the uploaded file, such as `image/jpg`.

MIME TYPES

A MIME (Multipurpose Internet Mail Extensions) type indicates the type of the content being transmitted. For instance, the MIME type of a JPEG file is `image/jpg`, and the MIME type of a Microsoft Word document is `application/msword`.

The goal of this script is to take the uploaded file and copy it to the document root of the Web server and return a confirmation to the user containing values for all the variables in the preceding list.

1. Open a new file in your text editor and start a PHP block:

```
<?
```

2. Create an `if...else` statement that checks for a value in `$_FILES[img1]`.

```
if ($_FILES[img1] != "") {
```

3. If `$_FILES[img1]` is not empty, execute the copy function. Use `@` before the function name to suppress warnings and use the `die()` function to cause the script to end and a message to display if the `copy()` function fails.

```
@copy($_FILES[img1][tmp_name],
  "/usr/local/apache2/htdocs/".$_FILES[img1][name])
     or die("Couldn't copy the file.");
```

DIRECTORIES

If the document root of your Web server is not `/usr/local/apache2/htdocs/`, as shown in Step 3, change the path to match your own system. For example, a Windows user might use `/Program Files/Apache Group/Apache/htdocs/`. Also, please note that we are suppressing all internal PHP errors (using the `@` sign in front of the copy function), so we display the error in a `die()` function call.

4. Continue the `else` statement to handle the lack of a file for upload:

```
} else {
    die("No input file specified");
```

5. Close the `if...else` statement and then close your PHP block:

```
}
?>
```

6. Add this HTML:

```
<HTML>
<HEAD>
<TITLE>Successful File Upload</TITLE>
</HEAD>
<BODY>
<H1>Success!</H1>
```

7. Mingle HTML and PHP, printing a line that displays values for the various elements of the uploaded file (name, size, and type):

```
<P>You sent: <? echo $_FILES[img1][name]; ?>,
a <? echo $_FILES[img1][size]; ?> byte file with
a mime type of <? echo $_FILES[img1][type]; ?>.</P>
```

Figure 10.2 The upload script.

8. Add some more HTML so that the document is valid:

```
</BODY>
</HTML>
```

9. Save the file with the name do_upload.php.

The code should look something like this (see Figure 10.2).

In the next section, you finally get to upload a file!

Uploading a File Using Your Form and Script

This is the moment of truth, where you hold your breath and test the script.

1. Open your Web browser and type `http://127.0.0.1/upload_form.html`.

2. Use the Browse button to locate a file you want to upload.

FILENAMES

This example uses a file on my own machine, so the figures won't look quite the same as your results.

Figure 10.3 Form filled in with full path.

The full path to the file should appear in the form field (see Figure 10.3).

3. Click the Upload File button.

The results screen should appear, providing information about the file you just uploaded.

Figure 10.4 File type checking.

A WARNING ON FILE UPLOADS

Allow your file upload script to be used only by yourself or other trusted sources, unless you limit the types of files you want to upload by checking the file type before copying to the system (see Figure 10.4).

If something went wrong, verify that the output path exists (for example, that you have a valid /usr/local/apache2/htdocs/ directory, and that it does not already contain a file of that name.

There's nothing to it! You're now a file system wizard. In the next chapter, you'll become a database wizard as well.

PART IV

Getting to Know Your MySQL Database

11

Establishing a Connection and Poking Around

During the process of installing and testing MySQL in Chapter 1, "Installing and Configuring MySQL," you should have created a sample database as well as a sample table and even inserted and selected some data. The next several chapters focus on making the same types of connections and queries and using PHP scripts for the front end. In this chapter, you learn how to do the following:

- Connect to MySQL.
- List all databases on `localhost`.
- List all tables in a database.
- Create a database.
- Drop (delete) a database.

Working with User Privileges in MySQL

When you installed the MySQL database in Chapter 1, you were working as the anonymous or root user. Before you begin working regularly with databases, you should create a real user with a real password. To do this, you need to understand a bit about the MySQL privilege system.

MYSQL USERS

If you are accessing MySQL through an Internet service provider, you probably have only one user and one database available to you. By default, that one user has access to all tables in the database and is allowed to perform all commands. If this is the case, you can skip the information in this section and proceed to the script-creation sections. In all instances where a username and password are used, use the one given to you by your ISP.

Creating a New User

If you have proper permissions for adding a user, the simplest method for performing this task is the GRANT command. The basic syntax of the GRANT command follows, where [privilege list] is a placeholder for the privileges you want to give to the new user.

```
GRANT [privilege list] ON databasename.tablename TO
username@host IDENTIFIED BY "password";
```

You can grant many types of privileges, and for more information, please visit the MySQL Manual topic at http://dev.mysql.com/doc/refman/5.0/en/grant.html. For now, you will just grant all privileges to your new user on all tables in the database.

UNIX COMPATIBILITY

The following commands are exactly the same for MySQL on Windows and Linux/UNIX platforms.

---

1. Start the MySQL Monitor from the command line, using the path to the `mysql` executable file that is relevant to your file system.

2. Select the database called `mysql` by typing the following at the `mysql>` prompt:

   ```
   use mysql;
   ```

3. Type the following SQL statement, substituting your own username (replacing `spike@localhost`) and password (replacing `'9sj7En4'`) if you want. The wildcard (*) grants permissions on all databases and tables:

   ```
   GRANT ALL ON *.* TO spike@localhost IDENTIFIED BY "9sj7En4";
   ```

4. Exit the MySQL Monitor by typing the following at the `mysql>` prompt:

   ```
   exit
   ```

5. Issue the command to reload the `grant` tables using the `mysqladmin` program:

   ```
   mysqladmin reload
   ```

The new user (`spike`) will now have access to all databases and tables when using the password `9sj7En4`. This user will be the sample user in all database connectivity scripts from this point forward. Please substitute your own username and password where appropriate.

Connecting to MySQL

The goal of this script is simply to connect to MySQL, running on your machine (`localhost`).

1. Open a new file in your text editor and start a PHP block:

   ```
   <?
   ```

2. Create a variable to hold the result of the `mysql_connect()` function:

   ```
   $connection = mysql_connect("localhost", "spike", "9sj7En4")
   ```

> ## WORKING WITH THE `MYSQL_CONNECT()` FUNCTION
> The `mysql_connect()` function requires a hostname, username, and password (in that order).

3. Add a `die()` function to the `mysql_connect()` line to cause the script to end and a message to display if the connection fails. Within the `die()` function, use the `mysql_error()` function. The message that is printed upon error is the exact error as sent by MySQL. The new line should read as follows:

```
$connection = mysql_connect("localhost", "spike", "9sj7En4")
    or die(mysql_error());
```

4. Test the value of `$connection`. If it's true, the connection to MySQL was made, and a variable is created to hold a message:

```
if ($connection) {
    $msg = "success!";
}
```

> ## ERROR HANDLING
> If a connection cannot be made, the script will end with the `die()` function.

5. Close your PHP block and then add HTML:

```
?>
<HTML>
<HEAD>
<TITLE>MySQL Connection</TITLE>
</HEAD>
<BODY>
```

6. Print the message string:

```
<? echo "$msg"; ?>
```

7. Add some more HTML so that the document is valid:

```
</BODY>
</HTML>
```

Figure 11.1 The database connect script in action.

8. Save the file with the name db_connect.php and place this file in the document root of your Web server.

9. Open your Web browser and type http://127.0.0.1/ db_connect.php. See Figure 11.1.

If you entered the correct username and password, you should have a successful result.

NEW FUNCTIONALITY WARNING!

With PHP 6.0, MySQL support is not enabled by default. If you want to use MySQL with version 6.0, you will need to edit the php.ini file and uncomment the line that includes the MySQL DLL:

```
extension=php_mysql.dll
```

Make sure there is no semi-colon (;) in front of the line. You may also need to configure the extensions directory setting:

```
; Directory in which the loadable extensions (modules) reside.
extension_dir = "c:\php6\ext\"
```

to be wherever your PHP install is done on your system. In my case, it is c:\php. Note that the trailing backslash (or forward slash on Linux) is extremely important. If you do not do these two things, you may see an error such as Fatal Error: Call to undefined function mysql_connect. If this happens, check the above settings.

Breaking Your Connection Script

Anytime you work with databases, you will have errors. It's inevitable. That's why I want to show you some common errors and how to handle them fairly gracefully.

You'll make a modification to the db_connect.php script that causes it to fail on connection, simply by changing the username.

1. Change the username to buffy (unless buffy is a real user!) so that the connection line reads as follows:

```
$connection = mysql_connect("localhost", "buffy", "9sj7En4")
    or die(mysql_error());
```

Figure 11.2 The connection script with an error.

2. Save the file and then open your Web browser to **http://127.0.01/ db_connect.php**. See Figure 11.2.

That is some kind of nasty response! At least it tells you exactly what is wrong and several times over: User buffy couldn't connect to MySQL. You can suppress one of the ugly warnings and just go with the message from the die() function by placing a @ before the mysql_connect() function name. Try it.

1. Add a @ before the mysql_connect() function, keeping the bad username:

```
$connection = @mysql_connect("localhost", "buffy", "9sj7En4")
    or die(mysql_error());
```

Figure 11.3 Suppressing error messages.

2. Save the file, and then open your Web browser to `http://127.0.0.1/ db_connect.php`. See Figure 11.3.

With this change, the warning is suppressed, and only the message from the `die()` function is displayed, which is a meaningful error message output from the `mysql_error()` function.

If you can keep nasty errors and warnings to a minimum, it will make the overall user experience much more pleasant if your database decides to render itself unavailable during peak Web-surfing hours.

Listing Databases on a Server

Now that you've successfully used PHP to make a connection to MySQL, it's time to familiarize yourself with some of the built-in MySQL-related functions. In this section, you use the following functions:

- `mysql_list_dbs()`—Used to list the databases on a MySQL server.
- `mysql_num_rows()`—Returns the number of rows in a result set.
- `mysql_tablename()`—Despite its name, can extract the name of a table or a database from a result.

The goal of this script is to list all the databases on the local MySQL server.

1. Open a new file in your text editor and start a PHP block:

```
<?
```

2. Create a variable to hold the result of the `mysql_connect()` function. Include the `@` to suppress warnings, as well as the `die()` function to cause the script to end and a message to display if the connection fails:

```
$connection = @mysql_connect("localhost", "spike", "9sj7En4")
    or die(mysql_error());
```

3. Create a variable to hold the result of the `mysql_list_dbs()` function. Include the `@` to suppress warnings, as well as the `die()` function to cause the script to end and a message to display if the script can't get the list:

```
$dbs = @mysql_list_dbs($connection) or die(mysql_error());
```

THE `MYSQL_LIST_DBS()` FUNCTION

The only argument necessary for the `mysql_list_dbs()` function is the link identifier for the current connection.

---

4. You'll be looping through a result and dynamically populating a bulleted list. Start that bulleted list outside the loop:

```
$db_list = "<ul>";
```

5. Start a counter. You'll need it for your loop:

```
$i = 0;
```

6. Begin a `while` loop. This loop will continue for as long as the value of `$i` is less than the number of rows in the `$dbs` result value:

```
while ($i < mysql_num_rows($dbs)) {
```

7. Once you're within the `while` loop, get the name of the database reflected in the current row of the result:

```
$db_names[$i] = mysql_tablename($dbs, $i);
```

VARIABLE SUBSTITUTION IN PHP

The variable `$i` is replaced by its value, so during the first loop, this line would be something like `$db_names[0] = mysql_tablename($dbs, 0);`

Counting starts at 0, not 1, so this would reflect the first row in the result. As the counter increments, so does the row number.

---

8. Add the current database name to the bulleted list:

```
$db_list .= "<li>$db_names[$i]";
```

9. Increment your count before you close the `while` loop:

```
$i++;
```

10. Close the `while` loop, the bulleted list, and your PHP block:

```
}
$db_list .= "</ul>";
?>
```

11. Add this HTML:

```
<HTML>
<HEAD>
<TITLE>MySQL Databases</TITLE>
</HEAD>
<BODY>
<P><strong>Databases on localhost</strong>:</P>
```

12. Print the message string:

```
<? echo "$db_list"; ?>
```

13. Add some more HTML so that the document is valid:

```
</BODY>
</HTML>
```

14. Save the file with the name `db_listdb.php`.

All together, your code should look like this:

```
<?
$connection = @mysql_connect("localhost", "spike", "9sj7En4")
     or die(mysql_error());

$dbs = @mysql_list_dbs($connection)or die(mysql_error());
$db_list ="<ul>";
$i =0;

while ($i < mysql_num_rows($dbs)){
     $db_names[$i] = mysql_tablename($dbs,$i);
     $db_list .= "<li>$db_names[$i]";
     $i++;
}
$db_list .="</ul>";
?>
<HTML>
<HEAD>
<TITLE>MySQL Databases</TITLE>
</HEAD>
<BODY>
<P><strong>Databases on localhost</strong>:</P>
<? echo "$db_list"; ?>
</BODY>
</HTML>
```

Figure 11.4 The database list script in action.

Place this file in the document root of your Web server; then open your Web browser and type **http://127.0.0.1/ db_listdb.php**. See Figure 11.4.

Your list might vary, depending on how much you played around with things in the first chapter, but you should at least see the MySQL system database (mysql) and the database created in Chapter 1 (testDB). Next, you add another loop to this script to print the tables within each database.

NOTES ON PERMISSIONS AND USERS

If the user you use to log in to the database does not have permission to see a given database, it will not be listed.

Listing Tables in a Database

A few additions to the `db_listdb.php` script are all you need to list the tables in the databases as well. The only new function you'll see is `mysql_list_tables()`, which is used to list tables within a MySQL database.

The goal of this script is to list all of the databases, including the tables within those databases, on the local MySQL server.

1. Open a new file in your text editor and start a PHP block:

```
<?
```

2. Add the connection information as you have been:

```
$connection = @mysql_connect("localhost", "spike", "9sj7En4")
    or die(mysql_error());
```

3. Create a variable to hold the result of the `mysql_list_dbs()` function. Include the @ to suppress warnings, as well as the `die()` function to cause the script to end and a message to display if the script can't get the list:

```
$dbs = @mysql_list_dbs($connection) or die(mysql_error());
```

4. You'll be looping through a result and dynamically populating a bulleted list. Start that bulleted list outside the loop:

```
$db_list = "<ul>";
```

5. Start a counter. You'll need it for your loop:

```
$db_num = 0;
```

WATCH YOUR COUNTERS

Use `$db_num` instead of `$i` as the counter because at one point in this script, you'll have two counters going at the same time.

---

6. Begin a `while` loop. This loop will continue for as long as the value of `$db_num` is less than the number of rows in the `$dbs` result value:

```
while ($db_num < mysql_num_rows($dbs)) {
```

7. Once you're within the `while` loop, get the name of the database reflected in the current row of the result:

```
$db_names[$db_num] = mysql_tablename($dbs, $db_num);
```

8. Add the current database name to the bulleted list:

```
$db_list .= "<li>$db_names[$db_num]";
```

9. Create a variable to hold the result of the `mysql_list_tables()` function. Include the `@` to suppress warnings, as well as the `die()` function to cause the script to end and a message to display if the script can't get the list:

```
$tables = @mysql_list_tables($db_names[$db_num]) or die(mysql_error());
```

USING THE MYSQL_LIST_TABLES() FUNCTION

The only argument necessary for the `mysql_list_tables()` function is the name of the current database.

---

10. You'll be looping through a result and dynamically populating a bulleted list. Start that bulleted list outside the loop:

```
$table_list = "<ul>";
```

11. Start a counter. You'll need it for your second loop:

```
$table_num = 0;
```

12. Begin a `while` loop. This loop will continue for as long as the value of `$table_num` is less than the number of rows in the `$tables` result value.

```
while ($table_num < mysql_num_rows($tables)) {
```

13. Once you're within the `while` loop, get the name of the table reflected in the current row of the result:

```
$table_names[$table_num] = mysql_tablename($tables, $table_num);
```

14. Add the current table name to the bulleted list:

```
$table_list .= "<li>$table_names[$table_num]";
```

15. Increment your count before you close the `while` loop:

```
$table_num++;
```

16. Close the inner `while` loop and the bulleted list of tables:

```
}
$table_list .= "</ul>";
```

17. Add the value of `$table_list` to `$db_list`, and then increment your count before you close the outer `while` loop:

```
$db_list .= "$table_list";
$db_num++;
}
```

18. Close the bulleted list of databases and then close your PHP block:

```
$db_list .= "</ul>";
?>
```

19. Add this HTML:

```
<HTML>
<HEAD>
<TITLE>MySQL Tables</TITLE>
</HEAD>
<BODY>
<P><strong>Databases and tables on localhost</strong>:</P>
```

20. Print the message string:

```
<? echo "$db_list"; ?>
```

21. Add some more HTML so that the document is valid:

```
</BODY>
</HTML>
```

22. Save the file with the name db_listtables.php.

Your code should look something like this:

```
<?
//connection code
$connection = @mysql_connect("localhost", "spike", "9sj7En4")
    or die(mysql_error());

//get database list
$dbs = @mysql_list_dbs($connection) or die(mysql_error());

//start first bullet list
$db_list = "<ul>";
$db_num = 0;

//loop through results of function
while ($db_num < mysql_num_rows($dbs)) {
    //get database names and make each a bullet point
$db_names[$db_num] = mysql_tablename($dbs, $db_num);
    $db_list .= "<li>$db_names[$db_num]";

    //get table names and start another bullet list
    $tables = @mysql_list_tables($db_names[$db_num]) or die(mysql_error());
    $table_list = "<ul>";
    $table_num = 0;

    //loop through results of function
    while ($table_num < mysql_num_rows($tables)) {
        //get table names and make each a bullet point
        $table_names[$table_num] = mysql_tablename($tables, $table_num);
        $table_list .= "<li>$table_names[$table_num]";
        $table_num++;
    }
    //close inner bullet list and increment number to continue loop
    $table_list .= "</ul>";
    $db_list .= "$table_list";
    $db_num++;
}
```

```
//close outer bullet list
$db_list .= "</ul>";
?>
<HTML>
<HEAD>
<TITLE>MySQL Tables</TITLE>
</HEAD>
<BODY>
<P><strong>Databases and tables on localhost</strong>:</P>
<? echo "$db_list"; ?>
</BODY>
</HTML>
```

Figure 11.5 The table list script in action.

It's time to see if this script lists the databases on your server, including their tables, so place this file in the document root of your Web server and open your Web browser to http://127.0.0.1/db_listtables.php. See Figure 11.5.

Because all privileges on all tables were granted to the test user, you should see a list of all tables and databases, including those reserved by the system. Your mileage might vary, depending on your server setup and your databases and tables.

In the next section, you'll attempt to create new databases on your server.

Creating a New Database

The complex elements of the previous scripts are nowhere to be found in this next script. The goal of this script is to create a new database on the MySQL server.

1. Open a new file in your text editor and start a PHP block:

```
<?
```

2. Create a variable to hold the query to issue, which will create the new database:

```
$sql = "CREATE database testDB2";
```

3. Add the connection information as you have been:

```
$connection = @mysql_connect("localhost", "spike", "9sj7En4")
    or die(mysql_error());
```

4. Issue the query, using the `mysql_query()` function. Include the `@` to suppress warnings, as well as the `die()` function to cause the script to end and a message to display if the query fails:

```
$result = @mysqlquery($sql, $connection) or die(mysql_error());
```

5. Test the value of `$result`. If it's true, the query was successful, and a variable is created to hold a message:

```
if ($result) {
    $msg = "<P>Database has been created!</P>";
}
```

6. Close your PHP block, and then add HTML:

```
?>
<HTML>
<HEAD>
<TITLE>Create a MySQL Database</TITLE>
</HEAD>
<BODY>
```

7. Print the message string:

```
<? echo "$msg"; ?>
```

8. Add some more HTML so that the document is valid:

```
</BODY>
</HTML>
```

9. Save the file with the name `db_createdb.php` and place this file in the document root of your Web server.

10. Open your Web browser and type `http://127.0.0.1/db_createdb.php`.

Figure 11.6 The database creation script in action.

If the database creation was successful, you'll see this message, as in Figure 11.6.

If the database creation failed, you may not see any message at all. This is due to the fact that we suppressed all errors from the connection and query functions. If you see nothing at all, remove the @ sign from the functions above to see what is going on.

Figure 11.7 The updated database list.

Verify that the new database is present by opening your Web browser to http://127.0.01/db_listdb.php. You should see your new database in the list, as shown in Figure 11.7.

> **WARNING**
>
> If you happen to have pages cached in the browser, you may not see the new database listed. If this happens, press the Refresh button (or hit Ctrl+R on most browsers) to re-run the script. The database should then appear.

In the next section, you'll drop (delete) the database you just created.

Deleting a Database

The goal of this script is to delete a database on the MySQL server. To do so, you simply have to modify the query used in the previous script.

1. Open `db_createdb.php` in your text editor.

2. Change the value of the `$sql` variable to:

```
$sql = "DROP DATABASE testDB2";
```

3. Change the error message and the HTML title to reflect that you want to delete a database and not create one.

Your code should look something like this:

```
<?
$sql = "DROP DATABASE testDB2";

$connection = @mysql_connect("localhost","spike","9sj7En4")
or die(mysql_error());
$result = @mysql_query($sql,$connection) or die(mysql_error());
if ($result) {
    $msg ="<P>Database has been deleted!</P>";
}
?>
```

```
<HTML>
<HEAD>
<TITLE>Delete a MySQL Database</TITLE>
</HEAD>
<BODY>
<? echo "$msg"; ?>
</BODY>
</HTML>
```

4. Save the file with the new name `db_dropdb.php` and place this file in the document root of your Web server.

Figure 11.8 Deleting a database.

5. Open your Web browser and type **http://127.0.0.1/db_dropdb.php**. See Figure 11.8.

If the database deletion was successful, you'll see the message in Figure 11.8.

Once again, you can verify this by running the `db_listdb.php` script to see if your database has been successfully removed.

In the next chapter, you'll create a database table for keeps, and you'll eventually populate that table with some data.

12

Creating a Database Table

You have this great database server and only a table called test_table sitting in a database called testDB. Where's the fun? In this chapter, you'll learn how to do the following:

- Plan for a database table.
- Recognize the pitfalls of certain data types.
- Recognize the importance of unique fields.
- Follow a two-step process for table creation.
- Create a table to hold your personal music catalog.

Planning for Your Tables

Creating a table is easy—it's the planning that takes some brainpower. To create a simple table, you only need to give it a name. But that would make for a boring table, because it wouldn't contain any columns (fields) and couldn't hold any data. So besides the name, you should know the number of fields and the types of fields you want to have in your table.

Basic MySQL Data Types

All fields in a table are given a particular data type definition. The *data type* defines the type of data that's allowed in the field. With some data type definitions, you must also define the maximum length you want to allow in the field, but others are assumed to have one specific length for its particular type.

It's very important to define fields appropriately. For example, if you have a field to hold the name of a recording, and it's a 50-character `varchar` field, yet you try to stuff a 100-character string into the field, your string will truncate at 50 characters.

Not only is it important to define the fields correctly so that the data fits inside the fields, but if you define a field with an incorrect SQL syntax, the table won't be created, period. For example, if you want to use the text data type for a field, you cannot specify a length: It's automatically assumed to have a particular length.

Table 12.1 shows some of the more common types you will use. For a complete list, please read the MySQL manual.

Defining Your Fields

The overall goal of this chapter is to create a table to hold data from your own personal music collection. Take a moment to think about the kinds of things you'd want to know: the title and artist, obviously, and maybe the record label, the date it was acquired, and your own personal notes regarding the recording. I thought about what I wanted for my own table, which I've decided to call `my_music`, as shown in Table 12.2.

Table 12.1 Some MySQL Data Types

Data Type	Definition
TINYINT	A very small integer that can be signed or unsigned. If signed, the allowable range is from –128 to 127. If unsigned, the allowable range is from 0 to 255.
SMALLINT	A small integer that can be signed or unsigned. If signed, the allowable range is from –32768 to 32767. If unsigned, the allowable range is from 0 to 65535.
BOOL	A Boolean true or false value. This value type is an alias for TINYINT.
MEDIUMINT	A medium-sized integer that can be signed or unsigned. If signed, the allowable range is from –8388608 to 8388607. If unsigned, the allowable range is from 0 to 16777215.
INT	A normal-size integer that can be signed or unsigned. If signed, the allowable range is from –2147483648 to 2147483647. If unsigned, the allowable range is from 0 to 4294967295.
BIGINT	A large integer that can be signed or unsigned. If signed, the allowable range is from –9223372036854775808 to 9223372036854775808. If unsigned, the allowable range is from 0 to 18446744073709551615.
FLOAT	A floating-point number that cannot be unsigned. You can define the display length (M) and the number of decimals (D). This is not required and will default to 10,2, where 2 is the number of decimals. Decimal precision can go to 24 places for a FLOAT.
DOUBLE	A normal-size (double-precision) floating-point number. Allowable values are –1.7976931348623157E+308 to –2.2250738585072014E-308, 0, and 2.2250738585072014E-308 to 1.7976931348623157E+308.
DATE	A date in YYYY-MM-DD format, between 1000-01-01 and 9999-12-31. For example, December 30, 1973, would be stored as 1973-12-30.
DATETIME	A date in YYYY-MM-DD format, between 1000-01-01 and 9999-12-31, plus hour and minute information in HH:MM:SS format. For example, 12:01 AM on December 30, 1973, would be stored as 1973-12-30 00:01:00.

Table 12.1 Some MySQL Data Types (continued)

Data Type	Definition
TIMESTAMP	A timestamp between midnight, January 1, 1970, and sometime in 2037. You can define multiple lengths to the TIMESTAMP field, which directly correlate to what is stored in it. The default length for TIMESTAMP is 14, which stores YYYYMMDDHHMMSS. This looks like the DATETIME format, only without the hyphens between numbers; 3:30 in the afternoon on December 30, 1973, would be stored as 19731230153000. Other definitions of TIMESTAMP are 12 (YYMMDDHHMMSS), 8 (YYYYMMDD), and 6 (YYMMDD).
CHAR	A fixed-length string between 1 and 255 characters in length, right-padded with spaces to the specified length when stored. Defining a length is not required, but the default is 1.
BINARY	The BINARY type is pretty much the same as the CHAR type, except that you can store binary values in it, rather than plain character values.
VARBINARY	This type is the same as the VARCHAR type, except that it stores binary values rather than character strings.
VARCHAR	A variable-length string between 1 and 255 characters in length. You must define a length when creating a VARCHAR field.
BLOB or TEXT	A field with a maximum length of 65,535 characters. BLOBs are "Binary Large Objects" and are used to store large amounts of binary data, such as images or other types of files. Fields defined as TEXT also hold large amounts of data; the difference between the two is that sorts and comparisons on stored data are case sensitive in BLOBs and case insensitive in TEXT fields. You do not specify a length with BLOB or TEXT.
ENUM	An enumeration (list). When defining an ENUM, you are creating a list of items from which the value must be selected (or it can be NULL). For example, if you wanted your field to contain either "A" or "B" or "C", you would define your ENUM as ENUM ('A', 'B', 'C'), and only those values (or NULL) could ever populate that field. ENUMs can have 65,535 different values.

Table 12.2 Fields for `my_music`

Field Name	Description
`id`	Creates a unique ID number for the entry
`format`	Is it a CD, cassette, or even an LP?
`title`	The title of the recording
`artist_fn`	The artist's first name
`artist_ln`	The artist's last name or the name of the group
`rec_label`	The record label
`my_notes`	My own thoughts about the recording
`date_acq`	Date acquired

In the next section, you'll create a sequence of forms that will take your table information and send it to your MySQL database. In the first step, you'll submit the name of the table and the number of fields you want to include. The second step will display additional form fields so that you can define the properties of your table columns. A third step will send the request to MySQL, verify that the table was created, and display a "Success!" message.

The Importance of Unique Fields

Using unique ID numbers not only helps you keep track of your data, but also down the road, helps you attempt to establish relationships between multiple tables. In the `my_music` table, there will be an ID field. Using this field as the unique field instead of the title field will allow you to have two recordings in your table that have the same name. For example, if you own the album *Strange Fire* by Indigo Girls, you could have two entries in your table: one for the version released in 1987 and one for the version re-released in 1989 (just trust me on that one).

Without using a unique identifier, you would have to pick only one version to put in your table, and your table wouldn't be very accurate. I hope this simple example conveys the importance of having a unique identifier in each record in your table. The usage of the unique identifier will become more apparent throughout the remainder of this book as you create more database-driven elements.

A Two-Step Form Sequence

A two-step form sequence for creating a database table might seem like overkill. After all, you saw a basic table-creation SQL statement in Chapter 1, "Installing and Configuring MySQL,"when you created `test_table`:

```
create table test_table (test_id int, test_note text);
```

When using a PHP script to create a table, all you're doing is sending the exact same query to MySQL. However, you can tie a pretty ribbon around the process (creating a form-based interface) and call it an administrative interface!

In the process of creating the administrative interface, you'll start with an HTML form and then create a PHP script that takes information from that form and dynamically creates another form. Finally, you'll create a script that sends the actual SQL query.

Step 1: Number of Fields

This HTML form will contain two input fields: one for the name of the table and one for the number of fields you want your table to contain.

1. Open a new file in your text editor and type the following HTML:

```
<HTML>
<HEAD>
<TITLE>Create a Database Table: Step 1</TITLE>
</HEAD>
<BODY>
<H1>Step 1: Name and Number</H1>
```

2. Begin your form. Assume that the method is POST and the action is a script called `do_showfielddef.php`:

```
<FORM METHOD="POST" ACTION="do_showfielddef.php">
```

3. Create an input field for the table name with a text label:

```
<P><strong>Table Name:</strong><br>
<INPUT TYPE="text" NAME="table_name" SIZE=30></P>
```

4. Create an input field for the number of fields in the table with a text label:

```
<P><strong>Number of Fields:</strong><br>
<INPUT TYPE="text" NAME="num_fields" SIZE=5></P>
```

5. Add a submit button, and then close your form and add some more HTML so that the document is valid:

```
<P><INPUT TYPE="submit" NAME="submit" VALUE="Go to Step 2"></P>
</FORM>
</BODY>
</HTML>
```

Figure 12.1 The table creation form.

6. Save the file with the name `show_createtable.html` and place this file in the document root of your Web server.

7. Open your Web browser and type `http://127.0.0.1/show_createtable.html`. See Figure 12.1.

In the next section, you'll follow Step 2 of the process and create the script that dynamically creates another form based on the values of `$_POST[table_name]` and `$_POST[num_fields]`.

Step 2: Defining Your Fields

In Step 1, you created variables to hold the name of the table (`$_POST[table_name]`) and the number of fields you want to place in the table (`$_POST[num_fields]`). In this step, you'll create a PHP script to display additional form elements needed for further definition of the fields: name, type, and length.

1. Open a new file in your text editor and start a PHP block:

```
<?
```

2. Check that values were actually entered for $_POST[table_name] and
$_POST[num_fields]. If they weren't, direct the user back to the form and exit
the script:

```
if ((!$_POST[table_name]) || (!$_POST[num_fields])) {
    header( "Location: show_createtable.html");
    exit;
}
```

3. Start building a string called $form_block, starting with the form action and
method. Assume that the method is POST and the action is a script called
do_createtable.php. Remember to escape your quotation marks!

```
$form_block = "
<FORM METHOD=\"POST\" ACTION=\"do_createtable.php\">
```

STRING CREATION

Because the script is creating the next form on-the-fly (dynamically), build
one big string so that you can echo just the string after the complicated
parsing has taken place. This way you won't be stuck with a half-built page
that won't display if an error occurs.

---

4. Add a hidden field to hold the value of $_POST[table_name], which you'll use at
the end of the sequence just to show the user that the proper table has been
created:

```
<INPUT TYPE=\"hidden\" NAME=\"table_name\" VALUE=\"$_POST[table_name]\">
```

5. Display your form in an HTML table so that fields line up nicely. Start with a row
of column headings and close the $form_block string for now:

```
<TABLE CELLSPACING=5 CELLPADDING=5>
<TR>
<TH>FIELD NAME</TH><TH>FIELD TYPE</TH><TH>FIELD LENGTH</TH></TR>";
```

6. Start a `for` loop to handle the creation of the form fields. Like a `while` loop, a `for` loop continues as long as a condition is true. In this case, the `for` loop starts out with the variable `$i` having a value of 0, and it continues for as long as `$i` is less than the value of `$_POST[num_fields]`. After each loop, `$i` is incremented by 1:

```
for ($i = 0; $i <$_POST[num_fields]; $i++) {
```

7. Within the `for` loop, you'll add to the original `$form_block`. You'll add one row for each field you want to have in your database table. Start with the table row tag and a table data cell containing an input type for the field name:

```
$form_block .= "
<TR>
<TD ALIGN=CENTER><INPUT TYPE=\"text\" NAME=\"field_name[]\"
SIZE=\"30\"></TD>
```

BRACKETS IN PHP

The use of brackets (the `[]`) after `field_name` in your input field indicates an array. For each field you define in this form, you'll be adding a value to the `$_POST[field_name]` array.

An array holds many variables in numbered slots, beginning with 0. Slots are added automatically as the array grows. For example, if you are creating a database table with six fields, the `$_POST[field_name]` array will be made up of six field name variables: `$_POST[field_name][0]`, `$_POST[field_name][1]`, `$_POST[field_name][2]`, `$_POST[field_name][3]`, `$_POST[field_name][4]`, and `$_POST[field_name][5]`.

---

8. In the next table data cell, create a drop-down list containing some common field types:

```
<TD ALIGN=CENTER>
<SELECT NAME=\"field_type[]\">
    <OPTION VALUE=\"char\">char</OPTION>
    <OPTION VALUE=\"date\">date</OPTION>
    <OPTION VALUE=\"float\">float</OPTION>
    <OPTION VALUE=\"int\">int</OPTION>
```

```
        <OPTION VALUE=\"text\">text</OPTION>
        <OPTION VALUE=\"varchar\">varchar</OPTION>
</SELECT>
</TD>
```

9. In the final table data cell, create a text field for the length of the field and close your table row. Also close the `$form_block` string because you're done with it for now:

```
<TD ALIGN=CENTER><INPUT TYPE=\"text\" NAME=\"field_length[]\"
SIZE=\"5\"></TD>
</TR>";
```

10. Close the `for` loop:

```
}
```

11. Add the final chunk of HTML to the `$form_block` string. You'll add one row that holds the submit button and then close your table and form:

```
$form_block .= "
<TR>
<TD ALIGN=CENTER COLSPAN=3><INPUT TYPE=\"submit\" VALUE=\"Create
Table\"></TD>
</TR>
</TABLE>
</FORM>";
```

12. Close the PHP block and type the following HTML:

```
?>
<HTML>
<HEAD>
<TITLE>Create a Database Table: Step 2</TITLE>
</HEAD>
<BODY>
```

13. Add a nice heading so that the users know what they are viewing. Mingle HTML and PHP to include the value of the `$_POST[table_name]` variable:

```
<H1>Define fields for <? echo "$_POST[table_name]"; ?></H1>
```

14. Display the contents of `$form_block`:

```
<? echo "$form_block"; ?>
```

15. Add some more HTML so that the document is valid:

```
</BODY>
</HTML>
```

16. Save the file with the name `do_showfielddef.php` and place this file in the document root of your Web server.

Your code should look something like this:

```
<?
//validate important input
if ((!$_POST[table_name]) || (!$_POST[num_fields])) {
    header( "Location: show_createtable.html");
    exit;
}


//begin creating form for display
$form_block = "
<FORM METHOD=\"POST\" ACTION=\"do_createtable.php\">
<INPUT TYPE=\"hidden\" NAME=\"table_name\" VALUE=\"$_POST[table_name]\">
<TABLE CELLSPACING=5 CELLPADDING=5>
<TR>
<TH>FIELD NAME</TH><TH>FIELD TYPE</TH><TH>FIELD LENGTH</TH></TR>";


//count from 0 until you reach the number of fields
for ($i = 0; $i <$_POST[num_fields]; $i++) {
    //add to the form, one row for each field
    $form_block .= "
    <TR>
    <TD ALIGN=CENTER>
    <INPUT TYPE=\"text\" NAME=\"field_name[]\" SIZE=\"30\"></TD>
    <TD ALIGN=CENTER>
    <SELECT NAME=\"field_type[]\">
        <OPTION VALUE=\"char\">char</OPTION>
        <OPTION VALUE=\"date\">date</OPTION>
        <OPTION VALUE=\"float\">float</OPTION>
        <OPTION VALUE=\"int\">int</OPTION>
        <OPTION VALUE="text\">text</OPTION>
        <OPTION VALUE=\"varchar\">varchar</OPTION>
    </SELECT>
    </TD>
    <TD ALIGN=CENTER>
    <INPUT TYPE=\"text\" NAME=\"field_length[]\" SIZE=\"5\"></TD>
    </TR>";
}
```

```
//finish up the form
$form_block .= "
<TR>
<TD ALIGN=CENTER COLSPAN=3><INPUT TYPE=\"submit\" VALUE=\"Create Table\"></TD>
</TR>
</TABLE>
</FORM>";
?>
<HTML>
<HEAD>
<TITLE>Create a Database Table: Step 2</TITLE>
</HEAD>
<BODY>
<H1>Define fields for <? echo "$_POST[table_name]"; ?></H1>
<? echo "$form_block"; ?>
</BODY>
</HTML>
```

In the next section, you'll go from Step 1 to Step 2, preparing to create the table.

Starting the Table Creation Process

You should be able to go from Step 1 (naming the table and providing the number of fields) to Step 2 (defining the fields) without any problems. Let's try it out.

1. Open your Web browser to `http://127.0.0.1/show_createtable.html`.

2. In the Table Name field, type `my_music`.

Figure 12.2 Create database form Step 2.

3. In the Number of Fields field, type **8**.

4. Click the Go to Step 2 button. You should see the form in Figure 12.2.

There are eight rows, corresponding to the eight fields you want to create in the `my_music` table. Populate those fields, but hold off on pressing the Create Table button, because you haven't created the script yet!

1. In the first row, type `id` for the Field Name, select `int` from the Field Type drop-down menu, and specify a Field Length of 5.

2. In the second row, type `format` for the Field Name, select `char` from the Field Type drop-down menu, and specify a Field Length of 2.

3. In the third row, type `title` for the Field Name, select `varchar` from the Field Type drop-down menu, and specify a Field Length of 150.

4. In the fourth row, type `artist_fn` for the Field Name, select `varchar` from the Field Type drop-down menu, and specify a Field Length of 100.

5. In the fifth row, type `artist_ln` for the Field Name, select `varchar` from the Field Type drop-down menu, and specify a Field Length of 100.

6. In the sixth row, type `rec_label` for the Field Name, select `varchar` from the Field Type drop-down menu, and specify a Field Length of 50.

7. In the seventh row, type `my_notes` for the Field Name and select `text` from the Field Type drop-down menu.

8. In the eighth row, type `date_acq` for the Field Name and select `date` from the Field Type drop-down menu.

TEXT FIELDS AND LENGTH IN MYSQL

No field length is specified for the `my_notes` field because it is a `text` field, and thus no length is used in its definition, as you learned. Similarly, no length is specified for the `date_acq` field because data in these fields is stored in the specific `0000-00-00` format.

Figure 12.3 The completed database schema form.

The completed form should look like Figure 12.3.

In the next section, you'll create the back-end script for this form so that you can click that button and create the table.

Creating the Table-Creation Script

This script will build a SQL statement and then send it to MySQL to create the my_music table.

1. Open a new file in your text editor and start a PHP block:

```
<?
```

2. Create a variable to hold the name of the database on which the table should reside:

```
$db_name = "testDB";
```

3. Add the connection information as you have been:

```
$connection = @mysql_connect("localhost", "spike", "9sj7En4")
    or die(mysql_error());
```

4. Create a variable to hold the result of the mysql_select_db() function. Include the @ to suppress warnings, as well as the die() function to cause the script to end and a message to display if the selection of the database fails:

```
$db = @mysql_select_db($db_name, $connection) or die(mysql_error());
```

THE MYSQL_SELECT_DB() FUNCTION

The `mysql_select_db()` function requires a database name and the link identifier for the current connection.

---

5. Start building the query by placing the initial syntax in a variable called `$sql`:

```
$sql = "CREATE TABLE $_POST[table_name] (";
```

6. Create a `for` loop to create the remainder of the SQL statement. The loop should repeat for the number of fields contained as elements in the `$_POST[field_name]` array:

```
for ($i = 0; $i < count($_POST[field_name]); $i++) {
```

ARRAY COUNT

The `count()` function counts the number of elements in an array.

---

7. For each new field, you'll need to add the field name and type to the SQL statement:

```
$sql .= $_POST[field_name][$i]." ".$_POST[field_type][$i];
```

8. Because some field definitions will have a specific length and others will not, start an `if...else` block to handle this aspect. If a length is present, it must go inside parentheses, followed by a comma to start the next field definition:

```
if ($_POST[field_length][$i] != "") {
    $sql .= " (".$_POST[field_length][$i]."),";
```

9. If no length is present, just print the comma to separate the field definitions. Then close the `if...else` block:

```
} else {
    $sql .= ",";
}
```

10. Close the `for` loop:

```
}
```

11. The SQL statement held in `$sql` still needs some help. It should have an extraneous comma at the end of it, and the parentheses must be closed. Use the `substr()` function to return the entire string, with the exception of the last character:

```
$sql = substr($sql, 0, -1);
```

LOOPING THROUGH CHARACTERS IN A STRING

The 0 in the `substr()` argument list tells the function to begin at the first character, and the –1 tells the function to stop at the next-to-last character.

---

12. Close the parentheses:

```
$sql .= ")";
```

13. Create a variable to hold the result of the `mysql_query()` function. Include the @ to suppress warnings, as well as the `die()` function to cause the script to end and a message to display if the query fails:

```
$result = mysql_query($sql,$connection) or die(mysql_error());
```

14. Test the value of `$result`. If it's true, the query was successful, and a variable is created to hold a message:

```
if ($result) {
    $msg = "<P>".$_POST[table_name]." has been created!</P>";
}
```

15. Close your PHP block and add HTML:

```
?>
<HTML>
<HEAD>
<TITLE>Create a Database Table: Step 3</TITLE>
</HEAD>
<BODY>
```

16. Add a nice heading so that the users know what they are viewing. Mingle HTML and PHP to include the value of the $_POST[db_name] variable:

```
<h1>Adding table to <? echo "$db_name"; ?>...</h1>
```

17. Print the message string:

```
<? echo "$msg"; ?>
```

18. Add some more HTML so that the document is valid:

```
</BODY>
</HTML>
```

19. Save the file with the name do_createtable.php and place this file in the document root of your Web server.

Your code should look something like this:

```
<?
//indicate the database you want to use
$db_name = "testDB";
//connect to database
$connection = @mysql_connect("localhost", "spike", "9sj7En4")
    or die(mysql_error());
$db = @mysql_select_db($db_name, $connection) or die(mysql_error());

//start creating the SQL statement
$sql = "CREATE TABLE $_POST[table_name] (";

//continue the SQL statement for each new field
for ($i = 0; $i < count($_POST[field_name]); $i++) {
    $sql .= $_POST[field_name][$i]." ".$_POST[field_type][$i];

    if ($_POST[field_length][$i] != "") {
        $sql .= " (".$_POST[field_length][$i]."),";
    } else {
        $sql .= ",";
    }
}
//clean up the end of the string
$sql = substr($sql, 0, -1);
$sql .= ")";

//execute the query
$result = mysql_query($sql,$connection) or die(mysql_error());
```

```
//get a good message for display upon success
if ($result) {
    $msg = "<P>".$_POST[table_name]." has been created!</P>";
}
?>
<HTML>
<HEAD>
<TITLE>Create a Database Table: Step 3</TITLE>
</HEAD>
<BODY>
<h1>Adding table to <? echo "$db_name"; ?>...</h1>
<? echo "$msg"; ?>
</BODY>
</HTML>
```

Go on to the next step, where you get to click a button and create a table.

Create That Table!

Figure 12.4 Successful table creation.

You should still have your Web browser opened to the field definition form, with the fields complete and ready for submission. Go ahead and click the Create Table button. If everything goes smoothly, you'll see the response shown in Figure 12.4.

Figure 12.5 The updated table list.

To prove that the `my_music` table has really been created in the `testDB` database, access the `db_listtables.php` script you created in the previous chapter. You should see the `my_music` table in the list (see Figure 12.5).

In the next chapter, you'll create an HTML form interface to a script that adds entries to the `my_music` table.

13

Inserting Data into the Table

The my_music database table is just sitting there, waiting for you to add information about your music collection. In this chapter, you'll learn how to do the following:

- Create an administrative interface for adding a record.
- Create a script to insert the record into your table.

Creating the Record Addition Form

The HTML form will contain an input field for each column in the my_music database table. In the previous chapter, you created eight fields, which correspond to eight columns. Your record addition interface should have a space for each of these fields.

DATABASE FIELD NAMES

Use the database field names as the value of the NAME attribute in the HTML form fields. Also, where appropriate, use the size of the database field as the value of the MAXLENGTH attribute in the HTML form fields.

---

1. Open a new file in your text editor and type the following HTML:

```
<HTML>
<HEAD>
<TITLE>Add a Record</TITLE>
</HEAD>
<BODY>
<H1>Adding a Record to my_music</H1>
```

2. Begin your form. Assume that the method is POST and the action is a script called do_addrecord.php:

```
<FORM METHOD="POST" ACTION="do_addrecord.php">
```

3. Begin an HTML table to assist in layout. Start a new table row and table data cell, and then create an input field for the ID, with a text label:

```
<TABLE CELLSPACING=3 CELLPADDING=3>
<TR>
<TD VALIGN=TOP>
<P><STRONG>ID:</STRONG><BR>
<INPUT TYPE="text" NAME="id" SIZE=5 MAXLENGTH=5></P>
```

4. Create an input field for the date acquired with a text label. Close the table data cell after the input field:

```
<P><STRONG>Date Acquired (YYYY-MM-DD):</STRONG><BR>
<INPUT TYPE="text" NAME="date_acq" SIZE=10 MAXLENGTH=10></P>
</TD>
```

MONTH, DATE, YEAR FORMAT

The date type used in MySQL uses the YYYY-MM-DD format. An example of a date using this format is 2004-03-02 (March 2, 2004).

---

5. In a new table data cell, create a set of radio buttons to select the format of the recording. Close the table data cell and the table row after the set of radio buttons:

```
<TD VALIGN=TOP>
<P><STRONG>Format:</STRONG><BR>
<INPUT TYPE="radio" NAME="format" VALUE="CD" checked> CD
<INPUT TYPE="radio" NAME="format" VALUE="CS"> cassette
<INPUT TYPE="radio" NAME="format" VALUE="LP"> LP
</P>
</TD>
</TR>
```

6. Start a new table row and table data cell, and then create an input field for the title with a text label. Close the table data cell after the input field:

```
<TR>
<TD VALIGN=TOP>
<P><STRONG>Title:</STRONG><BR>
<INPUT TYPE="text" NAME="title" SIZE=35 MAXLENGTH=150></P>
</TD>
```

7. In a new table data cell, create an input field for the record label information with a text label. Close the table data cell and the table row after the input field:

```
<TD VALIGN=TOP>
<P><STRONG>Record Label:</STRONG><BR>
<INPUT TYPE="text" NAME="rec_label" SIZE=35 MAXLENGTH=50></P>
</TD>
</TR>
```

8. Start a new table row and table data cell, and then create an input field for the artist's first name with a text label. Close the table data cell after the input field:

```
<TR>
<TD VALIGN=TOP>
<P><STRONG>Artist's First Name:</STRONG><BR>
<INPUT TYPE="text" NAME="artist_fn" SIZE=35 MAXLENGTH=100></P>
</TD>
```

9. In a new table data cell, create an input field for the artist's last name (or group name) with a text label. Close the table data cell and the table row after the input field:

```
<TD VALIGN=TOP>
<P><STRONG>Artist's Last Name (or Group Name):</STRONG><BR>
<INPUT TYPE="text" NAME="artist_ln" SIZE=35 MAXLENGTH=100></P>
</TD>
</TR>
```

10. Start a new table row and a table data cell that spans two columns. Create a TEXTAREA field with a text label to hold your notes regarding the recording:

```
<TR>
<TD VALIGN=TOP COLSPAN=2 ALIGN=CENTER>
<P><STRONG>My Notes:</STRONG><BR>
<TEXTAREA NAME="my_notes" COLS=35 ROWS=5 WRAP=virtual></TEXTAREA></P>
```

11. Add a submit button, and then close the table data cell, the table row, and the table itself:

```
<P><INPUT TYPE="SUBMIT" NAME="submit" VALUE="Add Record"></P>
</TD>
</TR>
</TABLE>
```

12. Close your form and add some more HTML so that the document is valid:

```
</FORM>
</BODY>
</HTML>
```

Figure 13.1 The Add Record form.

13. Save the file with the name `show_addrecord.html` and place this file in the document root of your Web server.

14. Open your Web browser and type `http://127.0.0.1/show_addrecord.html`. See Figure 13.1.

In the next section, you'll create the script that takes the form input, creates a SQL statement, and adds the record to the database table.

Creating the Record Addition Script

The script you'll create for a record addition is a lot simpler than the script for table creation!

1. Open a new file in your text editor and start a PHP block:

```
<?
```

2. Check that values were actually entered for $_POST[id], $_POST[format], and $_POST[title]. If they weren't, direct the user back to the form and exit the script:

```
if ((!$_POST[id]) || (!$_POST[format]) || (!$_POST[title])) {
    header( "Location: /show_addrecord.html");
    exit;
}
```

REQUIRED FIELDS

You can have as many (or as few) required fields as you want.

---

3. Create a variable to hold the name of the database on which the table resides:

```
$db_name = "testDB";
```

4. Create a variable to hold the name of the table you're populating with this script:

```
$table_name = "my_music";
```

5. Add the connection information as you have been:

```
$connection = @mysql_connect("localhost", "spike", "9sj7En4")
    or die(mysql_error());
```

6. Select the database as you have learned:

```
$db = @mysql_select_db($db_name, $connection) or die(mysql_error());
```

7. Create the SQL statement. The first parenthetical statement gives the names of the fields to populate (in order), and the second parenthetical statement sends the actual strings:

```
$sql = "INSERT INTO $table_name
   (id, format, title, artist_fn, artist_ln, rec_label,
   my_notes, date_acq) VALUES
   ('$_POST[id]', '$_POST[format]', '$_POST[title]',
   '$_POST[artist_fn]',  '$_POST[artist_ln]', '$_POST[rec_label]',
   '$_POST[my_notes]','$_POST[date_acq]')";
```

8. Create a variable to hold the result of the `mysql_query()` function, as you have learned:

```
$result = @mysql_query($sql,$connection) or die(mysql_error());
```

9. Close your PHP block and add HTML:

```
?>
<HTML>
<HEAD>
<TITLE>Add a Record</TITLE>
</HEAD>
<BODY>
```

10. Add a nice heading so that the users know what they are viewing. Mingle HTML and PHP to include the value of the `$table_name` variable:

```
<H1>Adding a Record to <? echo "$table_name"; ?></H1>
```

11. Next, you'll re-create the layout used in `show_addrecord.html`, only it won't contain form fields. Instead, you'll mingle HTML and PHP to show the values that were entered. Start a new table row and table data cell, and then display a text label and value for ID:

```
<TABLE CELLSPACING=3 CELLPADDING=3>
<TR>
<TD VALIGN=TOP>
<P><STRONG>ID:</STRONG><BR>
<? echo "$_POST[id]"; ?></P>
```

12. Display a text label and value for the date acquired, and then close the table data cell:

```
<P><STRONG>Date Acquired (YYYY-MM-DD):</STRONG><BR>
<? echo "$_POST[date_acq]"; ?></P>
</TD>
```

13. Display a text label and the format of the recording, and then close the table data cell and table row:

```
<TD VALIGN=TOP>
<P><STRONG>Format:</STRONG><BR>
<? echo "$_POST[format]"; ?>
</P>
</TD>
</TR>
```

14. Start a new table row and table data cell, display a text label and value for the title, and close the table data cell:

```
<TR>
<TD VALIGN=TOP>
<P><STRONG>Title:</STRONG><BR>
<? echo "$_POST[title]"; ?></P>
</TD>
```

15. In a new table data cell, display a text label and value for the record label information, and then close the table data cell and table row:

```
<TD VALIGN=TOP>
<P><STRONG>Record Label:</STRONG><BR>
<? echo "$_POST[rec_label]"; ?></P>
</TD>
</TR>
```

16. Start a new table row and table data cell, and then create an input field for the artist's first name with a text label. Close the table data cell after the input field:

```
<TR>
<TD VALIGN=TOP>
<P><STRONG>Artist's First Name:</STRONG><BR>
<? echo "$_POST[artist_fn]"; ?></P>
</TD>
```

17. In a new table data cell, display a text label and value for the artist's last name (or group name), and then close the table data cell and table row:

```
<TD VALIGN=TOP>
<P><STRONG>Artist's Last Name (or Group Name):</STRONG><BR>
<? echo "$_POST[artist_ln]"; ?></P>
</TD>
</TR>
```

18. Start a new table row and a table data cell that spans two columns. Display a text label and value for your notes regarding the recording:

```
<TR>
<TD VALIGN=TOP COLSPAN=2 ALIGN=CENTER>
<P><STRONG>My Notes:</STRONG><BR>
<? echo stripslashes($_POST[my_notes]); ?></P>
```

STRIPPING EXTRANEOUS CHARACTERS

The `stripslashes()` function will remove any slashes automatically added to your form data, which is turned on by default in PHP. It will add slashes where necessary to escape special characters such as single quotes and double quotes. You can turn it off by modifying your `php.ini` file, but if you leave it on, it's one less thing you have to worry about.

19. Add a link back to the original form and then close the table data cell, the table row, and the table itself:

```
<P><a href="show_addrecord.html">Add Another</a></P>
</TD>
</TR>
</TABLE>
```

20. Add some more HTML so that the document is valid:

```
</BODY>
</HTML>
```

21. Save the file with the name `do_addrecord.php` and place it in the document root of your Web server.

Your code should look something like this:

```
<?
//check for required fields
if ((!$_POST[id]) || (!$_POST[format]) || (!$_POST[title])) {
    header( "Location: /show_addrecord.html");
    exit;
}

//set up database and table names
$db_name = "testDB";
$table_name = "my_music";

//connect to MySQL and select database to use
$connection = @mysql_connect("localhost", "spike", "9sj7En4")
    or die(mysql_error());
$db = @mysql_select_db($db_name, $connection) or die(mysql_error());

//create SQL statement and issue query
$sql = "INSERT INTO $table_name
   (id, format, title, artist_fn, artist_ln, rec_label,
   my_notes, date_acq) VALUES
   ('$_POST[id]', '$_POST[format]', '$_POST[title]',
   '$_POST[artist_fn]', '$_POST[artist_ln]', '$_POST[rec_label]',
   '$_POST[my_notes]','$_POST[date_acq]')";
```

```
$result = @mysql_query($sql,$connection) or die(mysql_error());
?>
<HTML>
<HEAD>
<TITLE>Add a Record</TITLE>
</HEAD>
<BODY>
<H1>Adding a Record to <? echo "$table_name"; ?></H1>
<TABLE CELLSPACING=3 CELLPADDING=3>
<TR>
<TD VALIGN=TOP>
<P><STRONG>ID:</STRONG><BR>
<? echo "$_POST[id]"; ?></P>
<P><STRONG>Date Acquired (YYYY-MM-DD):</STRONG><BR>
<? echo "$_POST[date_acq]"; ?></P>
</TD>
<TD VALIGN=TOP>
<P><STRONG>Format:</STRONG><BR>
<? echo "$_POST[format]"; ?>
</P>
</TD>
</TR>
<TR>
<TD VALIGN=TOP>
<P><STRONG>Title:</STRONG><BR>
<? echo "$_POST[title]"; ?></P>
</TD>
<TD VALIGN=TOP>
<P><STRONG>Record Label:</STRONG><BR>
<? echo "$_POST[rec_label]"; ?></P>
</TD>
</TR>
<TR>
<TD VALIGN=TOP>
<P><STRONG>Artist's First Name:</STRONG><BR>
<? echo "$_POST[artist_fn]"; ?></P>
</TD>
<TD VALIGN=TOP>
<P><STRONG>Artist's Last Name (or Group Name):</STRONG><BR>
<? echo "$_POST[artist_ln]"; ?></P>
</TD>
</TR>
<TR>
<TD VALIGN=TOP COLSPAN=2 ALIGN=CENTER>
<P><STRONG>My Notes:</STRONG><BR>
<? echo stripslashes($_POST[my_notes]); ?></P>
<P><a href="show_addrecord.html">Add Another</a></P>
</TD>
</TR>
</TABLE>
</BODY>
</HTML>
```

Go on to the next step where you get to click a button and add a record.

A PROBLEM WITH DATA

Here's a potential problem with the script. If you enter a string such as "He's the best!" to the comment field, you will get an error when you try to insert the record into the database. Why? Because SQL does not allow a string with a single quotation mark in the middle of the string. You must escape the string. This is accomplished with the `mysql_escape_string()` function. You will need to escape each of the SQL parameters:

```
//create SQL statement and issue query
$id = mysql_escape_string($_POST[id]);
$format = mysql_escape_string($_POST[format]);
$title = mysql_escape_string($_POST[title]);
$artist_fn=mysql_escape_string($_POST[artist_fn]);
$artist_ln=mysql_escape_string($_POST[artist_ln]);
$rec_label=mysql_escape_string($_POST[rec_label]);
$my_notes=mysql_escape_string($_POST[my_notes]);
$date_acq=mysql_escape_string($_POST[date_acq]);

$sql = "INSERT INTO $table_name
    (id, format, title, artist_fn, artist_ln, rec_label,
    my_notes, date_acq) VALUES
    ('$id', '$format', '$title', '$artist_fn', '$artist_ln',
'$rec_label', '$my_notes',
    '$date_acq')";

$result = @mysql_query($sql,$connection) or die(mysql_error());
```

This will fix your problem.

Populating Your Table

Now the fun begins! If you didn't close your Web browser after the first part of this chapter, `show_addrecord.html` should still be visible in your browser window. If it's not, open http://127.0.0.1/show_addrecord.html now.

Figure 13.2 A sample album entry.

Complete the addition form for an album you have lying around. Here's an example from my collection (see Figure 13.2).

Figure 13.3 The album record added.

Click the Add Record button, and you should see a confirmation screen, as shown in Figure 13.3.

Add several of your own recordings to the database table. Unless you changed the script on your own, the only required fields are ID, format, and title.

AUTO-INCREMENTING FIELDS

In later chapters, you'll learn to make modifications to your table so that the ID field really is unique and increments automatically so that you don't have to keep entering a number and hoping it works.

14

Selecting and Displaying Data

By now, you've happily and repeatedly populated the my_music table with all the items in your music collection—or at least a few. In this chapter, you will learn how to do the following:

- Select records from a table using the SQL ORDER BY clause.
- Format and display records from a database table.

Planning and Creating Your Administrative Menu

You could just write one script that says "Select all my data; I don't care about the order," but that would be boring. In this chapter, you'll see four ways to select records from the my_music table. To facilitate easy navigation, create an administration menu—fancy words for "a list of links to scripts."

1. Open a new file in your text editor and type the following HTML:

```
<HTML>
<HEAD>
<TITLE>My Menu</TITLE>
</HEAD>
<BODY>
<H1>My Menu</H1>
<P><strong>My Music</strong></P>
```

2. Start a bulleted list and create the first link to a script called sel_byid.php. This script will display the records ordered by ID number:

```
<ul>
<li><a href="sel_byid.php">ordered by ID</a>
```

3. Add a link to a script called sel_bydateacq.php. This script will display the records ordered by date acquired. The most recently acquired item is listed first:

```
<li><a href="sel_bydateacq.php">ordered by date acquired</a>
   (most recent first)
```

4. Add a link to a script called sel_bytitle.php. This script will display the records ordered by title:

```
<li><a href="sel_bytitle.php">ordered by title</a>
```

5. Add a link to a script called sel_byartist.php. This script will display the records ordered by artist:

```
<li><a href="sel_byartist.php">ordered by artist</a>
```

6. Close the bulleted list, and then add some HTML so that the document is valid:

```
</ul>
</BODY>
</HTML>
```

Figure 14.1 The menu Web page.

7. Save the file with the name `my_menu.html` and place this file in the document root of your Web server.

8. Open your Web browser and type `http://127.0.0.1/my_menu.html`. You should see the display shown in Figure 14.1.

In the next sections, you'll create the scripts that do all the aforementioned selecting.

Selecting Data from the `my_music` Table

The next four sections contain scripts that are variations on a theme: selecting and displaying data. A large portion of the scripts is exactly the same, but repetition makes perfection, I was always told.

The only new function in these scripts is the `mysql_fetch_array()` function. This function takes the result of a SQL query and places the rows in array format. Using a simple `while` loop, you can extract and display these elements.

Hang on to your hat, and start with the first script, which just returns the results ordered by their ID number.

Displaying Records Ordered by ID

One of the required fields in the record addition script is ID. In this script, you'll select all the records in the `my_music` table, ordered by the ID number. The default value of the `ORDER BY` clause is `ASC` (ascending), so the records are returned with ID #1 first, followed by #2, #3, and so on.

1. Open a new file in your text editor and start a PHP block:

```
<?
```

2. Create a variable to hold the name of the database on which the table resides:

```
$db_name = "testDB";
```

3. Create a variable to hold the name of the table you're selecting from, using this script:

```
$table_name = "my_music";
```

4. Add the connection information as you have been doing:

```
$connection = @mysql_connect("localhost", "spike", "9sj7En4")
    or die(mysql_error());
```

5. Select the database as you have learned:

```
$db = @mysql_select_db($db_name, $connection) or die(mysql_error());
```

6. Create the SQL statement:

```
$sql = "SELECT id, format, title, artist_fn, artist_ln, rec_label,
   my_notes, date_acq FROM $table_name ORDER BY id";
```

SELECTING ALL FIELDS IN A SQL STATEMENT

Because you're selecting all the fields, you could use a * in the SQL statement instead of naming all the fields. In this case, the line would look like this:

```
$sql = "SELECT * FROM $table_name ORDER BY id";
```

7. Create a variable to hold the result of the `mysql_query()` function, as you have learned:

```
$result = @mysql_query($sql,$connection) or die(mysql_error());
```

8. Start the `while` loop. The `while` loop will create an array called `$row` for each record in the result set (`$result`):

```
while ($row = mysql_fetch_array($result)) {
```

9. Get the individual elements of the record and give them good names. Add the `stripslashes()` function around any free text field that might have had slashes added to it:

```
$id = $row['id'];
$format = $row['format'];
$title = stripslashes($row['title']);
$artist_fn = stripslashes($row['artist_fn']);
$artist_ln = stripslashes($row['artist_ln']);
$rec_label = stripslashes($row['rec_label']);
$my_notes = stripslashes($row['my_notes']);
$date_acq = $row['date_acq'];
```

10. Do a little formatting with the artists' names. Because some artists have only a first name, some artists use both first and last names, and group names are thrown into the `artist_ln` field, start an `if...else` block to deal with this. Start by looking for groups:

```
if ($artist_fn != "") {
```

11. Create a variable called `$artist_fullname`, which will contain a string with `$artist_fn`, followed by a space, followed by `$artist_ln`, all within the `trim()` function:

```
$artist_fullname = trim("$artist_fn $artist_ln");
```

THE TRIM() FUNCTION IN PHP

The `trim()` function gets rid of extraneous space at the beginning and end of a string.

---

12. Continue the block, assigning the trimmed value of `$artist_ln` to `$artist_fullname`:

```
} else {
    $artist_fullname = trim("$artist_ln");
}
```

13. Do a little more formatting. If you didn't enter a date in the `date_acq` field, MySQL will enter a default value of `0000-00-00`. Create an `if` block that looks for this value and then replaces it with something more friendly:

```
if ($date_acq == "0000-00-00") {
    $date_acq = "[unknown]";
}
```

14. Create a variable called `$display_block` to hold all the formatted records. The formatting in this block places the title of the recording in bold, followed by the name of the record label and the artist. Next comes a line break, and then your notes, and then an emphasized parenthetical statement that holds the date acquired and format:

```
$display_block .= "<P><strong>$title</strong> on $rec_label,
    by $artist_fullname<br>
$my_notes <em>(acquired:$date_acq, format:$format)</em></P>";
```

15. Close the `while` loop and then your PHP block:

```
}
?>
```

16. Add this HTML:

```
<HTML>
<HEAD>
<TITLE>My Music (Ordered by ID)</TITLE>
</HEAD>
<BODY>
<H1>My Music: Ordered by ID</H1>
```

17. Display the results:

```
<? echo "$display_block"; ?>
```

18. Add a link back to the main menu and then add some more HTML to make a valid document:

```
<P><a href="my_menu.html">Return to Menu</a></P>
</BODY>
</HTML>
```

19. Save the file with the name `sel_byid.php` and place this file in the document root of your Web server.

20. Open your Web browser and type **http://127.0.0.1/my_menu.html**.

21. Click the link called Ordered by ID.

Figure 14.2 The List script in action.

Your records will be different from mine, but you should see a screen like Figure 14.2, where the records are ordered by internal ID number.

In the next section, you will create the script that displays results ordered by date acquired.

Displaying Records Ordered by Date Acquired

Although it isn't a required field, the record addition script has a space for the date the recording made its way into your music collection. In this script, you'll select all the records in the `my_music` table, ordered by this date, with the most recent acquisition appearing first in the list.

1. Open the `sel_byID.php` file and change the SQL statement to:

```
$sql = "SELECT * FROM $table_name ORDER BY date_acq DESC";
```

2. Change the HTML title and heading to reflect the new ordering method:

```
<HTML>
<HEAD>
<TITLE>My Music (Ordered by Date Acquired)</TITLE>
</HEAD>
<BODY>
<H1>My Music: Ordered by Date Acquired</H1>
```

3. Save the file with the name `sel_bydateacq.php` and place this file in the document root of your Web server.

4. Open your Web browser and type `http://127.0.0.1/my_menu.html`.

5. Click the link called Ordered by Date Acquired.

Figure 14.3 The ordered by date script running.

Your records will be different from mine, but you should see a screen similar to Figure 14.3, where the records are ordered by the date the recordings were acquired. Those without dates would appear at the end of the list.

In the next section, you'll create the script that displays results ordered by title.

Displaying Records Ordered by Title

As you might imagine, the recording title is a required field in the record addition script. In this script, you'll select all the records in the `my_music` table, ordered alphabetically by title.

1. Open the `sel_bydateacq.php` file and change the SQL statement to:

```
$sql = "SELECT * FROM $table_name ORDER BY title";
```

2. Change the HTML title and heading to reflect the new ordering method:

```
<HTML>
<HEAD>
<TITLE>My Music (Ordered by Title)</TITLE>
</HEAD>
<BODY>
<H1>My Music: Ordered by Title</H1>
```

3. Display the results:

```
<? echo "$display_block"; ?>
```

4. Add a link back to the main menu and then add some more HTML to make a valid document:

```
<P><a href="my_menu.html">Return to Menu</a></P>
</BODY>
</HTML>
```

5. Save the file with the name `sel_bytitle.php` and place this file in the document root of your Web server.

6. Open your Web browser and type **http://127.0.0.1/my_menu.html**.

Figure 14.4 The ordered by title script running.

7. Click the link called Ordered by Title.

Your records will be different from mine, but you should see a screen similar to Figure 14.4, where the records are ordered by title of the recording.

In the final section, you'll create the script that displays results ordered by artist name.

Displaying Records Ordered by Artist

This script is a bit trickier because you have to take into consideration issues associated with artist names: Some have only a first name, some have first and last names, and group names are thrown into the artist_ln field as well. In this script, you'll select all the records in the my_music table, ordered alphabetically by the full name of the artist.

1. Open a new file in your text editor and start a PHP block:

```
<?
```

2. Create a variable to hold the name of the database in which the table resides:

```
$db_name = "testDB";
```

3. Create a variable to hold the name of the table you're selecting from, using this script:

```
$table_name = "my_music";
```

4. Add the connection information as you have been:

```
$connection = @mysql_connect("localhost", "spike", "9sj7En4")
    or die(mysql_error());
```

5. Select the database as you have learned:

```
$db = @mysql_select_db($db_name, $connection) or die(mysql_error());
```

6. Create the SQL statement. Go back to the method that names all the fields in the SELECT statement:

```
$sql = "SELECT id, format, title, trim(concat(artist_fn,' ',artist_ln)) as
    artist_fullname, rec_label, my_notes, date_acq FROM $table_name
    ORDER BY artist_fullname";
```

USING THE CONCAT() FUNCTION IN MYSQL

Within this SQL statement, you're essentially creating a new field from two fields that already exist, using the concat() function (a MySQL string function) to combine artist_fn and artist_ln, with a space in between. Using as artist_fullname assigns this new value to a field called artist_fullname. For example, suppose you own the album "White Ladder" by David Gray. The artist's first name (David) and last name (Gray) would go in their respective areas of the form but would be output as one string (David Gray).

The trim() function still strips the white space. The phrase trim(concat(artist_fn,' ',artist_ln)) as artist_fullname replaces the if...else block usually seen within the while loop in previous scripts.

7. Create a variable to hold the result of the mysql_query() function, as you have learned:

```
$result = @mysql_query($sql,$connection) or die(mysql_error());
```

8. Start the while loop. The while loop will create an array called $row for each record in the result set ($result):

```
while ($row = mysql_fetch_array($result)) {
```

9. Get the individual elements of the record and give them good names. Remember, you have a new field called artist_fullname. Add the stripslashes() function around any free text field that might have had slashes added to it:

```
$id = $row['id'];
$format = $row['format'];
$title = stripslashes($row['title']);
$artist_fullname = stripslashes($row['artist_fullname']);
$rec_label = stripslashes($row['rec_label']);
$my_notes = stripslashes($row['my_notes']);
$date_acq = $row['date_acq'];
```

10. If you didn't enter a date in the `date_acq` field, MySQL will enter a default value of `0000-00-00`. Create an `if` block that looks for this value and then replaces it with something more friendly:

```
if ($date_acq == "0000-00-00") {
    $date_acq = "[unknown]";
}
```

11. Create a variable called `$display_block` to hold all the formatted records. The formatting in this block places the title of the recording in bold, followed by the artist's name in parentheses. Next comes a line break, and then your notes, and then an emphasized parenthetical statement that holds the date acquired and format:

```
$display_block .= "
<P><strong>$title</strong> ($artist_fullname)<br>
$my_notes <em>(acquired: $date_acq, format: $format)</em></P>";
```

12. Close the `while` loop and then your PHP block:

```
}
?>
```

13. Add this HTML:

```
<HTML>
<HEAD>
<TITLE>My Music (Ordered by Artist)</TITLE>
</HEAD>
<BODY>
<H1>My Music: Ordered by Artist</H1>
```

14. Display the results:

```
<? echo "$display_block"; ?>
```

15. Add a link back to the main menu and then add some more HTML to make a valid document:

```
<P><a href="my_menu.html">Return to Menu</a></P>
</BODY>
</HTML>
```

16. Save the file with the name `sel_byartist.php` and place this file in the document root of your Web server.

Figure 14.5 The ordered by artist script in action.

17. Open your Web browser and type `http://127.0.0.1/my_menu.html`.

18. Click the link called Ordered by Artist.

Your records will be different from mine, but you should see a screen like Figure 14.5, where the records are ordered by the name of the artist.

Displaying Records Ordered by Multiple Criteria

You might wonder how you can order things by multiple columns. For example, you might have several albums by the same artist and want to display them in order by artist name and then within artist name by the date the album was acquired. SQL provides a method for doing just this. You can modify the existing SQL statement in the selection script as follows:

1. Open the `sel_byartist.php` file and change the SQL statement to:

```
$sql = "SELECT id, format, title, trim(concat(artist_fn,' ',artist_ln)) as
    artist_fullname, rec_label, my_notes, date_acq FROM $table_name
    ORDER BY artist_fullname, date_acq";
```

2. Change the HTML title and heading to reflect the new ordering method:

```
<HTML>
<HEAD>
<TITLE>My Music (Ordered by Title and Acquisition Date)</TITLE>
</HEAD>
```

```
<BODY>
<H1>My Music: Ordered by Title and Acquisition Date</H1>
```

3. Display the results:

```
<? echo "$display_block"; ?>
```

4. Add a link back to the main menu and then add some more HTML to make a valid document:

```
<P><a href="my_menu.html">Return to Menu</a></P>
</BODY>
</HTML>
```

5. Save the file with the name `sel_bytitle.php` and place this file in the document root of your Web server.

6. Open your Web browser and type **http://127.0.0.1/my_menu.html**.

7. Click the link called Ordered by Title.

Figure 14.6 The select by title script in action.

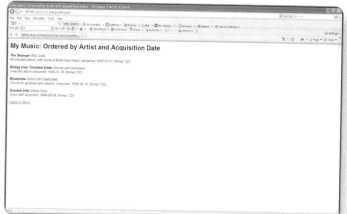

Your records will be different from mine, but you should see a screen like Figure 14.6, where the records are ordered by title of the recording.

The next chapters give you a break from database work, as you will learn a bit about user authentication, cookies, and sessions.

PART V

User Authentication and Tracking

15

Database-Driven User Authentication

Everyone has secrets they don't want to share with the entire world. But some secrets *can* be shared—with certain people. In this chapter, you will learn how to do the following:

- Create a database table for authorized users.
- Create a login form and script sequence that authenticate users before displaying any secrets.

Why Authenticate Anyone?

When initially developing a Web site, you might want to restrict access to certain members of your development team. If your corporate Web site contains sensitive financial data, you might want to restrict your financial statements to a particular list of investors. Or maybe you just don't want people poking around in your personal things.

A common type of user authentication is *database-driven*, in which usernames and passwords are kept in a database table and accessed via a login form and script. In the next section, you'll create this database table and add some users to it.

Creating the User Table

In Chapter 12, "Creating a Database Table," you followed a two-step table-creation process. You can use that same process to create the authorized users table.

1. Open your Web browser to `http://127.0.0.1/show_createtable.html`.

2. In the Table Name field, type `auth_users`.

3. In the Number of Fields field, type `4`.

4. Click the Go to Step 2 button. You should see a form with four rows, corresponding to the four fields that will be in the `auth_users` table.

5. In the first row, type `f_name` for the Field Name, select `varchar` from the Field Type drop-down menu, and specify a Field Length of `50`. This field will hold the user's first name.

6. In the second row, type `l_name` for the Field Name, select `varchar` from the Field Type drop-down menu, and specify a Field Length of `50`. This field will hold the user's last name.

7. In the third row, type `username` for the Field Name, select `varchar` from the Field Type drop-down menu, and specify a Field Length of `25`. This field will hold the user's username.

8. In the fourth row, type **password** for the Field Name, select `varchar` from the Field Type drop-down menu, and specify a Field Length of `100`. This field will hold a hash of the password.

HASHES AND STRINGS

If you recall from Chapter 7, "Displaying Dynamic Content," a *hash* is like a digital summary of the string. It can be used to compare versions of strings (or files) to determine whether the versions differ.

Figure 15.1 Creating the authorization table.

The completed form should look like Figure 15.1.

Click the Create Table button. You should see a confirmation screen stating that your table has been created. In the next section, you'll create a record addition form and script and add users to the `auth_users` table.

Adding Users to Your Table

An empty `auth_users` table does you no good. In this section, you'll create a simple record addition form and script, similar to those you created in Chapter 13, "Inserting Data into the Table."

Creating the User Addition Form and Script

The HTML form will contain an input field for each column in the `auth_users` table.

1. Open a new file in your text editor and type the following HTML:

```
<HTML>
<HEAD>
<TITLE>Add a User</TITLE>
</HEAD>
<BODY>
<H1>Adding a Record to auth_users</H1>
```

2. Begin your form. Assume that the method is POST and the action is a script called `do_adduser.php`:

```
<FORM METHOD="POST" ACTION="do_adduser.php">
```

3. Create an input field for the user's first name with a text label:

```
<P><STRONG>First Name:</STRONG><BR>
<INPUT TYPE="text" NAME="f_name" SIZE=25 MAXLENGTH=50></p>
```

4. Create an input field for the user's last name with a text label:

```
<P><STRONG>Last Name:</STRONG><BR>
<INPUT TYPE="text" NAME="l_name" SIZE=25 MAXLENGTH=50></p>
```

5. Create an input field for the username with a text label:

```
<P><STRONG>Username:</STRONG><BR>
<INPUT TYPE="text" NAME="username" SIZE=25 MAXLENGTH=25></p>
```

6. Create an input field for the password with a text label:

```
<P><STRONG>Password:</STRONG><BR>
<INPUT TYPE="text" NAME="password" SIZE=25 MAXLENGTH=25></p>
```

SETTING MAXIMUM INPUT LENGTH FOR A FIELD IN HTML

The MAXLENGTH of the password form field is 25, whereas the database field maximum length is 100. This discrepancy in length takes into consideration the encryption that will occur. A 25-character plain-text password, such as that entered in this form field, will probably be longer than 25 characters when encrypted. Because only the encrypted password is stored in the database, the greater maximum length will handle the extra data.

7. Add a submit button and then close your form and add some more HTML so that the document is valid:

```
<P><INPUT TYPE="SUBMIT" NAME="submit" VALUE="Add User"></P>
</FORM>
</BODY>
</HTML>
```

Figure 15.2 The add user form.

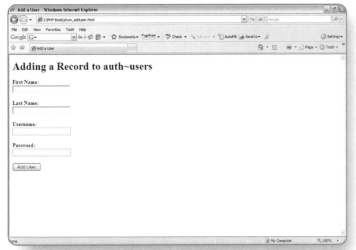

8. Save the file with the name show_adduser.html and place this file in the document root of your Web server.

9. Open your Web browser and type http://127.0.0.1/ show_adduser.html. (See Figure 15.2.)

You will see a form for adding a user, with four fields for name and password information, as well as a submit button. Next, you will create the back-end script for the record-addition form.

1. Open a new file in your text editor and start a PHP block:

```
<?
```

2. Check that values were actually entered for all four fields. If they weren't, direct the user back to the form and exit the script:

```
if ((!$_POST[f_name]) || (!$_POST[l_name]) ||
(!$_POST[username]) || (!$_POST[password])) {
    header( "Location: show_adduser.html");
    exit;
}
```

3. Create a variable to hold the name of the database on which the table resides:

```
$db_name = "testDB";
```

4. Create a variable to hold the name of the table you're populating with this script:

```
$table_name = "auth_users";
```

5. Add the connection information as you have been:

```
$connection = @mysql_connect("localhost", "spike", "9sj7En4")
    or die(mysql_error());
```

6. Select the database as you have learned:

```
$db = @mysql_select_db($db_name, $connection) or die(mysql_error());
```

7. Create the SQL statement. The first parenthetical statement gives the names of the fields to populate (in order), and the second parenthetical statement sends the actual strings:

```
$sql = "INSERT INTO $table_name (f_name, l_name, username, password)
VALUES ('$_POST[f_name]', '$_POST[l_name]', '$_POST[username]',
password('$_POST[password]'))";
```

THE PASSWORD() FUNCTION IN PHP

The PASSWORD() function inserts a hash of the password, not the password itself. This alleviates the security risk of having plain-text passwords sitting in your database, because all the script needs to do is match the two hashes.

---

8. Create a variable to hold the result of the mysql_query() function, as you have learned:

```
$result = @mysql_query($sql,$connection) or die(mysql_error());
```

9. Close your PHP block and then add HTML:

```
?>
<HTML>
<HEAD>
<TITLE>Add a User</TITLE>
</HEAD>
<BODY>
<H1>Added to auth_users:</H1>
```

10. Mingle HTML and PHP to show the values entered for each field, starting with the first name field:

```
<P><STRONG>First Name:</STRONG><BR>
<? echo "$_POST[f_name]"; ?></p>
<P><STRONG>Last Name:</STRONG><BR>
<? echo "$_POST[l_name]"; ?></p>
<P><STRONG>Username:</STRONG><BR>
<? echo "$_POST[username]"; ?></p>
<P><STRONG>Password:</STRONG><BR>
<? echo "$_POST[password]"; ?></p>
```

11. Add a link back to the original form:

```
<P><a href="show_adduser.html">Add Another</a></p>
```

12. Add some more HTML so that the document is valid:

```
</BODY>
</HTML>
```

13. Save the file with the name do_adduser.php and place this file in the document root of your Web server.

Your code should look like this:

```
<?
//check for required fields
if ((!$_POST[f_name]) || (!$_POST[l_name]) || (!$_POST[username]) ||
(!$_POST[password])) {
    header( "Location: show_adduser.html");
    exit;
}
//set up the names of the database and table
$db_name = "testDB";
$table_name = "auth_users";

//connect to the server and select the database
$connection = @mysql_connect("localhost", "spike", "9sj7En4")
    or die(mysql_error());
$db = @mysql_select_db($db_name, $connection) or die(mysql_error());

//create and issue query
$sql = "INSERT INTO $table_name (f_name, l_name, username, password)
VALUES ('$_POST[f_name]', '$_POST[l_name]', '$_POST[username]',
password('$_POST[password]'))";
$result = @mysql_query($sql,$connection) or die(mysql_error());
?>
<HTML>
<HEAD>
<TITLE>Add a User</TITLE>
</HEAD>
<BODY>
<H1>Added to auth_users:</H1>
<P><STRONG>First Name:</STRONG><BR>
<? echo "$_POST[f_name]"; ?></p>

<P><STRONG>Last Name:</STRONG><BR>
<? echo "$_POST[l_name]"; ?></p>
<P><STRONG>Username:</STRONG><BR>
<? echo "$_POST[username]"; ?></p>
```

```
<P><STRONG>Password:</STRONG><BR>
<? echo "$_POST[password]"; ?></p>
<P><a href="show_adduser.html">Add Another</a></p>
</BODY>
</HTML>
```

Next, you'll test this code by adding some sample users to your table.

Adding Some Users

The next examples are based on fake users on my server. Your results will vary, depending on what you enter in your table. To get to the user addition form, open your Web browser and type `http://127.0.0.1/show_adduser.html`.

Figure 15.3 The completed add user form.

In my user addition form, I typed information for a user named Joe Webby, with a username of `joe` and a password of `ilikecheese`. The completed form looks like Figure 15.3.

Figure 15.4 The add user confirmation screen.

After I clicked the Add User button, the confirmation screen was displayed (see Figure 15.4).

Figure 15.5 MySQL Monitor showing table entry.

To see an example of how the password hash is stored, use the command-line interface to the MySQL Monitor to view your record. You would see that the password entry says 127493710101bb5a (Figure 15.5), not ilikecheese. Note that your entry may be slightly different based on your machine and settings or the time you created it.

Continue adding some users on your own, until you have a nice family of users.

Creating the Login Form

The HTML form will contain just two fields: username and password. Both are required.

1. Open a new file in your text editor and type the following HTML:

```
<HTML>
<HEAD>
<TITLE>Login</TITLE>
</HEAD>
<BODY>
<H1>Login to Secret Area</H1>
```

2. Begin your form. Assume that the method is POST and the action is a script called do_authuser.php:

```
<FORM METHOD="POST" ACTION="do_authuser.php">
```

3. Create an input field for the username with a text label:

```
<P><STRONG>Username:</STRONG><BR>
<INPUT TYPE="text" NAME="username" SIZE=25 MAXLENGTH=25></p>
```

4. Create an input field for the password with a text label:

```
<P><STRONG>Password:</STRONG><BR>
<INPUT TYPE="password" NAME="password" SIZE=25 MAXLENGTH=25></p>
```

5. Add a submit button and then close your form and add some more HTML so that the document is valid:

```
<P><INPUT TYPE="SUBMIT" NAME="submit" VALUE="Login"></P>
</FORM>
</BODY>
</HTML>
```

6. Save the file with the name show_login.html and place this file in the document root of your Web server.

7. Open your Web browser and type http://127.0.0.1/show_login.html.

Figure 15.6 The login form.

You will see the login form, with text fields for the username and password as well as a submit button (see Figure 15.6).

Next, you create the back-end script for the login form.

Creating the Authentication Script

The goal of this script is to match the username and password entered in the form with a username and password (in the same record) in the auth_users table.

1. Open a new file in your text editor and start a PHP block:

```
<?
```

2. Check that values were actually entered for both. If they weren't, direct the user back to the form and exit the script:

```
if ((!$_POST[username]) || (!$_POST[password])) {
    header("Location: show_login.html");
    exit;
}
```

3. Create a variable to hold the name of the database in which the table resides:

```
$db_name = "testDB";
```

4. Create a variable to hold the name of the table you're populating with this script:

```
$table_name = "auth_users";
```

5. Add the connection information as you have been:

```
$connection = @mysql_connect("localhost", "spike", "9sj7En4")
    or die(mysql_error());
```

6. Select the database as you have learned:

```
$db = @mysql_select_db($db_name, $connection) or die(mysql_error());
```

7. Create the SQL statement. The statement is looking for all fields in a record where the username in the table matches the username entered in the form, and the password hash in the table matches a hash of the password entered in the form:

```
$sql = "SELECT * FROM $table_name WHERE username = '$_POST[username]'
AND password = password('$_POST[password]')";
```

8. Create a variable to hold the result of the `mysql_query()` function, as you have learned:

```
$result = @mysql_query($sql,$connection) or die(mysql_error());
```

9. Check for any results from the query by counting the number of rows returned in the result set:

```
$num = mysql_num_rows($result);
```

10. Start an `if...else` block to deal with your result. If the number of returned rows is more than 1, a match is found. Create a variable to hold an appropriate message:

```
if ($num != 0) {
    $msg = "<P>Congratulations, you're authorized!</p>";
```

11. If the number of returned rows is 0, no matches are found. In that case, direct the user back to the login form and then close the `if...else` block:

```
} else {
    header("Location: show_login.html");
    exit;
}
```

12. Close your PHP block and add HTML:

```
?>
<HTML>
<HEAD>
<TITLE>Secret Area</TITLE>
</HEAD>
<BODY>
```

13. Display the message:

```
<? echo "$msg"; ?>
```

14. Add some more HTML so that the document is valid:

```
</BODY>
</HTML>
```

15. Save the file with the name do_authuser.php and place this file in the document root of your Web server.

Your code should look like this:

```
<?
//check for required fields
if ((!$_POST[username]) || (!$_POST[password])) {
    header( "Location: show_login.html");
    exit;
}

//set up names of database and table to use
$db_name = "testDB";
$table_name = "auth_users";

//connect to server and select database
$connection = @mysql_connect("localhost", "spike", "9sj7En4")
    or die(mysql_error());
$db = @mysql_select_db($db_name, $connection) or die(mysql_error());

//build and issue the query
$sql = "SELECT * FROM $table_name WHERE username = '$_POST[username]'
    AND password = password('$_POST[password]')";

$result = @mysql_query($sql,$connection) or die(mysql_error());
```

```
//get the number of rows in the result set
$num = mysql_num_rows($result);

//print a message or redirect elsewhere, based on result
if ($num != 0) {
    $msg = "<P>Congratulations, you're authorized!</p>";
} else {
    header("Location: show_login.html");
    exit;
}
?>
<HTML>
<HEAD>
<TITLE>Secret Area</TITLE>
</HEAD>
<BODY>
<? echo "$msg"; ?>
</BODY>
</HTML>
```

Next, you get to test the login form.

Trying to Authenticate Yourself

In this section, you'll attempt to log in as one of the users you added to the auth_users table. Your results will vary, depending on the usernames and passwords you're using. To get to the login form, open your Web browser and type **http://127.0.0.1/show_login.html**.

Figure 15.7 An invalid attempt to log in.

I first tried to break the authentication routine by entering a bad username and a bad password (see Figure 15.7).

After I clicked on the Login button, I was directed back to the login page, because both the username and password were invalid.

SECURITY NOTE

Any combination of bad username and bad password will cause the authentication to fail. You should never tell someone exactly what he did that was wrong, as it helps hackers to break into a system.

Figure 15.8 Successful login!

Then I entered correct values in the Username and Password fields, and after I clicked the Login button, I saw the success message (Figure 15.8).

In the next chapter, you'll be introduced to cookies, and you'll see how to use them in an authentication scheme or just for general user tracking.

16

Using Cookies

Cookies are great little tools, but they get a bad rap in the press when nasty people misuse them. These little bits of text can make your development life much easier if you use them properly. In this chapter, you will learn how to do the following:

- Set a cookie.
- Extract data from a cookie.
- Amend your user authentication routines to use a cookie.

What Are Cookies?

Cookies are pieces of text that are sent to a user's Web browser. Cookies can help you create shopping carts, user communities, and personalized sites. It's not recommended that you store sensitive data in a cookie, but you can store a unique identification string that will match a user with data held securely in a database.

Take the shopping example. Suppose that you assign an identification variable to a user so that you can track what he does when he visits your site. First, the user logs in, and you send a cookie with variables designed to say, "This is Joe, and Joe is allowed to be here." While Joe is surfing around your site, you can say, "Hello, Joe!" on each and every page. If Joe clicks through your catalog and chooses 14 items to buy, you can keep track of these items and display them all in a bunch when Joe goes to the checkout area.

Setting Cookies

Before you start setting cookies, determine how you will use them and at what point you will set them. Whatever cookies you decide to set, remember that you absolutely must set a cookie before sending any other content to the browser because a cookie is actually part of the header information.

The `setcookie()` function is the one we will be using to create cookies. For example, we might create a cookie for a simple test if we had an HTML file that looked like this:

```
<HTML>
<HEAD>
<TITLE>I'm a Cookie</TITLE>
</HEAD>
<BODY>

<?
setcookie("test", "ok", "", "/", "localhost", 0);
?>

<H1>I'm a Cookie</H1>

</BODY>
</HTML>
```

Figure 16.1 The cookie script in action.

Loading that HTML file into a browser produces the display shown in Figure 16.1.

Obviously, we aren't doing much with the cookie, but we will get there.

The `setcookie()` function, used to set one cookie at a time, expects six arguments:

- **Name.** Holds the name of the variable that is kept in the global `$_COOKIE` and is accessible in subsequent scripts.

- **Value.** The value of the variable passed in the name parameter.

- **Expiration.** Sets a specific time at which the cookie value is no longer accessible. Cookies without a specific expiration time expire when the Web browser closes.

- **Path.** Determines for which directories the cookie is valid. If a single slash is in the path parameter, the cookie is valid for all files and directories on the Web server. If a specific directory is named, this cookie is valid only for pages within that directory.

- **Domain.** Cookies are valid only for the host and domain that set them. If no domain is specified, the default value is the hostname of the server that generated the cookie. The domain parameter must have at least two periods in the string in order to be valid.

- **Security.** If the security parameter is 1, the cookie will only be transmitted via HTTPS, which is to say, over a secure Web server.

This next line is an example of a cookie called `id` with a value of `55sds809892jjsj2`. This particular cookie expires in four hours (the current time plus 14,400 seconds), and it is valid for any page below the document root on the domain `yourdomain.com`.

```
setcookie("id", "55sds809892jjsj2", time()+14400, "/" ,".yourdomain.com",0);
```

In the next section, I'll give you a cheat sheet for common values of time. Then you'll move into using cookie variables.

Counting Time

If you want to specify an expiration date or time, the easiest way to do that is to tell PHP to count forward for you and then place a value in the expiration slot within the `setcookie()` function. This value should be a UNIX time integer (the number of seconds since January 1, 1970), which you can get using the `time()` function with additional seconds added to it.

Setting an expiration date on your cookies builds in some extra assurances of the validity of your users. If you set your cookie without a time limit, it will automatically expire when users close their browsers. This is useful when users are sharing computers; you don't want the next user to have all the access afforded by the previous user's cookie. Similarly, you might want to set a cookie for only 15 minutes, if you are building an online store that allows you to receive a discount on everything purchased in the first 15 minutes of your users' visits.

Table 16.1 shows some common uses of `time()+n` within the `setcookie()` function.

Setting a Test Cookie

The goal of this little script is just to set a test cookie and then print a message to the screen. Before you start, ensure that you do not have any personal firewall settings blocking incoming cookies. Also, modify your Web browser preferences to prompt you before setting cookies.

Table 16.1 Common Times

Value	Definition
`time()+60`	One minute from the current time
`time()+900`	15 minutes from the current time
`time()+1800`	30 minutes from the current time
`time()+3600`	One hour from the current time
`time()+14400`	Four hours from the current time
`time()+43200`	12 hours from the current time
`time()+86400`	24 hours from the current time
`time()+259200`	Three days from the current time
`time()+604800`	One week from the current time
`time()+2592000`	30 days from the current time

This is the only way to watch a cookie as the server attempts to send it to your browser.

1. Open a new file in your text editor and start a PHP block; then create a set of variables called $cookie_name, $cookie_value, $cookie_expire, and $cookie_domain and give them the following values:

```
<?
$cookie_name = "test_cookie";
$cookie_value = "test string!";
$cookie_expire = time()+86400;
$cookie_domain = "127.0.0.1";
```

USING COOKIE DOMAINS

Substitute your own domain name for the value of $cookie_domain, if you are not using 127.0.0.1 (localhost) as your domain.

2. Use the `setcookie()` function to set this test cookie and then close the PHP block:

```
setcookie($cookie_name, $cookie_value, $cookie_expire, "/" ,
$cookie_domain, 0);
?>
```

3. Type the following HTML:

```
<HTML>
<HEAD>
<TITLE>Set Test Cookie</TITLE>
</HEAD>
<BODY>
<h1>Mmmmmmmm...cookie!</h1>
</BODY>
</HTML>
```

4. Save the file with the name `setcookie.php` and place this file in the document root of your Web server.

Figure 16.2 The `setcookie` script in action.

5. Open your Web browser and type **http://127.0.0.1/ setcookie.php**. You should see the display shown in Figure 16.2.

You may see a dialog box prompting you to accept the cookie, depending on your security settings. The actual dialog box will differ from browser to browser, as will the action buttons. If so, click Allow to accept the cookie. You should see the HTML text.

Using Cookie Variables

There's an element to using cookies that most people forget about until they spend a few hours trying to debug something that isn't even wrong (I've done this). When a Web browser accepts a cookie, you can't extract its value until the next HTTP request is made.

In other words, if you set a cookie called name with a value of Julie on page 1, you can't extract that value until the user reaches page 2 (or page 5 or page 28—just some other page that isn't the page on which the cookie is initially set).

Using Cookies with Authentication

In the authentication script in the previous chapter, you had a login form and a results page. However, the authentication was valid only for the results page because it dynamically displayed the secret content (in this case, a Congratulations! message). If you want to require authentication for a series of static pages, you have to make some minor adjustments.

1. Open do_authuser.php in your text editor.

2. Scroll down to the if...else block that deals with the result of the authentication. Add a block that sets a cookie:

```
if ($num != 0) {
    $cookie_name = "auth";
    $cookie_value = "ok";
    $cookie_expire = "0";
    $cookie_domain = "127.0.0.1";
    setcookie($cookie_name, $cookie_value, $cookie_expire,
    "/" , $cookie_domain, 0);
```

COOKIES AND EXPIRATION DATES

The setcookie() function will send a cookie called auth with a value of ok. It will expire at the end of the browser session and will be valid for all directories on 127.0.0.1. Use your own domain name if appropriate.

3. Delete this line:

```
$msg = "<P>Congratulations, you're authorized!</p>";
```

4. Add this string:

```
$display_block = "
<p><strong>Secret Menu:</strong></p>
<ul>
<li><a href=\"secretA.php\">secret page A</a>
<li><a href=\"secretB.php\">secret page B</a>
</ul>";
```

COMPLETING THE MENU

Don't worry; you'll create the pages in this menu soon enough.

---

5. Scroll until you see the following code:

```
<? echo "$msg"; ?>
```

6. Replace it with this:

```
<? echo "$display_block"; ?>
```

7. Save the file.

Your new code should look like this:

```
<?
//check for required fields
if ((!$_POST[username]) || (!$_POST[password])) {
    header("Location: /show_login.html");
    exit;
}

//setup names of database and table to use
$db_name = "testDB";
$table_name = "auth_users";
//connect to server and select database
$connection = @mysql_connect("localhost", "spike", "9sj7En4")
    or die(mysql_error());
```

```
$db = @mysql_select_db($db_name, $connection) or die(mysql_error());

//build and issue query
$sql = "SELECT * FROM $table_name WHERE
username = \"$_POST[username]\" AND
password = password(\"$_POST[password]\")";

$result = @mysql_query($sql) or die (mysql_error());

//get the number of rows in the result set
$num = mysql_numrows($result);

//print a message and set a cookie if authorized,
//or redirect elsewhere if unauthorized
if ($num != 0) {
    $cookie_name = "auth";
    $cookie_value = "ok";
    $cookie_expire = "0";
    $cookie_domain = "127.0.0.1";
    setcookie($cookie_name, $cookie_value, $cookie_expire,
    "/" , $cookie_domain, 0);

    $display_block = "
    <p><strong>Secret Menu:</strong></p>
    <ul>
    <li><a href=\"secretA.php\">secret page A</a>
    <li><a href=\"secretB.php\">secret page B</a>
    </ul>";
} else {
    header("Location: /show_login.html");
    exit;
}
?>
<HTML>
<HEAD>
<TITLE>Secret Area</TITLE>
</HEAD>
<BODY>
<? echo "$display_block"; ?>
</BODY>
</HTML>
```

Open your Web browser and type `http://127.0.0.1/show_login.html` to get to the login form, and then enter a valid username and password. If you still have your preferences set to warn before accepting cookies, you'll see a dialog box with cookie information in it.

Figure 16.3 The new menu form.

After you click Yes (or OK, depending on the dialog box), the new menu will display, as shown in Figure 16.3.

Checking for the Authentication Cookie

The secret menu contains links to two files: secretA.php and secretB.php. By adding a snippet of code to the beginning of these pages, you can check for an authorized user.

1. Open a new file in your text editor and start a PHP block:

```
<?
```

2. Start an if...else block to check the value of $_COOKIE[auth]. The value must be ok for the user to be an authorized user:

```
if ($_COOKIE[auth] == "ok") {
```

3. Create a value to hold a success message:

```
$msg = "<P>Welcome to secret page A, authorized user!</p>";
```

4. Continue the if...else statement to account for an unauthorized visitor. An unauthorized user will be redirected to the login form:

```
} else {
    header( "Location: /show_login.html");
    exit;
}
```

> ### UNAUTHORIZED USERS
> An unauthorized visitor is one who attempts to access `secretA.php` directly without going through the authentication process.

5. Close the PHP block and type the following HTML:

```
?>
<HTML>
<HEAD>
<TITLE>Secret Page A</TITLE>
</HEAD>
<BODY>
```

6. Display the message:

```
<? echo "$msg"; ?>
```

7. Add some more HTML so that the document is valid:

```
</BODY>
</HTML>
```

8. Save the file with the name `secretA.php` and place this file in the document root of your Web server.

The contents of `secretB.php` should be nearly identical to `secretA.php`, so create another file just like `secretA.php`, only change "A" to "B" in the messaging.

It's time for some tests. Unless your browser crashed, you should still be logged in (the `auth` cookie hasn't expired), and you should have the secret menu in front of you.

Figure 6.4 The success message for secret page A.

Click the link for secret page A. You should see the success message (see Figure 6.4).

Now exit completely out of your Web browser. This includes closing all browser windows and your mail client (if it's integrated). The auth cookie should now have expired. (There's nothing to see; it just goes away.)

1. Reopen your Web browser and attempt to directly access secretB.php by typing **http://127.0.0.1/secretB.php**.

Figure 6.5 The success message for secret page B.

2. Because you are not an authorized user anymore, you should be redirected to the login screen. Go ahead and log back in as an authorized user and accept the cookie.

3. Click the link for secret page B.

You should see the success message now (see Figure 6.5).

EXPIRATIONS AND AUTHORIZATIONS

If you had remained in the browser and returned to the menu page, you would have been able to go directly to the secret B page. This is because our session cookie would not have expired and would have "thought" you were still logged in.

Thus concludes a brief yet useful introduction to user authentication and cookies.

17

Session Basics

Sessions are like cookies on steroids. Using sessions, you can maintain user-specific information without setting multiple cookies or even using a database. In this chapter, you'll learn how to do the following:

- ● Start a session.
- ● Add a variable to the $_SESSION superglobal.
- ● Enable a per-user access count.
- ● Maintain user preferences throughout multiple pages.

Before You Begin…Checking `php.ini`

Before you start working with sessions, check a value in your `php.ini` file. Look for this section of text and read it carefully:

```
; Argument passed to save_handler. In the case of files, this is the path
; where data files are stored. Note: Windows users have to change this
; variable in order to use PHP's session functions.
[much more explanatory text skipped]
session.save_path = /tmp
```

What the text in the `php.ini` file says is, essentially, that you must modify the value of `session.save_path` so that the file can be written to a directory that exists. This change primarily affects Windows users, and the modification is simple.

Enter a directory name after the = for `session.save_path`. For example, my `php.ini` file on Windows contains this:

```
session.save_path = c:\temp
```

After making the change, restart Apache so that the changes take effect. If you are using Linux/UNIX, `/tmp` is a standard directory, and you can leave this alone unless you want to change it for some compelling reason.

What's a Session?

In terms of time, a *session* is the amount of time during which a user visits a site. In the programming world, a session is kind of like a big blob that can hold all sorts of variables and values.

- This blob has an identification string, such as `940f8b05a40d5119c030c9c7745aead9`.

- This identification string is automatically sent to the user when a session is initiated, in a cookie called `PHPSESSID` (accessible via `$_COOKIE[PHPSESSID]`).

- On the server side, a matching temporary file is created with the same name (`940f8b05a40d5119c030c9c7745aead9`).

Understanding Session Variables

In the temporary session file on the Web server, session variables (and their values) are stored. Because these values and variables are not kept in a database, no additional system resources are required to connect to and extract information from database tables. You can access session variables through the $_SESSION superglobal.

For example, a temporary session file might contain the following:

```
count|s:7:"76";
valid|s:7:"yes";
```

In this example, count and valid are the names of the session variables, and 76 and yes are their respective values. However, to use the variable in the session, you must first explicitly add it to the $_SESSION superglobal. Once it is added, you can extract the value (using $_SESSION[count] or $_SESSION[valid] in this example).

When you attempt to retrieve a session variable, the sequence goes something like this (say you're trying to get the value of $_SESSION[count]):

1. The PHP parser gets the value of $_COOKIE[PHPSESSID] from the user cookie.

2. The PHP parser finds a matching temporary session file.

3. Inside the session file, the PHP parser looks for count and then finds its value (say, 76).

4. $_SESSION[count] is equal to 76.

Next, you start your own per-user counter script using a session.

Starting a Session

Starting a session is a snap. You just call the `session_start()` function, and PHP takes care of the rest, sending the cookie and creating the temporary file.

1. Open a new file in your text editor and start a PHP block, and then call the `session_start()` function:

```
<?
session_start();
```

THE SESSION_START() FUNCTION

The `session_start()` function actually performs several important tasks. First, it determines whether a session has been started for the current user, and it starts one if necessary. It also alerts the PHP engine that session variables and other session-related functions will be used within the specific script.

Because of the dual purpose of `session_start()`, use it at the beginning of all session-related scripts.

---

2. Create a string to hold a message and then close the PHP block:

```
$msg = "started a session....";
?>
```

3. Type the following HTML:

```
<HTML>
<HEAD>
<TITLE>Start a Session</TITLE>
</HEAD>
<BODY>
```

4. Display the message string:

```
<? echo "$msg"; ?>
```

5. Add some more HTML so that the document is valid:

```
</BODY>
</HTML>
```

6. Save the file with the name `session.php` and place this file in the document root of your Web server.

7. Open your Web browser and type `http://127.0.0.1/session.php`.

Figure 17.1 Cookie warning dialog.

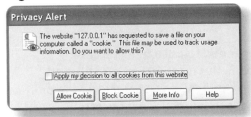

If you still have your preferences set to warn before accepting cookies, you'll see a dialog box, as shown in Figure 17.1 (or one appropriate to your browser).

Figure 17.2 Here's a screen showing a session starting. How inspiring is that?

After you click Allow, the message will display the screen shown in Figure 17.2.

In the next section, you'll register an actual value and watch it change during the course of your session.

Registering and Modifying Session Variables

The goal of this script is to register a variable and change its value during the course of a user session.

1. Open a new file in your text editor, start a PHP block, and call the `session_start()` function:

```
<?
session_start();
```

UPDATE NOTE!

In PHP systems before version 6.0, you needed to call a function called `session_register()`. Starting with version 5, this function was discouraged, and as of version 6.0, it has been removed entirely. If you are still relying on code that uses this function, simply remove it. It is no longer necessary.

---

2. We are going to be using a variable called `count` that will be stored in the `SESSION` array of variables.

3. Increment the value of `$_SESSION[count]` to account for the current access:

```
$_SESSION[count]++;
```

4. Create a string to hold a message, including the value of `$_SESSION[count]`:

```
$msg = "<P>You've been here $_SESSION[count] times. Thanks!</p>";
```

5. Close the PHP block and type the following HTML:

```
?>
<HTML>
<HEAD>
<TITLE>Count Me!</TITLE>
</HEAD>
<BODY>
```

6. Display the message string:

```
<? echo "$msg"; ?>
```

7. Add some more HTML so that the document is valid:

```
</BODY>
</HTML>
```

8. Save the file with the name `countme.php` and place this file in the document root of your Web server.

Figure 17.3 The session counting script in action!

9. Open your Web browser and type **http://127.0.0.1/ countme.php**.

Unless you closed your Web browser between the last script and now, your old session will still be active, and you won't see the cookie approval dialog box. You should just see the message displayed in Figure 17.3.

Figure 17.4 Reloading the page counting script.

Reload the page several times, and watch how the counter increments by one after each reload. For example, I reloaded the page seven times and finally saw the information displayed in Figure 17.4.

In the next section, you'll handle more than just an access count—you'll set and display user preferences during a user session.

Managing User Preferences with Sessions

Moving beyond the simple access counter, you can use sessions to manage your users' preferences when they visit your site. In this three-step example, you'll start a session, ask a user for her font family and base font size preferences, display those preferences on subsequent pages, and allow the user to change her mind and reset the values.

Starting a Session and Registering Defaults

In this script, you'll start a session and register the `font_family` and `font_size` variables. The displayed HTML will be a form that allows you to change your preferences.

1. Open a new file in your text editor, start a PHP block, and call the `session_start()` function:

```
<?
session_start();
```

2. Start an [if...else] block to check for any previous values for `font_family` and `font_size`. If values are not present in the current session, assign default values and add them:

```
if ((!$_SESSION[font_family]) || (!$_SESSION[font_size])) {
    $font_family = "sans-serif";
    $font_size = "10";
    $_SESSION[font_family] = $font_family;
    $_SESSION[font_size] = $font_size;
```

3. If previous values do exist, extract the values from the `$_SESSION` superglobal:

```
} else {
    $font_family = $_SESSION[font_family];
    $font_size = $_SESSION[font_size];
}
```

SAVING DATA IN SESSION VARIABLES

Because the user will come back to this script to reset her display preferences, you have to take into account the fact that the values of the variables must always be extracted from the session itself.

If you simply added the variables to a session without checking for previous values, each time the page were loaded, the value of these variables would be overwritten as an empty string.

4. Close the PHP block and type the following HTML:

```
?>
<HTML>
<HEAD>
<TITLE>My Display Preferences</TITLE>
```

5. Create a style sheet block, starting with the opening <STYLE> tag:

```
<STYLE type="text/css">
```

6. Add a style sheet entry for the BODY, P, and A tags. Mingle HTML and PHP to display the current values of $font_family and $font_size:

```
BODY, P, A {font-family:<? echo "$font_family"; ?>;
font-size:<? echo "$font_size"; ?>pt;font-weight:normal;}
```

7. Add a style sheet entry for the H1 tag. Mingle HTML and PHP to display the value of $font_family and a modified value of $font_size (base value plus 4):

```
H1 {font-family:<? echo "$font_family"; ?>;
font-size:<? echo $font_size + 4; ?>pt;font-weight:bold;}
```

8. Close the </STYLE> tag and continue with the HTML, adding a heading and beginning a form. Assume that the form method is POST and the action is session02.php:

```
</STYLE>
</HEAD>
<BODY>
<H1>Set Your Display Preferences</H1>
<FORM METHOD="POST" ACTION="session02.php">
```

9. Create a set of radio buttons from which the user can choose a new font family:

```
<P>Pick a Font Family:<br>
<input type="radio" name="sel_font_family" value="serif"> serif
<input type="radio" name="sel_font_family" value="sans-serif"
     checked> sans-serif
<input type="radio" name="sel_font_family" value="Courier"> Courier
<input type="radio" name="sel_font_family" value="Wingdings"> Wingdings
</p>
```

10. Create a set of radio buttons from which the user can choose a new base font size:

```
<P>Pick a Base Font Size:<br>
<input type="radio" name="sel_font_size" value="8"> 8pt
<input type="radio" name="sel_font_size" value="10" checked> 10pt
<input type="radio" name="sel_font_size" value="12"> 12pt
<input type="radio" name="sel_font_size" value="14"> 14pt
</p>
```

11. Add a submit button and close the form:

```
<P><input type="submit" name="submit" value="Set Display
Preferences"></p>
</FORM>
```

12. Add some more HTML so that the document is valid:

```
</BODY>
</HTML>
```

13. Save the file with the name `session01.php` and place this file in the document root of your Web server.

Your entire code should look like this:

```php
<?
//start a session
session_start();
//check for stored values and register defaults
if ((!$_SESSION[font_family]) || (!$_SESSION[font_size])) {
    $font_family = "sans-serif";
    $font_size = "10";
    $_SESSION[font_family] = $font_family;
    $_SESSION[font_size] = $font_size;
} else {
    //extract from $_SESSION superglobal if exist
    $font_family = $_SESSION[font_family];
    $font_size = $_SESSION[font_size];
}
?>
<HTML>
<HEAD>
<TITLE>My Display Preferences</TITLE>
<STYLE type="text/css">
BODY, P, A {font-family:<? echo "$font_family"; ?>;
font-size:<? echo "$font_size"; ?>pt;font-weight:normal;}
H1 {font-family:<? echo "$font_family"; ?>;
font-size:<? echo $font_size + 4; ?>pt;font-weight:bold;}
</STYLE>
</HEAD>
<BODY>
<H1>Set Your Display Preferences</H1>
<FORM METHOD="POST" ACTION="session02.php">
<P>Pick a Font Family:<br>
<input type="radio" name="sel_font_family" value="serif"> serif
<input type="radio" name="sel_font_family" value="sans-serif"
checked> sans-serif
<input type="radio" name="sel_font_family" value="Courier"> Courier
<input type="radio" name="sel_font_family" value="Wingdings"> Wingdings
</p>
<P>Pick a Base Font Size:<br>
<input type="radio" name="sel_font_size" value="8"> 8pt
<input type="radio" name="sel_font_size" value="10" checked> 10pt
<input type="radio" name="sel_font_size" value="12"> 12pt
<input type="radio" name="sel_font_size" value="14"> 14pt
</p>
<P><input type="submit" name="submit" value="Set Display Preferences"></p>
</FORM>
</BODY>
</HTML>
```

Now open your Web browser and type http://127.0.0.1/session01.php.

Figure 17.5 The login screen based on session variables.

Unless you closed your Web browser between the last script and now, your old session will still be active, and you won't see the cookie approval dialog box. You should just see the display shown in Figure 17.5.

In the next section, you'll create the script that handles the preference changes.

Making Preference Changes

In this script, you'll assign the new values for font_family and font_size and display a confirmation that the changes have been made.

1. Open a new file in your text editor, start a PHP block, and call the session_start() function:

```
<?
session_start();
```

2. Start an if...else block to check for the posted valued for font_family and font_size. If values are present, add them in the session.

```
if (($_POST[sel_font_family]) && ($_POST[sel_font_size])) {
    $font_family = $_POST[sel_font_family];
    $font_size = $_POST[sel_font_size];
    $_SESSION[font_family] = $font_family;
    $_SESSION[font_size] = $font_size;
```

3. Continue the block to check for previously stored values for font_family and font_size, but only if the posted values are not present.

```
} else if (((!$_POST[sel_font_family]) && (!$_POST[sel_font_size]))
    && ($_SESSION[font_family]) && ($_SESSION[font_size])) {
    $font_family = $_SESSION[font_family];
    $font_size = $_SESSION[font_size];
    $_SESSION[font_family] = $font_family;
    $_SESSION[font_size] = $font_size;
```

4. Finally, if values are not present from the form or from a previous session, define and add some defaults:

```
} else {
    $font_family = "sans-serif";
    $font_size = "10";
    $_SESSION[font_family] = $font_family;
    $_SESSION[font_size] = $font_size;
}
```

5. Close the PHP block and type the following HTML:

```
?>
<HTML>
<HEAD>
<TITLE>My Display Preferences</TITLE>
```

6. Create a style sheet block, starting with the opening <STYLE> tag:

```
<STYLE type="text/css">
```

7. Add a style sheet entry for the BODY, P, and A tags. Mingle HTML and PHP to display the current value of $font_family and $font_size:

```
BODY, P, A {font-family:<? echo "$font_family"; ?>;
font-size:<? echo "$font_size"; ?>pt;font-weight:normal;}
```

8. Add a style sheet entry for the H1 tag. Mingle HTML and PHP to display the value of $font_family and a modified value of $font_size (base value plus 4):

```
H1 {font-family:<? echo "$font_family"; ?>;
font-size:<? echo $font_size + 4; ?>pt;font-weight:bold;}
```

9. Close the `</STYLE>` tag and continue with the HTML, displaying the values of the two registered session variables:

```
</STYLE>
</HEAD>
<BODY>
<H1>Your Preferences Have Been Set</H1>
<P>As you can see, your selected font family is now
 <? echo "$font_family"; ?>, with a base size
of <? echo "$font_size" ?> pt.</p>
```

10. Provide a link back to `session01.php` in case the user wants to change preferences again, and then add some more HTML so that the document is valid:

```
<P>Please feel free to <a href="session01.php">change your
preferences</a> again.</p>
</BODY>
</HTML>
```

11. Save the file with the name `session02.php` and place this file in the document root of your Web server.

Your entire code should look like this:

```
<?
//start a session
session_start();
//check for posted values and register defaults
if (($_POST[sel_font_family]) && ($_POST[sel_font_size])) {
    $font_family = $_POST[sel_font_family];
    $font_size = $_POST[sel_font_size];
    $_SESSION[font_family] = $font_family;
    $_SESSION[font_size] = $font_size;
//check for stored values, extract from $_SESSION superglobal and register
} else if (((!$_POST[sel_font_family]) && (!$_POST[sel_font_size]))
    && ($_SESSION[font_family]) && ($_SESSION[font_size])) {
    $font_family = $_SESSION[font_family];
    $font_size = $_SESSION[font_size];
    $_SESSION[font_family] = $font_family;
    $_SESSION[font_size] = $font_size;
```

```
//register defaults
} else {
    $font_family = "sans-serif";
    $font_size = "10";
    $_SESSION[font_family] = $font_family;
    $_SESSION[font_size] = $font_size;
}
?>
<HTML>
<HEAD>
<TITLE>My Display Preferences</TITLE>
<STYLE type="text/css">
BODY, P, A {font-family:<? echo "$font_family"; ?>;
    font-size:<? echo "$font_size"; ?>pt;font-weight:normal;}
H1 {font-family:<? echo "$font_family"; ?>;
    font-size:<? echo $font_size + 4; ?>pt;font-weight:bold;}
</STYLE>
</HEAD>
<BODY>
<H1>Your Preferences Have Been Set</H1>
<P>As you can see, your selected font family is now <? echo "$font_family";
    ?>, with a base size of <? echo "$font_size" ?> pt.</p>
<P>Please feel free to <a href="session01.php">change your preferences</a>
        again.</p>
</BODY>
</HTML>
```

Unless you closed your Web browser between the last script and now, you should still be staring at the font family and font size selection form.

Figure 17.6 The preferences confirmation page.

1. Select sans-serif for the font family.

2. Select 14pt for the base font size.

3. Click the Set Display Preferences button.

The page is displayed using your selected font family and base font size, and the changes are confirmed. You can see the result of this in Figure 17.6.

Displaying Changes

This is getting fun! With your Web browser still open to the confirmation screen for the initial preference changes, click the Change Your Preferences link.

The selection form is also displayed using your new font family and base font size. Then follow these steps:

1. Select Courier for the font family.

2. Select 8pt for the base font size.

Figure 17.7 Confirmation screen showing selected font.

3. Click the Set Display Preferences button (see Figure 17.7).

The page is displayed using your selected font family and base font size, and accompanying text also indicates the changes have been made.

Figure 17.8 Confirmation screen with different font.

Again, click on the Change Your Preferences link to see that the selection form is displayed using your new font family and base font size, as shown in Figure 17.8.

Continue changing the font family and sizes, and you'll quickly discover which preferences you like and which are simply annoying! Play around with the script, changing the fonts to others available on your system, or even add other font attributes to your form and accompanying style sheet, such as italic, bold, underline, and so forth. Although the purpose of this script is to get a feel for how user-specific elements can be stored in session variables, you can also take the opportunity to explore more about the dynamic display of content.

PART VI

Creating Your Own Contact Management System

18

Planning Your System

The first step in good application design is having a plan. Although improvisation along the way is sometimes a good thing, it's best to start with a solid foundation and a series of goals. The next several chapters will help you create a simple contact-management system—basically, an online address book. In this chapter, you will learn how to:

- Define administrative tasks and create a menu.
- Modify the table-creation script sequence to account for primary keys and auto-incrementing fields.
- Define and create the my_contacts table.

Planning and Creating the Administration Menu

Not only will you be able to view data within your system, but you'll also be able to add, modify, and delete contacts. A menu would be a good idea—one that provides links to all your action scripts and adds some authentication to the mix so that only you can see the data. Now create all that in one script!

1. Open a new file in your text editor and start a PHP block. Then start a session or continue a session if a session currently exists:

```
<?
session_start();
```

2. Start an `if...else` block that checks for the value of the `$_POST[op]` variable, which will be a hidden variable in the login form you'll soon create:

```
if ($_POST[op] == "ds") {
```

3. If the value of `$_POST[op]` is `ds`, the user has completed the form. Start another `if...else` block that checks the validity of the username and password entered by the user:

```
if (($_POST[username] != "admin") || ($_POST[password] != "abc123")) {
```

> ### USERNAMES AND PASSWORDS
> You can use any username and password you want. This script is hard coded to check that the username is `admin` and the password is `abc123`.

4. If either the username or password is incorrect, create a variable called `$msg` to hold an error message:

```
$msg = "<P><font color=\"#FF0000\"><strong>Bad Login -
Try Again</strong></font></P>";
```

5. Create a variable called `$show_form` and give it a value of `yes`. This value will be checked later in the script to determine what to display:

```
$show_form = "yes";
```

6. Continue the `if...else` statement:

```
} else {
```

7. If the user makes it this far, the username and password are correct. So store a value of `yes` in the session variable called `$_SESSION[valid]`:

```
$_SESSION[valid] = "yes";
```

8. Create a variable called `$show_menu` and give it a value of `yes`. This value will be checked later in the script to determine what to display:

```
$show_menu = "yes";
```

9. Close the inner `if...else` block:

```
}
```

10. Continue the outer `if...else` block:

```
} else {
```

11. If the user is within this section of the outer `if...else` block, he has reached this script without going through the form. Check for the value of `$_SESSION[valid]` and determine what to show—menu or form:

```
if ($_SESSION[valid] == "yes") {
    $show_menu = "yes";
} else {
    $show_form = "yes";
}
```

12. Close the outer `if...else` block:

```
}
```

13. Create the form block, which will be shown if the user has not logged in or if the login is incorrect. Start by creating the variable and printing a header:

```
$form_block = "<h1>Login</h1>
```

14. Start the form. In this case, the method is POST, and the action is a variable called `$_SERVER[PHP_SELF]`:

```
<form method=POST action=\"$_SERVER[PHP_SELF]\">
```

WORKING WITH SERVER VARIABLES

`$_SERVER[PHP_SELF]` is a global variable whose value is equal to the name of the current script. By using `$_SERVER[PHP_SELF]` as a form action, you're essentially saying, "When the submit button is clicked, reload me!"

---

15. Print the value of `$msg`:

```
$msg
```

UNSET VARIABLES IN PHP

If the login is incorrect, `$msg` will contain a value, and that value will be printed in this space. If `$msg` was not created or a value was not given, nothing will print, so it doesn't hurt anything by being present all the time.

---

16. Create input fields for the username and password with text labels:

```
<P><strong>username:</strong><br>
<input type=\"text\" name=\"username\" size=15 maxlength=25></P>
<P><strong>password:</strong><br>
<input type=\"password\" name=\"password\" size=15 maxlength=25></P>
```

17. Add the hidden field for `op`:

```
<input type=\"hidden\" name=\"op\" value=\"ds\">
```

18. Add the submit button and close the form and string:

```
<P><input type=\"submit\" name=\"submit\" value=\"login\"></P>
</FORM>";
```

19. Create the menu block, which will be shown if a user has logged in and is valid. Start by creating the variable and printing a header:

```
$menu_block = "<h1>My Contact Administration System</h1>
```

20. Add several menu items and then close the string:

```
<P><strong>Administration</strong>
<ul>
<li><a href=\"show_addcontact.php\">Add a Contact</a>
<li><a href=\"pick_modcontact.php\">Modify a Contact</a>
<li><a href=\"pick_delcontact.php\">Delete a Contact</a>
</ul>
<P><strong>View Records</strong>
<ul>
<li><a href=\"show_contactsbyname.php\">Show Contacts, Ordered by
Name</a>
</ul>";
```

21. Use an `if...else` block to perform a final check to see which should be displayed—`$form_block` or `$menu_block`. Whichever should be displayed should be the value of a new variable called `$display_block`:

```
if ($show_form == "yes") {
    $display_block = $form_block;
} else if ($show_menu == "yes") {
    $display_block = $menu_block;
}
```

22. Close your PHP block and add HTML:

```
?>
<HTML>
<HEAD>
<TITLE>My Contact Management System</TITLE>
</HEAD>
<BODY>
```

23. Display the results:

```
<? echo "$display_block"; ?>
```

24. Add some more HTML to make a valid document:

```
</BODY>
</HTML>
```

25. Save the file with the name `contact_menu.php` and place this file in the document root of your Web server.

You just created a heck of a lot of code. It should look something like this:

```
<?
//start a session
session_start();

//check if user is coming from a form
if ($_POST[op] == "ds") {
    //check username and password
    if (($_POST[username] != "admin") || ($_POST[password] != "abc123")) {
        //handle bad login
        $msg = "<P><font color=\"#FF0000\"><strong>Bad Login -
        Try Again</strong></font></P>";
        $show_form = "yes";
    } else {


        //handle good login
        $_SESSION[valid] = "yes";
        $show_menu = "yes";
    }
} else {
    //determine what to show
    if ($valid == "yes") {
        $show_menu = "yes";
    } else {
        $show_form = "yes";
    }
}
//build form block
$form_block = "<h1>Login</h1>
<form method=POST action=\"$_SERVER[PHP_SELF]\">
$msg
<P><strong>username:</strong><br>
<input type=\"text\" name=\"username\" size=15 maxlength=25></P>
<P><strong>password:</strong><br>
<input type=\"password\" name=\"password\" size=15 maxlength=25></P>
<input type=\"hidden\" name=\"op\" value=\"ds\">
<P><input type=\"submit\" name=\"submit\" value=\"login\"></P>
</FORM>";
//build menu block
$menu_block = "<h1>My Contact Administration System</h1>
<P><strong>Administration</strong>
<ul>
<li><a href=\"show_addcontact.php\">Add a Contact</a>
<li><a href=\"pick_modcontact.php\">Modify a Contact</a>
<li><a href=\"pick_delcontact.php\">Delete a Contact</a>
</ul>
```

```
<P><strong>View Records</strong>
<ul>
<li><a href=\"show_contactsbyname.php\">Show Contacts, Ordered by Name</a>
</ul>";

//assign the block to show to the $display_block variable
if ($show_form == "yes") {
    $display_block = $form_block;
} else if ($show_menu == "yes") {
    $display_block = $menu_block;
}
?>
<HTML>
<HEAD>
<TITLE>My Contact Management System</TITLE>
</HEAD>
<BODY>
<? echo "$display_block"; ?>
</BODY>
</HTML>
```

Logging In to the Administration Menu

Now try to log in to the Administration menu, using the hard-coded username and password from the script.

Figure 18.1 The contact login screen.

1. Open your Web browser and type **http://127.0.0.1/ contact_menu.php**. See Figure 18.1.

You will see the login form with text fields for the username and password as well as a submit button.

Figure 18.2 Bad login display.

2. Type a bad username or a bad password in the appropriate fields and then click the Login button (see Figure 18.2).

You will see the login form again with a red error message displayed.

Figure 18.3 The main menu screen.

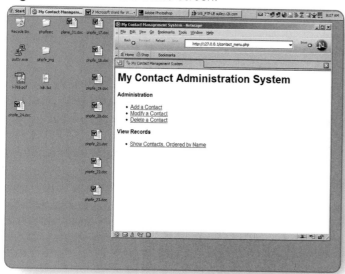

3. Type the correct username (admin) and the correct password (abc123); then click the Login button (see Figure 18.3).

You will see the Administration menu for your contact management system.

In the next section, you'll take a step back and create the my_contacts table so that you can perform all the tasks listed in this fancy Administration menu!

Defining the `my_contacts` Table

Take a moment to think about the kinds of things you'd want in a contact management system: names, addresses, telephone numbers of all sorts, e-mail addresses, and maybe even the person's birthday.

I thought about what I wanted for my own table, which I've decided to call `my_contacts`. This information appears in Table 18.1.

Table 18.1 Fields for `my_contacts`

Field Name	Description
id	Creates a unique ID number for the entry
f_name	The person's first name
l_name	The person's last name
address1	First line of the address
address2	Second line of the address
address3	Third line of the address
postcode	ZIP or postal code
country	Country in which the person resides
prim_tel	Primary telephone number
sec_tel	Secondary telephone number
email	E-mail address
birthday	The person's birthday

In the next section, you'll modify the table-creation scripts from Chapter 12, "Creating a Database Table." You'll add the capability to name primary keys and auto-incrementing fields.

Modifying the Table-Creation Scripts

With a few minor modifications to two of the three scripts in the table-creation sequence from Chapter 12, you can add check boxes to the form to handle primary keys and auto-incrementing fields. These types of fields are incredibly useful for ID fields.

1. Open `do_showfielddef.php` in your text editor and find the section of `$form_block` that prints table headings, and add the following before the end of the row:

```
<TH>PRIMARY KEY?</TH><TH>AUTO-INCREMENT?</TH>
```

2. In the `$form_block` within the `for` loop, the next-to-last line prints a text field with a name of `field_length[]`. After that line, and before the end of the table row, add these two lines:

```
<TD ALIGN=CENTER><INPUT TYPE=\"checkbox\" NAME=\"primary[]\"
VALUE=\"Y\"></TD>
<TD ALIGN=CENTER><INPUT TYPE=\"checkbox\" NAME=\"auto_increment[]\"
VALUE=\"Y\"></TD>
```

3. Save this file.

Your modified code for this script should look something like this:

```
<?
//validate important input
if ((!$_POST[table_name]) || (!$_POST[num_fields])) {
    header( "Location: http://127.0.0.1/show_createtable.html");
    exit;
}
//begin creating form for display
$form_block = "
<FORM METHOD=\"POST\" ACTION=\"do_createtable.php\">
<INPUT TYPE=\"hidden\" NAME=\"table_name\" VALUE=\"$_POST[table_name]\">
<TABLE CELLSPACING=5 CELLPADDING=5>
<TR>
<TH>FIELD NAME</TH><TH>FIELD TYPE</TH><TH>FIELD LENGTH</TH>
<TH>PRIMARY KEY?</TH><TH>AUTO-INCREMENT?</TH></TR>";
```

```
//count from 0 until you reach the number of fields
for ($i = 0; $i <$_POST[num_fields]; $i++) {
    //add to the form, one row for each field
    $form_block .= "<TR>
    <TD ALIGN=CENTER><INPUT TYPE=\"text\"
    NAME=\"field_name[]\" SIZE=\"30\"></TD>
    <TD ALIGN=CENTER>
    <SELECT NAME=\"field_type[]\">
        <OPTION VALUE=\"char\">char</OPTION>
        <OPTION VALUE=\"date\">date</OPTION>
        <OPTION VALUE=\"float\">float</OPTION>
        <OPTION VALUE=\"int\">int</OPTION>
        <OPTION VALUE=\"text\">text</OPTION>
        <OPTION VALUE=\"varchar\">varchar</OPTION>
    </SELECT>
    </TD>
    <TD ALIGN=CENTER><INPUT TYPE=\"text\"
    NAME=\"field_length[]\" SIZE=\"5\"></TD>
    <TD ALIGN=CENTER><INPUT TYPE=\"checkbox\"
    NAME=\"primary[]\" VALUE=\"Y\"></TD>
    <TD ALIGN=CENTER><INPUT TYPE=\"checkbox\"
    NAME=\"auto_increment[]\" VALUE=\"Y\"></TD>
    </TR>";
}


//finish up the form
$form_block .= "<TR>
<TD ALIGN=CENTER COLSPAN=3><INPUT TYPE=\"submit\" VALUE=\"Create Table\"></TD>
</TR>
</TABLE>
</FORM>";
?>
<HTML>
<HEAD>
<TITLE>Create a Database Table: Step 2</TITLE>
</HEAD>
<BODY>
<H1>Define fields for <? echo "$_POST[table_name]"; ?></H1>
<? echo "$form_block"; ?>
</BODY>
</HTML>
```

Next, you will modify the final part of the table-creation script.

1. Open do_createtable.php in your text editor.

2. Within the for loop, the first line appends text to the $sql variable, which holds the SQL statement for table creation. Because you've added two check boxes for additional elements of the SQL statement, you need to check for them.

Start by creating an `if...else` block that checks whether the `auto_increment` check box has been checked:

```
if ($_POST[auto_increment][$i] == "Y") {
```

3. If the `auto_increment` check box has been checked, create a variable to hold additional SQL options:

```
$additional = "NOT NULL auto_increment";
```

AUTO-INCREMENT

When you define a field as `auto_increment`, it must also be defined as NOT NULL.

---

4. If the `auto_increment` check box hasn't been checked, create the variable but do not place any text in it, and then close the block. This will assist in resetting the value of the string to an empty value as the looping continues:

```
} else {
    $additional = "";
}
```

5. Create an `if...else` block that checks whether the primary key check box has been checked:

```
if ($_POST[primary][$i] == "Y") {
```

6. If the primary key check box has been checked, append the primary key syntax to the `$additional` variable:

```
$additional .= ", primary key (".$_POST[field_name][$i].")";
```

PRIMARY KEY NAMING

The syntax for naming a field as a primary key is separated by a comma from the initial field definition. It looks something like this: `primary key (field_name)`.

---

7. If the primary key check box hasn't been checked, append an empty value to the $additional value, and then close the block:

```
} else {
    $additional = "";
}
```

8. The last change is to the preexisting loop that checks for field length and creates part of the SQL statement. Find the line that looks like this:

```
$sql .= " (".$_POST[field_length][$i]."),";
```

9. Change the line so that it looks like the following. This ensures that the $additional string is placed in the proper section of the SQL statement:

```
$sql .= " (".$_POST[field_length][$i].") $additional ,";
```

10. Similarly, find a line that looks like this:

```
$sql .= ",";
```

11. Change the line so that it looks like the following:

```
$sql .= " $additional ,";
```

12. Save the file.

Your modified code for this script should look something like this:

```
<?
//indicate the database you want to use
$db_name = "testDB";

//connect to database
$connection = @mysql_connect("localhost", "spike", "9sj7En4")
    or die(mysql_error());
$db = @mysql_select_db($db_name, $connection) or die(mysql_error());

//start creating the SQL statement
$sql = "CREATE TABLE $_POST[table_name] (";
```

```
//continue the SQL statement for each new field
for ($i = 0; $i < count($_POST[field_name]); $i++) {
    $sql .= $_POST[field_name][$i]." ".$_POST[field_type][$i];

    if ($_POST[auto_increment][$i] == "Y") {
        $additional = "NOT NULL auto_increment";
    } else {
        $additional = "";
    }

    if ($_POST[primary][$i] == "Y") {
        $additional .= ", primary key (".$_POST[field_name][$i].")";
    } else {
        $additional = "";
    }

    if ($_POST[field_length][$i] != "") {
        $sql .= " (".$_POST[field_length][$i].") $additional ,";
    } else {
        $sql .= " $additional ,";
    }

}


//clean up the end of the string
$sql = substr($sql, 0, -1);
$sql .= ")";


//execute the query
$result = mysql_query($sql,$connection) or die(mysql_error());


//get a good message for display upon success
if ($result) {
    $msg = "<P>".$_POST[table_name]." has been created!</P>";
}
?>
<HTML>
<HEAD>
<TITLE>Create a Database Table: Step 3</TITLE>
</HEAD>
<BODY>
<h1>Adding table to <? echo "$db_name"; ?>...</h1>
<? echo "$msg"; ?>
</BODY>
</HTML>
```

In the next section, you will use these new scripts to create the my_contacts table.

Creating the my_contacts Table

It's time to create the my_contacts table, complete with one primary key and auto-incrementing field.

1. Open your Web browser and type **http://127.0.0.1/show_createtable.html**.

Figure 18.4 The create table form.

2. In the Table Name field, type **my_contacts**.

3. In the Number of Fields field, type **12**.

4. Click the Go to Step 2 link (see Figure 18.4).

You will see a form with 12 rows, corresponding to the 12 fields you want to create in the my_contacts table. Populate the fields in these next steps:

1. In the first row, type **id** for the Field Name, select **int** from the Field Type drop-down menu, check the check box for Primary Key, and check the check box for Auto-Increment.

2. In the second row, type **f_name** for the Field Name, select varchar from the Field Type drop-down menu, and specify a Field Length of 75.

3. In the third row, type **l_name** for the Field Name, select varchar from the Field Type drop-down menu, and specify a Field Length of 75.

4. In the fourth row, type `address1` for the Field Name, select `varchar` from the Field Type drop-down menu, and specify a Field Length of 100.

5. In the fifth row, type `address2` for the Field Name, select `varchar` from the Field Type drop-down menu, and specify a Field Length of 100.

6. In the sixth row, type `address3` for the Field Name, select `varchar` from the Field Type drop-down menu, and specify a Field Length of 100.

7. In the seventh row, type `postcode` for the Field Name, select `varchar` from the Field Type drop-down menu, and specify a Field Length of 25.

8. In the eighth row, type `country` for the Field Name, select `varchar` from the Field Type drop-down menu, and specify a Field Length of 100.

9. In the ninth row, type `prim_tel` for the Field Name, select `varchar` from the Field Type drop-down menu, and specify a Field Length of 35.

10. In the tenth row, type `sec_tel` for the Field Name, select `varchar` from the Field Type drop-down menu, and specify a Field Length of 35.

11. In the eleventh row, type `email` for the Field Name, select `varchar` from the Field Type drop-down menu, and specify a Field Length of 100.

Figure 18.5 The completed create table form.

12. In the twelfth row, type **birthday** for the Field Name and select `date` from the Field Type drop-down menu.

The completed form should look like Figure 18.5.

Figure 18.6 The contacts table created!

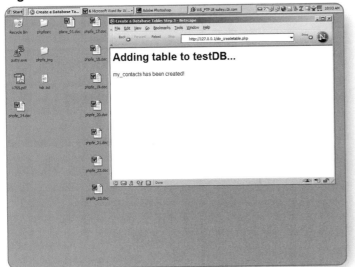

Click the Create Table button to create the my_contacts table (see Figure 18.6).

SCHEMAS

This is a very generic schema for an address book, and obviously you can see where it could be tightened up and made more specific. For example, if you knew your address book were United States-only, you could change the address fields to be two address fields: a two-character state field and a 10-character ZIP code field. The more you know about the data you want to hold in your table, the more precisely you can define it. In this case, the goal is simply to learn the process in general, and in general this is an adequate—if not a little loose—table structure. After mastering it, branch out on your own.

Congratulations! The table has been created. In the next chapter, you will create the record addition interface for this table. You are well on your way to creating a contact management system.

19

Adding Contacts

You've made it one step down the development path—you have the `my_contacts` table all created, waiting for contacts to be added. In this chapter, you'll learn how to:

- Create an administrative interface for adding a record.

- Create a script to insert the record into your table.

- Require session-based authentication before the script can be viewed or the record can be added.

Creating the Record-Addition Form

The HTML form will contain an input field for each column in the `my_contacts` table. In the previous chapter, you created 12 fields, which correspond to 12 columns. Your record-addition interface should have a space for each of these fields except the ID field, which can be left blank.

A NOTE ON AUTO-INCREMENTING

Because the ID field is an auto-incrementing field, if you add a record and leave the field blank, MySQL will place the next-highest available number in that field.

---

1. Open a new file in your text editor and start a PHP block; then start a session or continue a session if a session currently exists:

```
<?
session_start();
```

2. Start an `if...else` block that checks the value of `$_SESSION[valid]` and performs a particular action based on the result. If the value is not `yes`, the user didn't go through the proper authentication channels:

```
if ($_SESSION[valid] != "yes") {
```

3. Send the user back to the login form and exit this script:

```
header("Location: http://127.0.0.1/contact_menu.php");
exit;
```

4. Close your PHP block and then type this HTML to start building the record-addition form:

```
?>
<HTML>
<HEAD>
<TITLE>My Contact Management System: Add a Contact</TITLE>
</HEAD>
```

```
<BODY>
<h1>My Contact Management System</h1>
<h2><em>Add a Contact</em></h2>
```

5. Begin your form. Assume that the method is POST and the action is a script called do_addcontact.php:

```
<FORM METHOD="POST" ACTION="do_addcontact.php">
```

6. Begin an HTML table to assist in layout. Start a new table row, add two column headings, and then close that row:

```
<table cellspacing=3 cellpadding=5>
<tr>
<th>NAME & ADDRESS INFORMATION</th>
<th>OTHER CONTACT/PERSONAL INFORMATION</th>
</tr>
```

7. Start a new table row and table data cell, and then create an input field for the person's first name with a text label:

```
<tr>
<td valign=top>
<P><STRONG>First Name:</STRONG><BR>
<INPUT TYPE="text" NAME="f_name" SIZE=35 MAXLENGTH=75></P>
```

8. In the same table data cell, create an input field for the person's last name with a text label:

```
<P><STRONG>Last Name:</STRONG><BR>
<INPUT TYPE="text" NAME="l_name" SIZE=35 MAXLENGTH=75></P>
```

9. In the same table data cell, create an input field for the person's address (first line) with a text label:

```
<P><STRONG>Address Line 1:</STRONG><BR>
<INPUT TYPE="text" NAME="address1" SIZE=35 MAXLENGTH=100></P>
```

10. In the same table data cell, create an input field for the person's address (second line) with a text label:

```
<P><STRONG>Address Line 2:</STRONG><BR>
<INPUT TYPE="text" NAME="address2" SIZE=35 MAXLENGTH=100></P>
```

11. In the same table data cell, create an input field for the person's address (third line) with a text label:

```
<P><STRONG>Address Line 3:</STRONG><BR>
<INPUT TYPE="text" NAME="address3" SIZE=35 MAXLENGTH=100></P>
```

12. In the same table data cell, create an input field for the person's ZIP/postal code with a text label:

```
<P><STRONG>Zip/Postal Code:</STRONG><BR>
<INPUT TYPE="text" NAME="postcode" SIZE=35 MAXLENGTH=25></P>
```

13. In the same table data cell, create an input field for the person's country with a text label. Close the table data cell after this input field:

```
<P><STRONG>Country:</STRONG><BR>
<INPUT TYPE="text" NAME="country" SIZE=35 MAXLENGTH=100></P>
</td>
```

14. In a new table data cell, create an input field for the person's primary telephone number with a text label:

```
<td valign=top>
<P><STRONG>Primary Telephone Number:</STRONG><BR>
<INPUT TYPE="text" NAME="prim_tel" SIZE=35 MAXLENGTH=35></P>
```

15. In the same table data cell, create an input field for the person's secondary telephone number with a text label:

```
<P><STRONG>Secondary Telephone Number:</STRONG><BR>
<INPUT TYPE="text" NAME="sec_tel" SIZE=35 MAXLENGTH=35></P>
```

16. In the same table data cell, create an input field for the person's e-mail address with a text label:

```
<P><STRONG>E-mail Address:</STRONG><BR>
<INPUT TYPE="text" NAME="email" SIZE=35 MAXLENGTH=100></P>
```

17. In the same table data cell, create an input field for the person's birthday with a text label. Close the table data cell and the table row after this input field:

```
<P><STRONG>Birthday (YYYY-MM-DD):</STRONG><BR>
<INPUT TYPE="text" NAME="birthday" SIZE=10 MAXLENGTH=10></P>
</td>
</tr>
```

DATE TYPES IN MYSQL

The date type used in MySQL uses the YYYY-MM-DD format. An example of a date using this format is 2004-03-20 (March 20, 2004). In this example application, your date-related form fields are designed for you to enter the dates manually in this format. In Appendix C, "Writing Your Own Functions," you'll learn how to create code snippets that enable you to create dynamic lists for things like months, days, and years.

---

18. Start a new table row and table data cell that spans two columns. Inside, add a submit button as well as a link back to the main menu. Close the table data cell, the table row, and the table itself:

```
<tr>
<td align=center colspan=2><br>
<P><INPUT TYPE="SUBMIT" NAME="submit" VALUE="Add Contact to System"></P>
<p><a href="contact_menu.php">Return to Main Menu</a></p>
</TD>
</TR>
</TABLE>
```

19. Close your form and add some more HTML so that the document is valid:

```
</FORM>
</BODY>
</HTML>
```

20. Save the file with the name `show_addcontact.php`, and then place this file in the document root of your Web server.

Your code should look something like this:

```
<?
//start a session
session_start();

//validate user to see if they are allowed to be here
if ($_SESSION[valid] != "yes") {
    header("Location: http://127.0.0.1/contact_menu.php");
    exit;
}
?>
<HTML>
<HEAD>
<TITLE>My Contact Management System: Add a Contact</TITLE>
</HEAD>
<BODY>
<h1>My Contact Management System</h1>
<h2><em>Add a Contact</em></h2>
<FORM METHOD="post" ACTION="do_addcontact.php">
<table cellspacing=2 cellpadding=1>
<tr>
<th>NAME & ADDRESS INFORMATION</th>
<th>OTHER CONTACT/PERSONAL INFORMATION</th>
</tr>
<tr>
<td valign=top>
<P><STRONG>First Name:</STRONG><BR>
<INPUT TYPE="text" NAME="f_name" SIZE=35 MAXLENGTH=75></P>
<P><STRONG>Last Name:</STRONG><BR>
<INPUT TYPE="text" NAME="l_name" SIZE=35 MAXLENGTH=75></P>
<P><STRONG>Address Line 1:</STRONG><BR>
<INPUT TYPE="text" NAME="address1" SIZE=35 MAXLENGTH=100></P>
<P><STRONG>Address Line 2:</STRONG><BR>
<INPUT TYPE="text" NAME="address2" SIZE=35 MAXLENGTH=100></P>
<P><STRONG>Address Line 3:</STRONG><BR>
<INPUT TYPE="text" NAME="address3" SIZE=35 MAXLENGTH=100></P>
<P><STRONG>Zip/Postal Code:</STRONG><BR>
<INPUT TYPE="text" NAME="postcode" SIZE=35 MAXLENGTH=25></P>
<P><STRONG>Country:</STRONG><BR>
<INPUT TYPE="text" NAME="country" SIZE=35 MAXLENGTH=100></P>
</td>
<td valign=top>
<P><STRONG>Primary Telephone Number:</STRONG><BR>
<INPUT TYPE="text" NAME="prim_tel" SIZE=35 MAXLENGTH=35></P>
<P><STRONG>Secondary Telephone Number:</STRONG><BR>
<INPUT TYPE="text" NAME="sec_tel" SIZE=35 MAXLENGTH=35></P>
<P><STRONG>E-mail Address:</STRONG><BR>
<INPUT TYPE="text" NAME="email" SIZE=35 MAXLENGTH=100></P>
<P><STRONG>Birthday (YYYY-MM-DD):</STRONG><BR>
<INPUT TYPE="text" NAME="birthday" SIZE=10 MAXLENGTH=10></P>
</td>
```

```
</tr>
<tr>
<td align=center colspan=2><br><br>
<INPUT TYPE="SUBMIT" NAME="submit" VALUE="Add Contact to System">
<p><a href="contact_menu.php">Return to Main Menu</a></p>
</TD>
</TR>
</TABLE>
</FORM>
</BODY>
</HTML>
```

In the next section, you'll create the script that takes the form input, creates a SQL statement, and adds the record to the database table.

Creating the Record-Addition Script

This script will add your record to the `my_contacts` table, taking into consideration the auto-incrementing ID field.

1. Open a new file in your text editor and start a PHP block:

```
<?
```

2. Start an `if...else` block that checks for values in `$_POST[f_name]` and `$_POST[l_name]`. If they don't have values, direct the user back to the form and exit the script:

```
if ((!$_POST[f_name]) || (!$_POST[l_name])) {
    header( "Location: http://127.0.0.1/show_addcontact.php");
    exit;
```

REQUIRED FIELDS

You can have as many (or as few) required fields as you want; in this instance, you're only checking for the first and last names.

---

3. If the required fields have values, start a session, or continue a session if one currently exists. Then close the block:

```
} else {
    session_start();
}
```

4. Start an if...else block that checks the value of $_SESSION[valid] and performs a particular action based on the result. If the value is not yes, the user didn't go through the proper authentication channels:

```
if ($_SESSION[valid] != "yes") {
```

5. Send the user back to the login form and exit this script:

```
header("Location: http://127.0.0.1/contact_menu.php");
exit;
}
```

6. Create a variable to hold the name of the database in which the table resides:

```
$db_name = "testDB";
```

7. Create a variable to hold the name of the table you're populating with this script:

```
$table_name = "my_contacts";
```

8. Add the connection information as you have been:

```
$connection = @mysql_connect("localhost", "spike", "9sj7En4")
    or die(mysql_error());
```

9. Select the database as you have learned:

```
$db = @mysql_select_db($db_name, $connection) or die(mysql_error());
```

10. Create the SQL statement. The first parenthetical statement gives the names of the fields to populate (in order), and the second parenthetical statement sends the actual strings:

```
$sql = "INSERT INTO $table_name
(id, f_name, l_name, address1, address2, address3, postcode, country,
prim_tel, sec_tel, email, birthday) VALUES
('', '$_POST[f_name]', '$_POST[l_name]', '$_POST[address1]',
'$_POST[address2]', '$_POST[address3]', '$_POST[postcode]',
'$_POST[country]', '$_POST[prim_tel]', '$_POST[sec_tel]',
'$_POST[email]', '$_POST[birthday]')";
```

SETTING AUTO-INCREMENT FIELDS

Leaving a blank slot for the ID field will ensure that the field auto-increments on its own.

---

11. Create a variable to hold the result of the `mysql_query()` function, as you have learned:

```
$result = @mysql_query($sql,$connection) or die(mysql_error());
```

12. Close your PHP block and add this HTML:

```
?>
<HTML>
<HEAD>
<TITLE>My Contact Management System: Contact Added</TITLE>
</HEAD>
<BODY>
<h1>My Contact Management System</h1>
<h2><em>Add a Contact - Contact Added</em></h2>
```

13. Add a confirmation statement. Mingle HTML and PHP to include the value of the $table_name variable:

```
<P>The following information was successfully added to
<? echo "$table_name"; ?></P>
```

14. Next, you'll re-create the layout used in show_addcontact.php, only it won't contain form fields. Instead, you'll mingle HTML and PHP to show the values that were entered.

```
<table cellspacing=2 cellpadding=1>
<tr>
<th>NAME & ADDRESS INFORMATION</th>
<th>OTHER CONTACT/PERSONAL INFORMATION</th>
</tr>

<tr>
<td valign=top>
<P><STRONG>First Name:</STRONG><BR>
<? echo "$_POST[f_name]"; ?></P>

<P><STRONG>Last Name:</STRONG><BR>
<? echo "$_POST[l_name]"; ?></P>

<P><STRONG>Address Line 1:</STRONG><BR>
<? echo "$_POST[address1]"; ?></P>

<P><STRONG>Address Line 2:</STRONG><BR>
<? echo "$_POST[address2]"; ?></P>

<P><STRONG>Address Line 3:</STRONG><BR>
<? echo "$_POST[address3]"; ?></P>

<P><STRONG>Zip/Postal Code:</STRONG><BR>
<? echo "$_POST[postcode]"; ?></P>
```

```
<P><STRONG>Country:</STRONG><BR>
<? echo "$_POST[country]"; ?></P>
</td>

<td valign=top>
<P><STRONG>Primary Telephone Number:</STRONG><BR>
<? echo "$_POST[prim_tel]"; ?></P>

<P><STRONG>Secondary Telephone Number:</STRONG><BR>
<? echo "$_POST[sec_tel]"; ?></P>

<P><STRONG>E-mail Address:</STRONG><BR>
<? echo "$_POST[email]"; ?></P>

<P><STRONG>Birthday (YYYY-MM-DD):</STRONG><BR>
<? echo "$_POST[birthday]"; ?></P>
</td>
</tr>
```

15. Start a new table row and table data cell that spans two columns. Inside, add a link back to the main menu. Close the table data cell, the table row, and the table itself:

```
<tr>
<td align=center colspan=2><br>
<a href="contact_menu.php">Return to Main Menu</a>
</TD>
</TR>
</TABLE>
```

16. Add some more HTML so that the document is valid:

```
</BODY>
</HTML>
```

17. Save the file with the name do_addcontact.php and place this file in the document root of your Web server.

Go on to the next step and start adding contacts!

Populating Your Table

To start populating the my_contacts table, open http://127.0.0.1/ contact_menu.php. If you've already logged in, you'll see your Administration menu. Otherwise, log in using the username (admin) and password (abc123).

Figure 19.1 The add a contact form.

1. Select the Add a Contact menu item (see Figure 19.1).

You will see a blank form with numerous fields for adding contact information as well as a submit button and a link back to the main menu.

Figure 19.2 A sample contact.

2. Now complete the form! Only two fields are required (unless you changed that on your own): the first name and last name. Here's a sample contact shown in Figure 19.2.

Figure 19.3 Contact added confirmation.

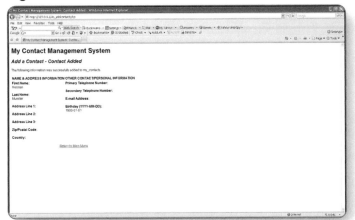

3. Click the Add Contact to System button. You should see a confirmation screen, as shown in Figure 19.3.

Add several of your own contacts to the system. Feel free to make some mistakes because in the next chapter, you create a set of record-modification scripts.

20

Modifying Contacts

Now that you have at least a few contacts in your database table, you need a simple way to modify information. People move, change e-mail accounts—you'll need to update your records sometimes. In this chapter, you'll learn how to:

- Create an administrative interface for modifying a record.
- Create a script to update the record in your table.
- Require session-based authentication before the script can be viewed or the record can be modified.

Creating the Record-Selection Form

You have a number of entries in the my_contacts table, so you'll need a quick way to select a single record for modification. The next script will create a drop-down menu of all the people in your database, from which you can select one record to modify.

1. Open a new file in your text editor and start a PHP block, and then start a session, or continue a session if one currently exists:

```
<?
session_start();
```

2. Start an if...else block that checks the value of $_SESSION[valid] and performs a particular action based on the result. If the value is not yes, the user didn't go through the proper authentication channels:

```
if ($_SESSION[valid] != "yes") {
```

3. Send the user back to the login form and exit this script:

```
header("Location: http://127.0.0.1/contact_menu.php");
exit;
}
```

4. Create variables to hold the name of the database on which the table resides, as well as the name of the table itself:

```
$db_name = "testDB";
$table_name = "my_contacts";
```

5. Add the connection information as you have been doing:

```
$connection = @mysql_connect("localhost", "spike", "9sj7En4")
    or die(mysql_error());
```

6. Select the database as you have learned:

```
$db = @mysql_select_db($db_name, $connection) or die(mysql_error());
```

7. Create the SQL statement. You want to select just the ID number, first name, and last name of each record in the table:

```
$sql = "SELECT id, f_name, l_name FROM $table_name ORDER BY l_name";
```

8. Create a variable to hold the result of the `mysql_query()` function, as you have learned:

```
$result = @mysql_query($sql,$connection) or die(mysql_error());
```

9. Check for results using the `mysql_num_rows()` function:

```
c$num = @mysql_num_rows($result);
```

10. Check the value returned by the `mysql_num_rows()` function and create a variable called `$display_block` to hold an error message if the number is less than 1 (in other words, if there are no rows returned and therefore no records in the table).

```
if ($num < 1) {
    $display_block = "<P><em>Sorry! No results.</em></p>";
```

11. Continue the `if...else` block, so the script continues if the count of rows is 1 or more:

```
} else {
```

12. Start the `while` loop. The `while` loop will create an array called `$row` for each record in the result set (`$result`):

```
while ($row = mysql_fetch_array($result)) {
```

13. Get the individual elements of the record and give them good names:

```
$id = $row['id'];
$f_name = $row['f_name'];
$l_name = $row['l_name'];
```

14. Create a variable called `$option_block`, which will contain the individual elements in the drop-down menu:

```
$option_block .= "<option value=\"$id\">$l_name, $f_name</option>";
```

15. Close the `while` loop:

```
}
```

16. Create a variable called `$display_block`, which will hold the form. Although this same variable was used to hold an error message in Step 10, it will not be used at that point unless there is an error. If there is an error, the script will never get to this step, so you have no worries about overwriting variables and can begin your form. For the form, assume that the method is POST and the action is a script called `show_modcontact.php`:

```
$display_block = "<FORM METHOD=\"POST\" ACTION=\"show_modcontact.php\">
```

17. Create a text label for the drop-down menu:

```
<P><strong>Contact:</strong>
```

18. Start the drop-down menu:

```
<select name=\"id\">
```

19. Place the `$option_block` string inside the `<select>` `</select>` tag pair. It should contain at least one `<option>` element:

```
$option_block
```

20. Finish the drop-down menu:

```
</select>
```

21. Add a submit button. Then close your form, the string, the if...else block, and the PHP block:

```
<INPUT TYPE=\"SUBMIT\" NAME=\"submit\" VALUE=\"Select this
Contact\"></P>
</form>";
}
?>
```

22. Add this HTML:

```
<HTML>
<HEAD>
<TITLE>My Contact Management System: Modify a Contact</TITLE>
</HEAD>
```

```
<BODY>
<h1>My Contact Management System</h1>
<h2><em>Modify a Contact - Select from List</em></h2>
<P>Select a contact from the list below, to modify the contact's
record.</P>
```

23. Display the contents of `$display_block`:

```
<? echo "$display_block"; ?>
```

24. Add a link back to the main menu:

```
<br><p><a href="contact_menu.php">Return to Main Menu</a></p>
```

25. Add some more HTML so that the document is valid:

```
</BODY>
</HTML>
```

26. Save the file with the name `pick_modcontact.php` and place this file in the document root of your Web server.

Your code should look something like this:

```
<?
//start a session
session_start();

//check validity of user
if ($_SESSION[valid] != "yes") {
    header("Location: http://127.0.0.1/contact_menu.php");
    exit;
}

//set up table and database names
$db_name = "testDB";
$table_name = "my_contacts";

//connect to server and select database
$connection = @mysql_connect("localhost", "spike", "9sj7En4")
or die(mysql_error());
$db = @mysql_select_db($db_name, $connection) or die(mysql_error());
```

```
//build and issue query
$sql = "SELECT id, f_name, l_name FROM $table_name ORDER BY l_name";
$result = @mysql_query($sql,$connection) or die(mysql_error());

//check the number of results
$num = @mysql_num_rows($result);

if ($num < 1) {
    //if there are no results, display message
    $display_block = "<P><em>Sorry! No results.</em></p>";
} else {
    //if results are found, loop through them
    //and make a form selection block
    while ($row = mysql_fetch_array($result)) {
        $id = $row['id'];
        $f_name = $row['f_name'];
        $l_name = $row['l_name'];
        $option_block .= "<option value=\"$id\">$l_name, $f_name</option>";
    }

    //create the entire form block
    $display_block = "
    <FORM METHOD=\"POST\" ACTION=\"show_modcontact.php\">
    <P><strong>Contact:</strong>
    <select name=\"id\">
    $option_block
    </select>
    <INPUT TYPE=\"SUBMIT\" NAME=\"submit\" VALUE=\"Select this Contact\"></P>
    </form>";
}
?>
<HTML>
<HEAD>
<TITLE>My Contact Management System: Modify a Contact</TITLE>
</HEAD>
<BODY>
<h1>My Contact Management System</h1>
<h2><em>Modify a Contact - Select from List</em></h2>
<P>Select a contact from the list below, to modify the contact's record.</P>
<? echo "$display_block"; ?>
<br>
<p><a href="contact_menu.php">Return to Main Menu</a></p>
</BODY>
</HTML>
```

In the next section, you will create the record-modification form, which looks strikingly similar to the record-addition form.

Creating the Record-Modification Form

The record-modification form is based on the record-addition form created in the previous chapter. The difference lies in the pre-population of values in the form fields. In other words, if there's already data in a record, you can see what you have before you change it.

1. Open a new file in your text editor and start a PHP block:

```
<?
```

2. Start an `if...else` block that checks for a value for `$_POST[id]`, the one variable sent from the record-selection form. If a value doesn't exist, the block directs the user back to the selection form and exits the script:

```
if (!$_POST[id]) {
    header( "Location: http://127.0.0.1/pick_modcontact.php");
    exit;
```

3. If the required field has a value, you start a session or continue a session if one currently exists. Then close the block:

```
} else {
    session_start();
}
```

4. Start an `if...else` block that checks the value of `$_SESSION[valid]` and performs a particular action based on the result. If the value is not `yes`, the user didn't go through the proper authentication channels:

```
if ($_SESSION[valid] != "yes") {
```

5. Send the user back to the login form and exit this script:

```
header("Location: http://127.0.0.1/contact_menu.php");
exit;
}
```

6. Create variables to hold the name of the database in which the table resides, as well as the table itself:

```
$db_name = "testDB";
$table_name = "my_contacts";
```

7. Add the connection information as you have been doing:

```
$connection = @mysql_connect("localhost", "spike", "9sj7En4")
    or die(mysql_error());
```

8. Select the database as you have learned:

```
$db = @mysql_select_db($db_name, $connection) or die(mysql_error());
```

9. Create the SQL statement. You want to select all the fields in the database except ID for the record with an ID equal to the value of $_POST[id]:

```
$sql = "SELECT f_name, l_name, address1, address2, address3,
postcode, country, prim_tel, sec_tel, email, birthday
FROM $table_name WHERE id = '$_POST[id]'";
```

ALTERNATE SQL APPROACHES

You could just as easily have written SELECT * FROM $table_name WHERE id = '$_POST[id]'; and simply not have done anything with the resulting value from the ID field in the database.

---

10. Create a variable to hold the result of the mysql_query() function, as you have learned:

```
$result = @mysql_query($sql,$connection) or die(mysql_error());
```

11. Start the while loop. The while loop will create an array called $row for each record in the result set ($result):

```
while ($row = mysql_fetch_array($result)) {
```

12. Get the individual elements of the record, and give them good names:

```
$f_name = $row['f_name'];
$l_name = $row['l_name'];
$address1 = $row['address1'];
$address2 = $row['address2'];
$address3 = $row['address3'];
$postcode = $row['postcode'];
$country = $row['country'];
$prim_tel = $row['prim_tel'];
$sec_tel = $row['sec_tel'];
$email = $row['email'];
$birthday = $row['birthday'];
```

USING RECORD VALUES

Now that you have the current values for the selected record, you will use them later in the script to populate the form fields.

---

13. Close the `while` loop and then close your PHP block:

```
}
?>
```

14. Type this HTML to start building the record-modification form:

```
<HTML>
<HEAD>
<TITLE>My Contact Management System: Modify a Contact</TITLE>
</HEAD>
<BODY>
<h1>My Contact Management System</h1>
<h2><em>Modify a Contact</em></h2>
```

15. Begin your form. Assume that the method is POST and the action is a script called do_modcontact.php:

```
<FORM METHOD="POST" ACTION="do_modcontact.php">
```

16. Add a hidden field to hold the value of `$_POST[id]` so it will be passed along to the script:

```
<INPUT TYPE="hidden" name="id" value="<? echo "$_POST[id]"; ?>">
```

17. Begin an HTML table to assist in layout. Start a new table row, add two column headings, and then close that row:

```
<table cellspacing=3 cellpadding=5>
<tr>
<th>NAME & ADDRESS INFORMATION</th>
<th>OTHER CONTACT/PERSONAL INFORMATION</th>
</tr>
```

18. Create rows and cells to hold input fields for all the items in the record. Use the `value` attribute in each input field and mingle HTML and PHP to echo the actual value:

```
<tr>
<td valign=top>
<P><STRONG>First Name:</STRONG><BR>
<INPUT TYPE="text" NAME="f_name" VALUE="<? echo "$f_name"; ?>"
SIZE=35 MAXLENGTH=75></P>
<P><STRONG>Last Name:</STRONG><BR>
<INPUT TYPE="text" NAME="l_name" VALUE="<? echo "$l_name"; ?>"
SIZE=35 MAXLENGTH=75></P>
<P><STRONG>Address Line 1:</STRONG><BR>
<INPUT TYPE="text" NAME="address1" VALUE="<? echo "$address1"; ?>"
SIZE=35 MAXLENGTH=100></P>
<P><STRONG>Address Line 2:</STRONG><BR>
<INPUT TYPE="text" NAME="address2" VALUE="<? echo "$address2"; ?>"
SIZE=35 MAXLENGTH=100></P>
<P><STRONG>Address Line 3:</STRONG><BR>
<INPUT TYPE="text" NAME="address3" VALUE="<? echo "$address3"; ?>"
SIZE=35 MAXLENGTH=100></P>
<P><STRONG>Zip/Postal Code:</STRONG><BR>
<INPUT TYPE="text" NAME="postcode" VALUE="<? echo "$postcode"; ?>"
SIZE=35 MAXLENGTH=25></P>
<P><STRONG>Country:</STRONG><BR>
```

```
<INPUT TYPE="text" NAME="country" VALUE="<? echo "$country"; ?>"
SIZE=35 MAXLENGTH=100></P>
</td>
<td valign=top>
<P><STRONG>Primary Telephone Number:</STRONG><BR>
<INPUT TYPE="text" NAME="prim_tel" VALUE="<? echo "$prim_tel"; ?>"
SIZE=35 MAXLENGTH=35></P>
<P><STRONG>Secondary Telephone Number:</STRONG><BR>
<INPUT TYPE="text" NAME="sec_tel" VALUE="<? echo "$sec_tel"; ?>"
SIZE=35 MAXLENGTH=35></P>
<P><STRONG>E-mail Address:</STRONG><BR>
<INPUT TYPE="text" NAME="email" VALUE="<? echo "$email"; ?>"
SIZE=35 MAXLENGTH=100></P>
<P><STRONG>Birthday (YYYY-MM-DD):</STRONG><BR>
<INPUT TYPE="text" NAME="birthday" VALUE="<? echo "$birthday"; ?>"
SIZE=10 MAXLENGTH=10></P>
</td>
</tr>
```

19. Start a new table row and table data cell that spans two columns. Inside, add a submit button as well as a link back to the main menu. Close the table data cell, the table row, and the table itself:

```
<tr>
<td align=center colspan=2><br>
<P><INPUT TYPE="SUBMIT" NAME="submit" VALUE="Update Contact Record"></P>
<br>
<p><a href="contact_menu.php">Return to Main Menu</a></p>
</TD>
</TR>
</TABLE>
```

20. Close your form and add some more HTML so that the document is valid:

```
</FORM>
</BODY>
</HTML>
```

21. Save the file with the name show_modcontact.php and place this file in the document root of your Web server.

In the next section, you'll create the script that takes the form input, creates a SQL statement, and updates the record in the database table.

Creating the Record-Modification Script

This script will update the record in the `my_contacts` table, using the value of `$_POST[id]` as the primary key (which it is).

1. Open a new file in your text editor and start a PHP block:

```
<?
```

2. Start an `if...else` block that checks for values in `$_POST[f_name]` and `$_POST[l_name]`. If they don't have values, direct the user back to the selection form and exit the script:

```
if ((!$_POST[f_name]) || (!$_POST[l_name])) {
    header( "Location: http://127.0.0.1/pick_modcontact.php");
    exit;
```

REQUIRED FIELDS

You can have as many (or as few) required fields as you want, but the requirements should match the required fields from the record-addition form.

---

3. If the required fields have values, start a session or continue a session if one currently exists. Then close the block:

```
} else {
    session_start();
}
```

4. Start an `if...else` block that checks the value of `$_SESSION[valid]` and performs a particular action based on the result. If the value is not `yes`, the user didn't go through the proper authentication channels:

```
if ($_SESSION[valid] != "yes") {
```

5. Send the user back to the login form and exit this script:

```
header("Location: http://127.0.0.1/contact_menu.php");
exit;
}
```

6. Create variables to hold the name of the database on which the table resides, as well as the table itself:

```
$db_name = "testDB";
$table_name = "my_contacts";
```

7. Add the connection information as you have been:

```
$connection = @mysql_connect("localhost", "spike", "9sj7En4")
    or die(mysql_error());
```

8. Select the database as you have learned:

```
$db = @mysql_select_db($db_name, $connection) or die(mysql_error());
```

9. Create the SQL statement. This statement uses UPDATE to set fields to specific values:

```
$sql = "UPDATE $table_name SET
    f_name = '$_POST[f_name]',
    l_name = '$_POST[l_name]',
    address1 = '$_POST[address1]',
    address2 = '$_POST[address2]',
    address3 = '$_POST[address3]',
    postcode = '$_POST[postcode]',
    country = '$_POST[country]',
    prim_tel = '$_POST[prim_tel]',
    sec_tel = '$_POST[sec_tel]',
    email = '$_POST[email]',
    birthday = '$_POST[birthday]'
    WHERE id = '$_POST[id]'";
```

10. Create a variable to hold the result of the mysql_query() function, as you have learned:

```
$result = @mysql_query($sql,$connection) or die(mysql_error());
```

11. Close your PHP block and add this HTML:

```
?>
<HTML>
<HEAD>
<TITLE>My Contact Management System: Contact Updated</TITLE>
</HEAD>
<BODY>
<h1>My Contact Management System</h1>
<h2><em>Modify a Contact - Contact Updated</em></h2>
```

12. Add a confirmation statement. Mingle HTML and PHP to include the value of the $table_name variable:

```
<P>The following information was successfully updated in
<? echo "$table_name"; ?></P>
```

13. Next, you re-create the layout used in show_modcontact.php, only it won't contain form fields. Instead, you'll mingle HTML and PHP to show the values that were entered. Start a new table row, add two column headings, and then close that row:

```
<table cellspacing=3 cellpadding=5>
<tr>
<th>NAME & ADDRESS INFORMATION</th>
<th>OTHER CONTACT/PERSONAL INFORMATION</th>
</tr>
```

14. Start a new table row and table data cell, and then display a text label and value for each field:

```
<tr>
<td valign=top>
<P><STRONG>First Name:</STRONG><BR>
<? echo "$_POST[f_name]"; ?></P>
<P><STRONG>Last Name:</STRONG><BR>
<? echo "$_POST[l_name]"; ?></P>
<P><STRONG>Address Line 1:</STRONG><BR>
<? echo "$_POST[address1]"; ?></P>
<P><STRONG>Address Line 2:</STRONG><BR>
```

```
<? echo "$_POST[address2]"; ?></P>
<P><STRONG>Address Line 3:</STRONG><BR>
<? echo "$_POST[address3]"; ?></P>
<P><STRONG>Zip/Postal Code:</STRONG><BR>
<? echo "$_POST[postcode]"; ?></P>
<P><STRONG>Country:</STRONG><BR>
<? echo "$_POST[country]"; ?></P>
</td>
<td valign=top>
<P><STRONG>Primary Telephone Number:</STRONG><BR>
<? echo "$_POST[prim_tel]"; ?></P>
<P><STRONG>Secondary Telephone Number:</STRONG><BR>
<? echo "$_POST[sec_tel]"; ?></P>
<P><STRONG>E-mail Address:</STRONG><BR>
<? echo "$_POST[email]"; ?></P>
<P><STRONG>Birthday (YYYY-MM-DD):</STRONG><BR>
<? echo "$_POST[birthday]"; ?></P>
</td>
</tr>
```

15. Start a new table row and table data cell that spans two columns. Inside, add a link back to the main menu. Close the table data cell, the table row, and the table itself:

```
<tr>
<td align=center colspan=2><br>
<p><a href="contact_menu.php">Return to Main Menu</a></p>
</TD>
</TR>
</TABLE>
```

16. Add some more HTML so that the document is valid:

```
</BODY>
</HTML>
```

17. Save the file with the name `do_modcontact.php` and place this file in the document root of your Web server.

You can now go on to the next step—modifying some of the contacts in your table.

Modifying Contacts

To start modifying contacts in the my_contacts table, open http://127.0.0.1/ contact_menu.php. If you've already logged in, you'll see your Administration menu. Otherwise, log in using the username (admin) and password (abc123).

Figure 20.1 The contact selection form.

1. Select the Modify a Contact menu item (see Figure 20.1).

You will see a drop-down menu of the contacts in the system, ordered by last name, as well as a submit button and a link back to the main menu.

Figure 20.2 The modify contact form.

2. Select a contact from the list and click the Select This Contact button. I selected a sample from my own list. It is not complete, needing us to fill in some information (see Figure 20.2).

Figure 20.3 The contact modification form.

You will see the contact modification form, with fields pre-populated with existing values (see Figure 20.3).

Figure 20.4 The contact modification confirmation screen.

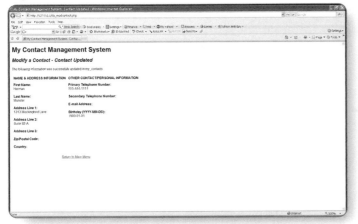

3. Change something in the record. In my sample, I changed the Address 1 and Address 2 fields to "1313 Mockingbird Lane" and "Suite 92-A." I also changed the primary telephone number to 555-444-1111. Click the Update Contact Record button. You should see a confirmation screen, shown in Figure 20.4.

Figure 20.5 The updated record.

4. Return to the selection form and select your contact again to see that the value has really changed, as shown in Figure 20.5.

Modify the records of some of your own contacts. In the next chapter, you will create the administrative scripts used to delete some records.

21

Deleting Contacts

There are plenty of times when I want to delete people from my address book for one reason or another. You should be able to delete people from your online contact management system, too! In this chapter, you'll learn how to:

- Create an administrative interface for deleting a record.
- Create a script to delete the record from your table.
- Require session-based authentication before the script can be viewed or the record can be deleted.

Using the Record-Selection Form

The script that creates a selection form for record deletion is virtually identical to the script used to select a record for modification. This section will be very easy for you to skim through. Repetition makes for perfection!

1. Open a new file in your text editor and start a PHP block. Then start a session or continue a session if one currently exists:

```
<?
session_start();
```

2. Start an `if...else` block that checks the value of `$_SESSION[valid]` and performs a particular action based on the result. If the value is not `yes`, the user didn't go through the proper authentication channels:

```
if ($_SESSION[valid] != "yes") {
```

3. Send the user back to the login form, and exit this script:

```
header("Location: http://127.0.0.1/contact_menu.php");
exit;
}
```

4. Create variables to hold the name of the database in which the table resides, as well as the table itself:

```
$db_name = "testDB";
$table_name = "my_contacts";
```

5. Add the connection information as you have been doing:

```
$connection = @mysql_connect("localhost", "spike", "9sj7En4")
      or die(mysql_error());
```

6. Select the database as you have learned:

```
$db = @mysql_select_db($db_name, $connection) or die(mysql_error());
```

7. Create the SQL statement. You want to select just the ID number, first name, and last name of each record in the table:

```
$sql = "SELECT id, f_name, l_name FROM $table_name ORDER BY l_name";
```

8. Create a variable to hold the result of the `mysql_query()` function, as you have learned:

```
$result = @mysql_query($sql,$connection) or die(mysql_error());
```

9. Check for results using the `mysql_num_rows()` function:

```
$num = @mysql_num_rows($result);
```

10. Check the value returned by the `mysql_num_rows()` function and create a variable called `$display_block` to hold an error message if the number is less than 1 (in other words, if there are no rows returned and therefore no records in the table).

```
if ($num < 1) {
    $display_block = "<P><em>Sorry! No results.</em></p>";
```

11. Continue the `if...else` block, so the script continues if the count of rows is 1 or more:

```
} else {
```

12. Start the `while` loop. The `while` loop will create an array called `$row` for each record in the result set (`$result`):

```
while ($row = mysql_fetch_array($result)) {
```

13. Get the individual elements of the record and give them good names:

```
$id = $row['id'];
$f_name = $row['f_name'];
$l_name = $row['l_name'];
```

14. Create a variable called `$option_block`, which will contain the individual elements in the drop-down menu:

```
$option_block .= "<option value=\"$id\">$l_name, $f_name</option>";
```

15. Close the `while` loop:

```
}
```

16. Create a variable called `$display_block`, which will hold the form. Although this same variable was used to hold an error message in Step 10, it will not be used at that point unless there is an error. If there is an error, the script will never get to this step, so you have no worries about overwriting variables and can begin your form. For the form, assume that the method is POST and the action is a script called `show_delcontact.php`:

```
$display_block = "<FORM METHOD=\"POST\" ACTION=\"show_delcontact.php\">
```

17. Create a text label for the drop-down menu:

```
<P><strong>Contact:</strong>
```

18. Start the drop-down menu:

```
<select name=\"id\">
```

19. Place the `$option_block` string inside the `<select>` `</select>` tag pair. It should contain at least one `<option>` element:

```
$option_block
```

20. Finish the drop-down menu:

```
</select>
```

21. Add a submit button:

```
<INPUT TYPE=\"SUBMIT\" NAME=\"submit\" VALUE=\"Select this
Contact\"></P>
```

22. Close your form, the string, the `if...else` block, and the PHP block:

```
</form>";
}
?>
```

23. Add this HTML:

```
<HTML>
<HEAD>
<TITLE>My Contact Management System: Delete a Contact</TITLE>
</HEAD>
```

```
<BODY>
<h1>My Contact Management System</h1>
<h2><em>Delete a Contact - Select from List</em></h2>
<P>Select a contact from the list below, to delete the contact's
record.</P>
```

24. Display the contents of `$display_block`:

```
<? echo "$display_block"; ?>
```

25. Add a link back to the main menu:

```
<br><p><a href="contact_menu.php">Return to Main Menu</a></p>
```

26. Add some more HTML so that the document is valid:

```
</BODY>
</HTML>
```

27. Save the file with the name `pick_delcontact.php` and place this file in the document root of your Web server.

Your code should look something like this:

```
<?
//start a session
session_start();

//check validity of user
if ($_SESSION[valid] != "yes") {
    header("Location: http://127.0.0.1/contact_menu.php");
    exit;
}

//set up table and database names
$db_name = "testDB";
$table_name = "my_contacts";

//connect to server and select database
$connection = @mysql_connect("localhost", "spike", "9sj7En4")
    or die(mysql_error());
$db = @mysql_select_db($db_name, $connection) or die(mysql_error());
```

```
//build and issue query
$sql = "SELECT id, f_name, l_name FROM $table_name ORDER BY l_name";
$result = @mysql_query($sql,$connection) or die(mysql_error());

//check the number of results
$num = @mysql_num_rows($result);

if ($num < 1) {
    //if there are no results, display message
    $display_block = "<P><em>Sorry! No results.</em></p>";
} else {
    //if results are found, loop through them
    //and make a form selection block
    while ($row = mysql_fetch_array($result)) {
        $id = $row['id'];
        $f_name = $row['f_name'];
        $l_name = $row['l_name'];
        $option_block .= "<option value=\"$id\">$l_name, $f_name</option>";
    }

    //create the entire form block
    $display_block = "
    <FORM METHOD=\"POST\" ACTION=\"show_delcontact.php\">
    <P><strong>Contact:</strong>
    <select name=\"id\">
    $option_block
    </select>
    <INPUT TYPE=\"SUBMIT\" NAME=\"submit\" VALUE=\"Select this Contact\"></P>
    </form>";
}
?>
<HTML>
<HEAD>
<TITLE>My Contact Management System: Delete a Contact</TITLE>
</HEAD>
<BODY>
<h1>My Contact Management System</h1>
<h2><em>Delete a Contact - Select from List</em></h2>
<P>Select a contact from the list below, to delete the contact's record.</P>
<? echo "$display_block"; ?>
<br>
<p><a href="contact_menu.php">Return to Main Menu</a></p>
</BODY>
</HTML>
```

In the next section, you will create a pre-deletion confirmation screen that shows all the current values of the selected record.

Creating the Record-Deletion Form

The record-deletion form isn't a form in the usual sense of the word—you aren't typing anything into a form field. Instead, this screen will display the existing record in read-only format and include hidden form fields and a submit button. By viewing the record before deleting it, you're certain to delete the correct record.

1. Open a new file in your text editor and start a PHP block:

```
<?
```

2. Start an `if...else` block that checks for a value for `$_POST[id]`, the one variable sent from the record-selection form. If a value doesn't exist, direct the user back to the selection form and exit the script:

```
if (!$_POST[id]) {
    header( "Location: http://127.0.0.1/pick_delcontact.php");
    exit;
```

3. If the required field has a value, start a session or continue a session if one currently exists. Then close the block:

```
} else {
    session_start();
}
```

4. Start an `if...else` block that checks the value of `$_SESSION[valid]` and performs a particular action based on the result. If the value is not `yes`, the user didn't go through the proper authentication channels:

```
if ($_SESSION[valid] != "yes") {
```

5. Send the user back to the login form and exit this script:

```
header("Location: http://127.0.0.1/contact_menu.php");
exit;
}
```

6. Create variables to hold the name of the database on which the table resides, as well as the table itself:

```
$db_name = "testDB";
$table_name = "my_contacts";
```

7. Add the connection information as you have been doing:

```
$connection = @mysql_connect("localhost", "spike", "9sj7En4")
    or die(mysql_error());
```

8. Select the database as you have learned:

```
$db = @mysql_select_db($db_name, $connection) or die(mysql_error());
```

9. Create the SQL statement. You want to select all the fields in the database except ID, for the record with an ID equal to the value of $_POST[id]:

```
$sql = "SELECT f_name, l_name, address1, address2, address3,
postcode, country, prim_tel, sec_tel, email, birthday
FROM $table_name WHERE id = '$_POST[id]'";
```

10. Create a variable to hold the result of the mysql_query() function, as you have learned:

```
$result = @mysql_query($sql,$connection) or die(mysql_error());
```

11. Start the while loop. The while loop will create an array called $row for each record in the result set ($result):

```
while ($row = mysql_fetch_array($result)) {
```

12. Get the individual elements of the record and give them good names:

```
$f_name = $row['f_name'];
$l_name = $row['l_name'];
$address1 = $row['address1'];
$address2 = $row['address2'];
$address3 = $row['address3'];
$postcode = $row['postcode'];
$country = $row['country'];
$prim_tel = $row['prim_tel'];
$sec_tel = $row['sec_tel'];
$email = $row['email'];
$birthday = $row['birthday'];
```

13. Close the `while` loop and then close your PHP block:

```
}
?>
```

14. Type this HTML to start building the record-confirmation screen:

```
<HTML>
<HEAD>
<TITLE>My Contact Management System: Delete a Contact</TITLE>
</HEAD>
<BODY>
<h1>My Contact Management System</h1>
<h2><em>Delete a Contact</em></h2>
```

15. Begin your form. Assume that the method is `POST` and the action is a script called `do_delcontact.php`:

```
<FORM METHOD="POST" ACTION="do_delcontact.php">
```

16. Add a hidden field to hold the value of `$_POST[id]`:

```
<INPUT TYPE="hidden" name="id" value="<? echo "$_POST[id]"; ?>">
```

17. Add two more hidden fields to hold the value of `$f_name` and `$1_name`. You'll use these fields for display purposes in the final confirmation screen, after the deletion has occurred:

```
<INPUT TYPE="hidden" name="f_name" value="<? echo "$f_name"; ?>">
<INPUT TYPE="hidden" name="l_name" value="<? echo "$l_name"; ?>">
```

18. Next, you'll re-create the layout used in the record-addition and -modification forms, mingling HTML and PHP to show the values for the selected record. Start a new table row, add two column headings, and then close that row:

```
<table cellspacing=3 cellpadding=5>
<tr>
<th>NAME & ADDRESS INFORMATION</th>
<th>OTHER CONTACT/PERSONAL INFORMATION</th>
</tr>
```

19. Start a new table row and table data cell, and then display a text label and value for the fields in the record:

```
<tr>
<td valign=top>
<P><STRONG>First Name:</STRONG><BR>
<? echo "$f_name"; ?></P>
<P><STRONG>Last Name:</STRONG><BR>
<? echo "$l_name"; ?></P>
<P><STRONG>Address Line 1:</STRONG><BR>
<? echo "$address1"; ?></P>
<P><STRONG>Address Line 2:</STRONG><BR>
<? echo "$address2"; ?></P>
<P><STRONG>Address Line 3:</STRONG><BR>
<? echo "$address3"; ?></P>
<P><STRONG>Zip/Postal Code:</STRONG><BR>
<? echo "$postcode"; ?></P>
<P><STRONG>Country:</STRONG><BR>
<? echo "$country"; ?></P>
</td>
<td valign=top>
<P><STRONG>Primary Telephone Number:</STRONG><BR>
<? echo "$prim_tel"; ?></P>
<P><STRONG>Secondary Telephone Number:</STRONG><BR>
<? echo "$sec_tel"; ?></P>
<P><STRONG>E-mail Address:</STRONG><BR>
<? echo "$email"; ?></P>
<P><STRONG>Birthday (YYYY-MM-DD):</STRONG><BR>
<? echo "$birthday"; ?></P>
</td>
</tr>
```

20. Start a new table row and table data cell that spans two columns. Inside, add a submit button and a link back to the main menu. Close the table data cell, the table row, and the table itself:

```
<tr>
<td align=center colspan=2><br>
<P><INPUT TYPE="SUBMIT" NAME="submit" VALUE="Delete this Contact"></P>
```

```
<p><a href="contact_menu.php">Return to Main Menu</a></p>
</TD>
</TR>
</TABLE>
```

21. Close the form and add some more HTML so that the document is valid:

```
</FORM>
</BODY>
</HTML>
```

22. Save the file with the name `show_delcontact.php` and place this file in the document root of your Web server.

In the next section, you will create the script that takes the value of `$_POST[id]` (currently held in a hidden form field) and deletes the corresponding record from the database table.

Creating the Record-Deletion Script

This script will delete the record in the `my_contacts` table, using the value of `$_POST[id]` as the primary key.

1. Open a new file in your text editor and start a PHP block:

```
<?
```

2. Start an `if...else` block that checks for a value for `$_POST[id]`. If no value is present, direct the user back to the selection form and exit the script:

```
if (!$_POST[id]) {
    header( "Location: http://127.0.0.1/pick_delcontact.php");
    exit;
```

3. If the required field has a value, start a session or continue a session if one currently exists. Then close the block:

```
} else {
    session_start();
}
```

4. Start an if...else block that checks the value of $_SESSION[valid] and performs a particular action based on the result. If the value is not yes, the user didn't go through the proper authentication channels:

```
if ($_SESSION[valid] != "yes") {
```

5. Send the user back to the login form and exit this script:

```
header("Location: http://127.0.0.1/contact_menu.php");
exit;
}
```

6. Create variables to hold the name of the database in which the table resides, as well as the table itself:

```
$db_name = "testDB";
$table_name = "my_contacts";
```

7. Add the connection information as you have been doing:

```
$connection = @mysql_connect("localhost", "spike", "9sj7En4")
    or die(mysql_error());
```

8. Select the database as you have learned:

```
$db = @mysql_select_db($db_name, $connection) or die(mysql_error());
```

9. Create the SQL statement to delete the record:

```
$sql = "DELETE FROM $table_name WHERE id = '$_POST[id]'";
```

10. Create a variable to hold the result of the mysql_query() function, as you have learned:

```
$result = @mysql_query($sql,$connection) or die(mysql_error());
```

11. Close your PHP block and add this HTML:

```
?>
<HTML>
<HEAD>
<TITLE>My Contact Management System: Contact Deleted</TITLE>
</HEAD>
```

```
<BODY>
<h1>My Contact Management System</h1>
<h2><em>Delete a Contact - Contact Deleted</em></h2>
```

12. Add a confirmation statement. Mingle HTML and PHP to include the values of the $_POST[f_name], $_POST[l_name], and $table_name variables:

```
<P><? echo "$_POST[f_name] $_POST[l_name]"; ?> has been deleted
from <? echo "$table_name"; ?></p>
```

13. Add a link back to the main menu and then add some more HTML so that the document is valid:

```
<br><p><a href="contact_menu.php">Return to Main Menu</a></p>
</BODY>
</HTML>
```

14. Save the file with the name do_delcontact.php and place this file in the document root of your Web server.

Your code should look something like this:

```
<?
//check for required form variables
if ((!$_POST[f_name]) || (!$_POST[l_name])) {
    header( "Location: http://127.0.0.1/pick_delcontact.php");
    exit;
} else {
    //if form variables are present, start a session
    session_start();
}

//check for validity of user
if ($_SESSION[valid] != "yes") {
    header("Location: http://127.0.0.1/contact_menu.php");
    exit;
}

//set up table and database names
$db_name = "testDB";
$table_name = "my_contacts";

//connect to server and select database
$connection = @mysql_connect("localhost", "spike", "9sj7En4")
or die(mysql_error());
$db = @mysql_select_db($db_name, $connection) or die(mysql_error());
```

```
//build and issue query
$sql = "DELETE FROM $table_name WHERE id = '$_POST[id]'";

$result = @mysql_query($sql,$connection) or die(mysql_error());
?>
<HTML>
<HEAD>
<TITLE>My Contact Management System: Contact Deleted</TITLE>
</HEAD>
<BODY>
<h2><em>Delete a Contact - Contact Deleted</em></h2>
<P><? echo "$_POST[f_name] $_POST[l_name]"; ?> has been deleted
from <? echo "$table_name"; ?></p>
<br><p><a href="contact_menu.php">Return to Main Menu</a></p>
</BODY>
</HTML>
```

Go on to the next step and delete some of the contacts in your database table.

Deleting Contacts

To start deleting contacts from the `my_contacts` table, open http://127.0.0.1/
contact_menu.php. If you've already logged in, you'll see your Administration
menu. Otherwise, log in using the username (`admin`) and password (`abc123`).

Figure 21.1 The delete contact screen.

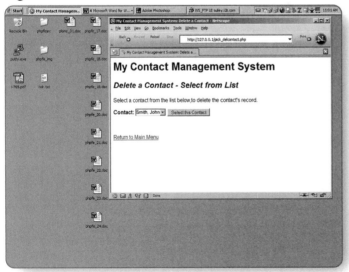

1. Select the Delete a Contact
menu item (see Figure 21.1).

You will see a drop-down
menu of the contacts in the
system, as well as a submit
button and a link back to the
main menu.

Figure 21.2 The contact selection screen.

2. Select a contact from the list and click the Select This Contact button. I selected a sample from my own list (see Figure 21.2).

DEFAULT DATES

If no birthday is entered in the record, the display will show 0000-00-00. MySQL uses a default date for date fields. Numeric fields should default to zero, while string fields will default to empty displays.

Figure 21.3 Delete contact confirmation.

3. Click the Delete This Contact button. You should see a confirmation screen, as shown in Figure 21.3.

4. Return to the selection form and select your contact again to see that the record no longer exists in the drop-down menu.

Delete a record or two and then move on to the next chapter, where you'll create the read-only contact information screens.

22

Working with Contacts

You have all this information in a table, but I haven't shown you how to create any scripts for selecting and displaying read-only data. It's time to remedy that! In this chapter, you learn how to:

- Count and display the number of contacts in your system.

- Display the current date.

- Check for birthdays in the current month and display special text.

- Display read-only contact details.

- Require session-based authentication before the script can be viewed or the record is deleted.

Modifying Your Administrative Menu

The next few sections show some modifications you can make to the original
contact_menu.php to display elements such as the current date, the number of
contacts in the database, and other pieces of information that make your system
more customized.

Showing the Number of Contacts

The following modifications should be made to the contact_menu.php script so that
it displays the current number of contacts in the my_contacts table.

1. Open contact_menu.php in your text editor.

2. Find this block of code, highlight it, and cut it out of the file (prepare to paste):

```
//build form block
$form_block = "<h1>Login</h1>
<form method=POST action=\"$_SERVER[PHP_SELF]\">
$msg
<P><strong>username:</strong><br>
<input type=\"text\" name=\"username\" size=15 maxlength=25></P>
<P><strong>password:</strong><br>
<input type=\"password\" name=\"password\" size=15 maxlength=25></P>
<input type=\"hidden\" name=\"op\" value=\"ds\">
<P><input type=\"submit\" name=\"submit\" value=\"login\"></P>
</FORM>";
```

3. Find the if[...]else block that looks like the following:

```
if ($show_form == "yes") {
    $display_block = $form_block;
} else if ($show_menu == "yes") {
    $display_block = $menu_block;
}
```

4. Replace the following line with the section you cut in Step 2:

```
$display_block = $form_block;
```

The `if...else` block should now look like this:

```
if ($show_form == "yes") {
    $form_block = "<h1>Login</h1>
    <form method=POST action=\"$_SERVER[PHP_SELF]\">
    $msg
    <P><strong>username:</strong><br>
    <input type=\"text\" name=\"username\" size=15 maxlength=25></P>
    <P><strong>password:</strong><br>
    <input type=\"password\" name=\"password\" size=15 maxlength=25></P>
    <input type=\"hidden\" name=\"op\" value=\"ds\">
    <P><input type=\"submit\" name=\"submit\" value=\"login\"></P>
    </FORM>";
} else if ($show_menu == "yes") {
    $display_block = $menu_block;
}
```

5. Change the name of the variable from `$form_block` to `$display_block`.

6. The `if...else` block should look like this:

```
if ($show_form == "yes") {
    //build form block
    $display_block = "<h1>Login</h1>

    <form method=POST action=\"$_SERVER[PHP_SELF]\">
    $msg
    <P><strong>username:</strong><br>
    <input type=\"text\" name=\"username\" size=15 maxlength=25></P>
    <P><strong>password:</strong><br>
    <input type=\"password\" name=\"password\" size=15 maxlength=25></P>
    <input type=\"hidden\" name=\"op\" value=\"ds\">
    <P><input type=\"submit\" name=\"submit\" value=\"login\"></P>
    </FORM>";
} else if ($show_menu == "yes") {
    $display_block = $menu_block;
}
```

7. Find the following block of code, highlight it, and cut it out of the file (prepare to paste):

```
$menu_block = "<h1>My Contact Management System</h1>

<P><strong>Administration</strong>
<ul>
<li><a href=\"show_addcontact.php\">Add a Contact</a>
<li><a href=\"pick_modcontact.php\">Modify a Contact</a>
<li><a href=\"pick_delcontact.php\">Delete a Contact</a>
</ul>
<P><strong>View Records</strong>
<ul>
<li><a href=\"show_contactsbyname.php\">Show Contacts, Ordered by Name</a>
</ul>";
```

8. Find the if[...]else block that contains the following:

```
} else if ($show_menu == "yes") {
     $display_block = $menu_block;
}
```

9. Replace the following line with the section you cut in Step 7:

```
$display_block = $menu_block;
```

The if...else block should now look like this:

```
if ($show_form == "yes") {
     $display_block = "<h1>Login</h1>
     <form method=POST action=\"$_SERVER[PHP_SELF]\">
     $msg
     <P><strong>username:</strong><br>
     <input type=\"text\" name=\"username\" size=15 maxlength=25></P>
     <P><strong>password:</strong><br>
     <input type=\"password\" name=\"password\" size=15 maxlength=25></P>
     <input type=\"hidden\" name=\"op\" value=\"ds\">
     <P><input type=\"submit\" name=\"submit\" value=\"login\"></P>
     </FORM>";
```

```
} else if ($show_menu == "yes") {
    $menu_block = "<h1>My Contact Administration System</h1>
        <P><strong>Administration</strong>
    <ul>
    <li><a href=\"show_addcontact.php\">Add a Contact</a>
    <li><a href=\"pick_modcontact.php\">Modify a Contact</a>
    <li><a href=\"pick_delcontact.php\">Delete a Contact</a>
    </ul>
    <P><strong>View Records</strong>
    <ul>
    <li><a href=\"show_contactsbyname.php\">Show Contacts, Ordered by
Name</a>
    </ul>";
}
```

10. Change the name of the variable from `$menu_block` to `$display_block`.

11. The complete `if...else` block should look like this:

```
if ($show_form == "yes") {
    $display_block = "    <h1>Login</h1>

    <form method=POST action=\"$_SERVER[PHP_SELF]\">
    $msg
    <P><strong>username:</strong><br>
    <input type=\"text\" name=\"username\" size=15 maxlength=25></P>
    <P><strong>password:</strong><br>
    <input type=\"password\" name=\"password\" size=15
maxlength=25></P>
    <input type=\"hidden\" name=\"op\" value=\"ds\">
    <P><input type=\"submit\" name=\"submit\" value=\"login\"></P>
    </FORM>";
} else if ($show_menu == "yes") {
    $display_block = "<h1>My Contact Administration System</h1>

    <P><strong>Administration</strong>
    <ul>
    <li><a href=\"show_addcontact.php\">Add a Contact</a>
```

```
<li><a href=\"pick_modcontact.php\">Modify a Contact</a>
<li><a href=\"pick_delcontact.php\">Delete a Contact</a>
</ul>
<P><strong>View Records</strong>
<ul>
<li><a href=\"show_contactsbyname.php\">Show Contacts, Ordered by
Name</a>
</ul>";
}
```

12. Save your changes before going any further.

None of those changes modified the display in any way. They simply organized your code a little bit better in preparation for the next changes.

These next changes will all take place within the second part of the `if...else` block you just modified.

1. Find this line, because the rest of the changes go right after it:

```
} else if ($show_menu == "yes") {
```

2. Create variables to hold the name of the database in which the table resides, as well as the table itself:

```
$db_name = "testDB";
$table_name = "my_contacts";
```

3. Add the connection information as you have been doing:

```
$connection = @mysql_connect("localhost", "spike", "9sj7En4")
    or die(mysql_error());
```

4. Select the database as you have learned:

```
$db = @mysql_select_db($db_name, $connection) or die(mysql_error());
```

5. Create a SQL statement counts the number of entries in the ID field:

```
$sql = "SELECT count(id) FROM $table_name";
```

6. Create a variable to hold the result of the `mysql_query()` function, as you have learned:

```
$result = @mysql_query($sql,$connection) or die(mysql_error());
```

7. Create a variable to hold the specific value within the result:

```
$count = @mysql_result($result,0,"count(id)") or die(mysql_error());
```

THE `MYSQL_RESULT` FUNCTION VERSUS FETCHING ROWS

If you're working with a one-field result, the `mysql_result()` function is simpler than fetching an entire row. This function requires the result of a valid query, a row (starting at 0), and the field name.

---

8. The next modification is primarily aesthetic. Take the string within `$display_block` and replace it with the following HTML, creating a two-column table for menu options:

```
$display_block = "<h1>My Contact Management System</h1>

<table cellspacing=3 cellpadding=3>
<tr>
<td valign=top>
<P><strong>Administration</strong>
<ul>
<li><a href=\"show_addcontact.php\">Add a Contact</a>
<li><a href=\"pick_modcontact.php\">Modify a Contact</a>
<li><a href=\"pick_delcontact.php\">Delete a Contact</a>
</ul>
<P><strong>View Records</strong>
<ul>
<li><a href=\"show_contactsbyname.php\">Show Contacts, Ordered by Name</a>
</ul>
</td>
```

```
<td valign=top>
<P><strong>Miscellaneous</strong></P>
</td>
</tr>
</table>";
```

9. In the new `$display_block` string, find the section for Miscellaneous. Start a bulleted list and then print a list item with a text label and a bold representation of the value of `$count`. After that list item, close the list itself:

```
<ul>
<li>Contacts in system: <strong>$count</strong>
</ul>
```

10. Save your changes.

Your new code should look like this:

```php
<?
//start a session
session_start();

//check if user is coming from a form
if ($_POST[op] == "ds") {
    //check username and password
    if (($_POST[username] != "admin") || ($_POST[password] != "abc123")) {
        //handle bad login
        $msg = "<P><font color=\"#FF0000\">
        <strong>Bad Login - Try Again</strong>
        </font></P>";
        $show_form = "yes";
    } else {
        //handle good login
        $_SESSION[valid] = "yes";
        $show_menu = "yes";
    }
} else {
    //determine what to show
    if ($_SESSION[valid] == "yes") {
        $show_menu = "yes";
    } else {
        $show_form = "yes";
    }
}
```

```
//assign the block to show to the $display_block variable
if ($show_form == "yes") {
     //build form block
     $display_block = "<h1>Login</h1>
     <form method=POST action=\"$_SERVER[PHP_SELF]\">
     $msg
     <P><strong>username:</strong><br>
     <input type=\"text\" name=\"username\" size=15 maxlength=25></P>
     <P><strong>password:</strong><br>
     <input type=\"password\" name=\"password\" size=15 maxlength=25></P>
     <input type=\"hidden\" name=\"op\" value=\"ds\">
     <P><input type=\"submit\" name=\"submit\" value=\"login\"></P>
     </FORM>";
} else if ($show_menu == "yes") {
     //set up table and database names
     $db_name = "testDB";
     $table_name = "my_contacts";

     //connect to server and select database
     $connection = @mysql_connect("localhost", "spike", "9sj7En4")
          or die(mysql_error());
     $db = @mysql_select_db($db_name, $connection) or die(mysql_error());

     //build and issue query
     $sql = "SELECT count(id) FROM $table_name";
     $result = @mysql_query($sql,$connection) or die(mysql_error());
     $count = @mysql_result($result,0,"count(id)") or die(mysql_error());

     //build menu block
     $display_block = "<h1>My Contact Management System</h1>
     <table cellspacing=3 cellpadding=3>
     <tr>
     <td valign=top>
     <P><strong>Administration</strong>
     <ul>
     <li><a href=\"show_addcontact.php\">Add a Contact</a>
     <li><a href=\"pick_modcontact.php\">Modify a Contact</a>
     <li><a href=\"pick_delcontact.php\">Delete a Contact</a>
     </ul>
     <P><strong>View Records</strong>
     <ul>
     <li><a href=\"show_contactsbyname.php\">Show Contacts, Ordered by Name</a>
     </ul>
     </td>
```

```
            <td valign=top>
            <P><strong>Miscellaneous</strong></P>
            <ul>
            <li>Contacts in system: <strong>$count</strong>
            </ul>
            </td>
            </tr>
            </table>";
    }
    ?>
    <HTML>
    <HEAD>
    <TITLE>My Contact Management System</TITLE>
    </HEAD>
    <BODY>
    <? echo "$display_block"; ?>
    </BODY>
    </HTML>
```

Figure 22.1 New contact menu with number of contacts.

Open http://127.0.0.1/
contact_menu.php. If you've
already logged in, you'll see
your Administrative menu.
Otherwise, log in using the
username (admin) and password
(abc123). You should now see a
new layout for the menu, as well
as the number of contacts in the
table, in the appropriate places
(see Figure 22.1).

In the next section, you'll display the current date on your menu.

Displaying Today's Date

Compared to the previous section, the changes needed to display the current date
are a snap! The date() function is highly customizable once you know all the
options.

DATE FUNCTION OPTIONS

You can find a list of `date()` function options in Appendix B, "Basic PHP Language Reference."

---

1. Open `contact_menu.php` in your text editor.

2. Find this line because the rest of the changes go in this block:

```
} else if ($show_menu == "yes") {
```

3. After the line that assigns a value to the `$count` variable, add this line to create a variable called `$today`, containing a formatted date string:

```
$today = @date("l, F jS, Y");
```

4. Find this line in the `$display_block` string:

```
<h1>My Contact Management System</h1>
```

5. After it, add the following to print the date string:

```
<p><em>Today is $today</em></p>
```

6. Save your file.

The date format options are interpreted, as shown in Table 22.1.

Table 22.1 Date Formatting Example

Format Option	Description
l,	Long name of day (literal comma)
F	Long name of month
j	Day of month (2-digit)
S	Ordinal suffix
Y	Year (4-digit)

Figure 22.2 Menu showing current date.

Open http://127.0.0.1/ contact_menu.php. If you've already logged in, you'll see your Administrative menu. Otherwise, log in using the username (`admin`) and password (`abc123`). You should now see a line of text that says "Today is [your date here]." See Figure 22.2.

In the next section, you'll do some neat SQL to find the number of contacts whose birthdays occur during the current month, and you'll print their names in a list. This is helpful for people like me, who can't remember their mother's birthday, let alone anyone else's!

Showing the Birthdays in the Current Month

One of the fields in your database is a field for the person's birthday. It's not required, but if you take the time to enter someone's birthday, chances are good that you actually want to remember it. This next section will print the number of contacts who have birthdays in the current month, as well as the person's name and birthday and a link to his or her contact details. Nifty!

1. Open `contact_menu.php` in your text editor.

2. Find this line because the rest of the changes go in this block:

```
} else if ($show_menu == "yes") {
```

3. Now find the line that assigns a value to the `$today` variable because you'll start typing things after this line:

```
$today = date("l, F jS Y");
```

4. Create a SQL statement that gets the number of people who have birthdays in the current month:

```
$get_birthday_count = "SELECT count(id) FROM $table_name
WHERE MONTH(birthday) = MONTH(NOW())";
```

MYSQL DATE FUNCTIONS

MONTH() and NOW() are MySQL functions used to get the month out of a date string (in this case, the value of the Birthday field) and the current date, respectively. You can learn more about MySQL functions in Appendix E, "Database Normalization and SQL Reference."

---

5. Create a variable to hold the result of the mysql_query() function, as you have learned:

```
$birthday_count_res = @mysql_query($get_birthday_count,$connection)
    or die(mysql_error());
```

6. Create a variable to hold the specific value within the result:

```
$birthday_count = mysql_result($birthday_count_res, 0, "count(id)");
```

Next, you'll have more fun with SQL. If the number of contacts who have birthdays in the current month is one or more, you'll create a string that includes the person's name and birthday and a link to his or her contact details.

1. Find the line in contact_menu.php that assigns a value to the $birthday_count variable, and after it create an if statement that will be executed if the value is true. In this case, it's looking for a positive value for $birthday_count:

```
if ($birthday_count > 0) {
```

2. You'll create a bulleted list within a while block in a moment. Start the bulleted list outside the while block:

```
$bd_string = "<ul>";
```

3. Create a SQL statement that selects the ID, first name, last name, month of the birthday, and day of the birthday. This SQL statement also orders the result set by birthday:

```
$get_contacts_bd = "SELECT id, f_name, l_name,
    MONTH(birthday) as month, DAYOFMONTH(birthday) as date
    FROM $table_name WHERE
    MONTH(birthday) = MONTH(NOW())ORDER BY birthday";
```

RENAMING FIELDS IN SQL

You can select fields or parts of fields and assign a new name to them using as [new name] within your SQL statement. In the previous statement, you're extracting the month of a birthday and giving it a name of month, and you're extracting the day of a birthday and giving it a name of date.

---

4. Create a variable to hold the result of the mysql_query() function, as you have learned:

```
$contacts_bd_res = @mysql_query($get_contacts_bd, $connection)
    or die(mysql_error());
```

5. Start the while loop. The while loop will create an array called $contacts_bd for each record in the result set ($contacts_bd_res):

```
while ($contacts_bd = mysql_fetch_array($contacts_bd_res)) {
```

6. Get the individual elements of the record and give them good names:

```
$contact_id = $contacts_bd['id'];
$contact_fname = $contacts_bd['f_name'];
$contact_lname = $contacts_bd['l_name'];
$contact_bd_month = $contacts_bd['month'];
$contact_bd_date = $contacts_bd['date'];
```

7. Append a list item to `$bd_string` that contains the person's name and birthday. Create a link to a script called `show_contact.php`, which you'll create in the next section:

```
$bd_string .= "<li><a
href=\"show_contact.php?id=$contact_id\">$contact_fname
$contact_lname</a> ($contact_bd_month"."-"."$contact_bd_date)";
```

8. Close the `while` loop, then the bulleted list, and finally the `if` statement:

```
}
$bd_string .= "</ul>";
}
```

9. Inside `$display_block`, within the bulleted list under the Miscellaneous heading and under a Birthdays This Month list item, add the following:

```
$bd_string
```

10. Save your file.

The final `contact_menu.php` script should look like this, with all modifications so far in this chapter:

```
<?
//start a session
session_start();

//check if user is coming from a form
if ($_POST[op] == "ds") {

    //check username and password
    if (($_POST[username] != "admin") || ($_POST[password] != "abc123")) {
        //handle bad login
        $msg = "<P><font color=\"#FF0000\">
        <strong>Bad Login - Try Again</strong>
        </font></P>";
        $show_form = "yes";
    } else {
        //handle good login
        $_SESSION[valid] = "yes";
        $show_menu = "yes";
    }
```

```php
} else {
    //determine what to show
    if ($_SESSION[valid] == "yes") {
        $show_menu = "yes";
    } else {
        $show_form = "yes";
    }
}


//assign the block to show to the $display_block variable
if ($show_form == "yes") {
    //build form block
    $display_block = "<h1>Login</h1>
    <form method=POST action=\"$_SERVER[PHP_SELF]\">
    $msg
    <P><strong>username:</strong><br>
    <input type=\"text\" name=\"username\" size=15 maxlength=25></P>
    <P><strong>password:</strong><br>
    <input type=\"password\" name=\"password\" size=15 maxlength=25></P>
    <input type=\"hidden\" name=\"op\" value=\"ds\">
    <P><input type=\"submit\" name=\"submit\" value=\"login\"></P>
    </FORM>";
} else if ($show_menu == "yes") {
    //set up table and database names
    $db_name = "testDB";
    $table_name = "my_contacts";

    //connect to server and select database
    $connection = @mysql_connect("localhost", "spike", "9sj7En4")
        or die(mysql_error());
    $db = @mysql_select_db($db_name, $connection) or die(mysql_error());

    //build and issue query
    $sql = "SELECT count(id) FROM $table_name";
    $result = @mysql_query($sql,$connection) or die(mysql_error());
    $count = @mysql_result($result,0,"count(id)") or die(mysql_error());

    //get current date
    $today = date("l, F jS, Y");

    //get birthday count
    $get_birthday_count = "SELECT count(id) FROM $table_name
    WHERE MONTH(birthday) = MONTH(NOW())";
    $birthday_count_res = @mysql_query($get_birthday_count,$connection)
        or die(mysql_error());
    $birthday_count = mysql_result($birthday_count_res, 0, "count(id)");
```

```php
//create a list, based on a positive result
if ($birthday_count > 0) {
    $bd_string = "<ul>";
    $get_contacts_bd = "SELECT id, f_name, l_name,
    MONTH(birthday) as month, DAYOFMONTH(birthday) as date
    FROM $table_name
    WHERE MONTH(birthday) = MONTH(NOW())ORDER BY birthday";
    $contacts_bd_res = @mysql_query($get_contacts_bd, $connection)
        or die(mysql_error());

    while ($contacts_bd = mysql_fetch_array($contacts_bd_res)) {
        $contact_id = $contacts_bd['id'];
        $contact_fname = $contacts_bd['f_name'];
        $contact_lname = $contacts_bd['l_name'];
        $contact_bd_month = $contacts_bd['month'];
        $contact_bd_date = $contacts_bd['date'];

        $bd_string .= "<li>
        <a href=\"show_contact.php?id=$contact_id\">
        $contact_fname $contact_lname</a>
        ($contact_bd_month"."-"."$contact_bd_date)";
    }

    $bd_string .= "</ul>";
}


//build menu block
$display_block = "<h1>My Contact Management System</h1>
<p><em>Today is $today</em></p>
<table cellspacing=3 cellpadding=3>
<tr>
<td valign=top>
<P><strong>Administration</strong>
<ul>
<li><a href=\"show_addcontact.php\">Add a Contact</a>
<li><a href=\"pick_modcontact.php\">Modify a Contact</a>
<li><a href=\"pick_delcontact.php\">Delete a Contact</a>
</ul>
<P><strong>View Records</strong>
<ul>
<li><a href=\"show_contactsbyname.php\">Show Contacts, Ordered by Name</a>
</ul>
</td>
```

```
        <td valign=top>
        <P><strong>Miscellaneous</strong></P>
        <ul>
        <li>Contacts in system: <strong>$count</strong>
        <li>Birthdays this month: <strong>$birthday_count</strong>
        $bd_string
        </ul>
        </td>
        </tr>
        </table>";
    }
    ?>
    <HTML>
    <HEAD>
    <TITLE>My Contact Management System</TITLE>
    </HEAD>
    <BODY>
    <? echo "$display_block"; ?>
    </BODY>
    </HTML>
```

Figure 22.3 Contact menu showing birthdays.

Open http://127.0.0.1/ contact_menu.php. If you've already logged in, you'll see your Administrative menu. Otherwise, log in using the username (admin) and password (abc123). If you have any contacts in your database table whose birthdays are in the current month, you should see their names and birthdays listed (see Figure 22.3).

In the next section, you'll create the contact details script to display all the contact information you've been putting in the my_contacts table.

Selecting Data from the `my_contacts` Table

Now that all the difficult scripting is out of the way, it's time to do some simple SQL selects to display the data in the `my_contacts` table. You'll start by listing the contacts, and then you'll show the contact details.

Displaying the Record List

The goal of this script is to display a bulleted list of the contacts in your database table, complete with a link to the `show_contact.php` script.

1. Open a new file in your text editor and start a PHP block. Then start a session or continue a session if one currently exists:

```
<?
session_start();
```

2. Start an `if...else` block that checks the value of `$_SESSION[valid]` and performs a particular action based on the result. If the value is not `yes`, the user didn't go through the proper authentication channels:

```
if ($_SESSION[valid] != "yes") {
```

3. Send the user back to the login form and exit this script:

```
header("Location: http://127.0.0.1/contact_menu.php");
exit;
}
```

4. Create variables to hold the name of the database in which the table resides, as well as the table itself:

```
$db_name = "testDB";
$table_name = "my_contacts";
```

5. Add the connection information as you have been doing:

```
$connection = @mysql_connect("localhost", "spike", "9sj7En4")
    or die(mysql_error());
```

6. Select the database as you have learned:

```
$db = @mysql_select_db($db_name, $connection) or die(mysql_error());
```

7. Create the SQL statement. You want to select just the ID number, first name, and last name of each record in the table:

```
$sql = "SELECT id, f_name, l_name FROM $table_name ORDER BY l_name";
```

8. Create a variable to hold the result of the `mysql_query()` function, as you have learned:

```
$result = @mysql_query($sql,$connection) or die(mysql_error());
```

9. You'll create a bulleted list within a `while` block in a moment. Start the bulleted list outside the `while` block:

```
$contact_list = "<ul>";
```

10. Start the `while` loop. The `while` loop will create an array called `$row` for each record in the result set (`$result`):

```
while ($row = mysql_fetch_array($result)) {
```

11. Get the individual elements of the record and give them good names:

```
$id = $row['id'];
$f_name = $row['f_name'];
$l_name = $row['l_name'];
```

12. Append a list item to `$contact_list` that contains the person's name within a link to a script called `show_contact.php`:

```
$contact_list .= "<li><a href=\"show_contact.php?id=$id\">$l_name,
    $f_name</a>";
```

13. Close the `while` loop, the bulleted list, and the PHP block:

```
}
$contact_list .= "</ul>";
?>
```

14. Add this HTML:

```
<HTML>
<HEAD>
<TITLE>My Contact Management System: Contacts Listed by Name</TITLE>
</HEAD>
<BODY>
<h1>My Contact Management System</h1>
<P>Select a contact from the list below, to view the contact's
record.</P>
```

15. Display the contents of $contact_list:

```
<? echo "$contact_list"; ?>
```

16. Add a link back to the main menu:

```
<br><p><a href="contact_menu.php">Return to Main Menu</a></p>
```

17. Add some more HTML so that the document is valid:

```
</BODY>
</HTML>
```

18. Save the file with the name show_contactsbyname.php and place this file in the document root of your Web server.

Your code should look something like this:

```
<?
//start a session
session_start();

//check for validity of user
if ($_SESSION[valid] != "yes") {
    header("Location: http://127.0.0.1/contact_menu.php");
    exit;
}

//set up table and database names
$db_name = "testDB";
$table_name = "my_contacts";
```

```
//connect to server and select database
$connection = @mysql_connect("localhost", "spike", "9sj7En4")
or die(mysql_error());
$db = @mysql_select_db($db_name, $connection) or die(mysql_error());

//build and issue query
$sql = "SELECT id, f_name, l_name FROM $table_name ORDER BY l_name";
$result = @mysql_query($sql,$connection) or die(mysql_error());

//create list block of results
$contact_list = "<ul>";
while ($row = mysql_fetch_array($result)) {
    $id = $row['id'];
    $f_name = $row['f_name'];
    $l_name = $row['l_name'];
    $contact_list .= "<li>
    <a href=\"show_contact.php?id=$id\">$l_name, $f_name</a>";
}
$contact_list .= "</ul>";
?>
<HTML>
<HEAD>
<TITLE>My Contact Management System: Contacts Listed by Name</TITLE>
</HEAD>
<BODY>
<h1>My Contact Management System</h1>
<P>Select a contact from the list below, to view the contact's record.</P>
<? echo "$contact_list"; ?>
<br><p><a href="contact_menu.php">Return to Main Menu</a></p>
</BODY>
</HTML>
```

Figure 22.4 Contacts ordered by name.

Open http://127.0.0.1/ contact_menu.php. When you log in, you'll see the Administrative menu. On that menu is a link called Contacts, Ordered by Name. If you click that, you'll see the display shown in Figure 22.4 (or something close to it anyway, depending on your data).

In the next section, you'll create the contact display page, show_contact.php.

Displaying Read-Only Records

It's the moment of truth: displaying your contacts!

1. Open a new file in your text editor and start a PHP block:

```
<?
```

2. Start an if...else block that checks for a value for $_GET[id], the one variable sent in the link's query string. If a value doesn't exist, direct the user back to the menu and exit the script:

```
if (!$_GET[id]) {
    header( "Location: http://127.0.0.1/contact_menu.php");
    exit;
```

3. If the required field has a value, start a session or continue a session if one currently exists, and then close the block:

```
} else {
    session_start();
}
```

4. Start an if...else block that checks the value of $_SESSION[valid] and performs a particular action based on the result. If the value is not yes, the user didn't go through the proper authentication channels:

```
if ($_SESSION[valid] != "yes") {
```

5. Send the user back to the login form and exit this script:

```
header("Location: http://127.0.0.1/contact_menu.php");
exit;
}
```

6. Create variables to hold the name of the database in which the table resides, as well as the table itself:

```
$db_name = "testDB";
$table_name = "my_contacts";
```

7. Add the connection information as you have been doing:

```
$connection = @mysql_connect("localhost", "spike", "9sj7En4")
    or die(mysql_error());
```

8. Select the database as you have learned:

```
$db = @mysql_select_db($db_name, $connection) or die(mysql_error());
```

9. Perform some validation on the value of $_GET[id]. You want to make sure that the number really exists in the system before you run SQL queries using a bad key.

```
$chk_id = "SELECT id FROM $table_name WHERE id = '$_GET[id]'";
```

10. Create a variable to hold the result of the mysql_query() function, as you have learned:

```
$chk_id_res = @mysql_query($chk_id,$connection) or die(mysql_error());
```

11. Create a variable to count the number of rows within the result. There should be one row:

```
$chk_id_num = mysql_num_rows($chk_id_res);
```

12. Start an if...else block to deal with the results of the validation. The first section checks the row count. You want there to be one and only one row:

```
if ($chk_id_num != 1) {
```

13. If the row count is anything other than 1, the id was invalid. Redirect the user to the menu and exit the script:

```
header("Location: http://127.0.0.1/contact_menu.php");
exit;
```

14. Continue the if...else statement, now preparing to act on a valid result:

```
} else {
```

15. Create the SQL statement. You want to select all the fields in the database except ID for the record that has an ID equal to the value of $_GET[id]:

```
$sql = "SELECT f_name, l_name, address1, address2, address3, postcode,
    country, prim_tel, sec_tel, email, birthday
    FROM $table_name WHERE id = '$_GET[id]'";
```

16. Create a variable to hold the result of the mysql_query() function, as you have learned:

```
$result = @mysql_query($sql,$connection) or die(mysql_error());
```

17. Start the while loop. The while loop will create an array called $row for each record in the result set ($result):

```
while ($row = mysql_fetch_array($result)) {
```

18. Get the individual elements of the record and give them good names:

```
$f_name = $row['f_name'];
$l_name = $row['l_name'];
$address1 = $row['address1'];
$address2 = $row['address2'];
$address3 = $row['address3'];
$postcode = $row['postcode'];
$country = $row['country'];
$prim_tel = $row['prim_tel'];
$sec_tel = $row['sec_tel'];
$email = $row['email'];
$birthday = $row['birthday'];
```

19. Close the while loop, the if...else loop, and the PHP block:

```
        }
    }
    ?>
```

20. Type this HTML to start building the record details screen:

```
<HTML>
<HEAD>
<TITLE>My Contact Management System: Read-Only Contact Details</TITLE>
</HEAD>
<BODY>
<h1>My Contact Management System</h1>
```

21. Mingle HTML and PHP to show a nice title with the contact's full name:

```
<h2>Contact Details for <? echo "$f_name $l_name"; ?></h2>
```

22. Start a paragraph with a text label:

```
<P><strong>Name & Address:</strong><br>
```

23. Display all the individual elements for name and address:

```
<? echo "$f_name $l_name"; ?><br>
<? echo "$address1"; ?><br>
<? echo "$address2"; ?><br>
<? echo "$address3"; ?><br>
<? echo "$postcode"; ?><br>
<? echo "$country"; ?></P>
```

24. Start a paragraph and print text labels and results for the telephone and e-mail fields:

```
<P><strong>Tel 1:</strong> <? echo "$prim_tel"; ?><br>
<strong>Tel 2:</strong> <? echo "$sec_tel"; ?><br>
<strong>E-Mail:</strong> <? echo "<a href=\"mailto:$email\">$email</a>";
?></P>
```

25. Start a paragraph and print a text label and result for the birthday:

```
<P><strong>Birthday:</strong> <? echo "$birthday"; ?></P>
```

26. Add a link back to the main menu and then add some more HTML so that the document is valid:

```
<p><a href="contact_menu.php">Return to Main Menu</a></p>
</BODY>
</HTML>
```

27. Save the file with the name show_contact.php and place this file in the document root of your Web server.

Figure 22.5 Contact form.

Open http://127.0.0.1/contact_menu.php. If you've already logged in, you'll see your Administrative menu. Otherwise, log in using the username (admin) and password (abc123). Select the Show Contacts, Ordered by Name link, and then select one of your contacts from the list (see Figure 22.5).

Figure 22.6 Incomplete contact form.

Looks good! This is a contact in my database table that's complete. But here's what happens when the contact isn't complete (see Figure 22.6).

Pretty ugly! Now you can make some modifications to show_contact.php to take into account the fact that only two fields (first name and last name) are required.

1. Open show_contact.php.

2. Scroll down to the Name & Address section.

3. Delete this section:

```
<? echo "$address1"; ?><br>
<? echo "$address2"; ?><br>
<? echo "$address3"; ?><br>
<? echo "$postcode"; ?><br>
<? echo "$country"; ?></P>
<P><strong>Tel 1:</strong> <? echo "$prim_tel"; ?><br>
<strong>Tel 2:</strong> <? echo "$sec_tel"; ?><br>
<strong>E-Mail:</strong> <? echo "<a href=\"mailto:$email\">$email</a>"; ?></P>
<P><strong>Birthday:</strong> <? echo "$birthday"; ?></P>
```

4. Type the following series of if statements, which look for a value of the specific variable and print the line only if a value is present:

```
<?
    if ($address1 != "") {
        echo "$address1 <br>";
    }
    if ($address2 != "") {
        echo "$address2 <br>";
    }
    if ($address3 != "") {
        echo "$address3 <br>";
    }
    if ($postcode != "") {
        echo "$postcode <br>";
    }
    if ($country != "") {
        echo "$country <br>";
    }
?>
</P>
```

```
<P>
<?
    if ($prim_tel != "") {
        echo "<strong>Tel 1:</strong> $prim_tel <br>";
    }
    if ($sec_tel != "") {
        echo "<strong>Tel 2:</strong> $sec_tel <br>";
    }
    if ($email != "") {
        echo "<strong>E-Mail:</strong>
        <a href=\"mailto:$email\">$email</a> <br>";
    }
?>
</P>
<?
    if ($birthday != "0000-00-00") {
        echo "<P><strong>Birthday:</strong> $birthday </P>";
    }
?>
```

5. Save this file.

Figure 22.7 Incomplete contact form updated.

Now when you view an incomplete record, you don't see all that white space, as shown in Figure 22.7.

BROWSER SECURITY

One note concerning the Internet Explorer Web browser and this application: Under certain scenarios, you may need to set your security level to low, rather than medium or better, or you will not get your variables passed along properly.

So there you have it—a complete online contact-management system utilizing sessions and user authentication. There are plenty of areas for modification and additional validation checks, so take some time and play with these scripts until you are comfortable with the concepts. For example, you might want a different set of fields to be required, or you might want to add more fields to your table (and thus your forms and display scripts). These simple concepts will help you to understand and build larger applications.

PART VII

Additional Project Examples

23

Managing a Simple Mailing List

Eventually, your Web site will have visitors, and someday you might even want to send a newsletter to them. You can create a very simple subscription and publication mechanism using PHP and MySQL. In this chapter, you'll learn how to:

- Create a subscribe/unsubscribe script.
- Create a front end to sending a newsletter.
- Create a script that mails your newsletter to all recipients in your database.

A Brief Word About Mailing List Software

Several very good mailing list applications are available to send mail to large numbers of e-mail addresses. The type of system you'll build in this chapter should be used only for small lists of less than a few hundred e-mail addresses.

The system described in this chapter was born from my own laziness one day when I didn't want to download and install any third-party software. I just made some very simple files that performed a task. That's the beauty of PHP: It's such a simple language that sometimes it's easier to write a few scripts than to download or install something. However, when your mailing list grows large enough, please move to a more robust mailing list application that's a bit easier on your outgoing mail server, and also on you, the administrator.

Developing a Subscription Mechanism

Before you can start sending mail to a mailing list, you need to build up that subscriber base. A simple subscribe/unsubscribe script will take care of that. All this script does is add or delete records in a MySQL database table, called *subscribers*, which you'll create in the next section.

Creating the `subscribers` Table

My `subscribers` table has three fields, as shown in Table 23.1. You can have as many or as few fields as you want.

Table 23.1 Fields for the `subscribers` Table

Field Name	Description
`id`	A primary key that holds the subscriber's auto-incrementing ID number
`email_addr`	Holds the subscriber's e-mail address
`date_added`	The date the user subscribed

Next, you'll actually create this table, using the table-creation scripts you're familiar with at this point.

1. Open your Web browser and type `http://127.0.0.1/show_createtable.html`.

Figure 23.1 The subscribers list table building.

2. In the Table Name field, type `subscribers`.

3. In the Number of Fields field, type 3.

4. Click the Go to Step 2 button, where you will see three rows, corresponding to the three fields you want to create in the subscribers table (see Figure 23.1).

Populate the fields in these next steps:

1. In the first row, type `id` for Field Name, select `int` from the Field Type drop-down menu, check the check box for Primary Key, and check the check box for Auto-Increment.

Figure 23.2 Completed subscribers list table form.

2. In the second row, type `email_addr` for Field Name, select `varchar` from the Field Type drop-down menu, and specify a Field Length of 100.

3. In the third row, type `date_added` for Field Name and select `date` from the Field Type drop-down menu.

The completed form should look like Figure 23.2.

Figure 23.3 Confirmation of table creation.

4. Click the Create Table button to create the `subscribers` table.

You will see a confirmation of the table creation as in Figure 23.3.

In the next section, you will create the subscribe/unsubscribe form mechanism.

Creating the Subscription Form

Like the "all-in-one" mail form in Chapter 8, "Sending E-Mail," the subscription form will be used for subscribing, unsubscribing, and error checking.

1. Open a new file in your text editor and start a PHP block:

```
<?
```

2. Create variables to hold the name of the database on which the table resides, as well as the table itself:

```
$db_name = "testDB";
$table_name = "subscribers";
```

Next, you'll check for a variable you haven't yet created. When you create the actual HTML form, you'll add a hidden field called `op` with a value of `ds`. The `$_POST[op]` variable will be present only if the form has been submitted.

3. Start an `if...else` block and first check if the value of `$_POST[op]` is `ds`:

```
if ($_POST[op] != "ds") {
```

4. If the value of $\texttt{\$\_POST[op]}$ is not $\texttt{ds}$, the user hasn't seen the form. If the user hasn't seen the form, you need to show it. Create a variable called $\texttt{\$text\_block}$ that will hold the entire form. Start with the form action and assume that the method is $\texttt{POST}$ and the action is $\texttt{\$\_SERVER[PHP\_SELF]}$:

```
$text_block = "
<form method=POST action=\"$_SERVER[PHP_SELF]\">
```

5. Add the hidden field:

```
<input type=hidden name=op value=ds>
```

6. Create an input field for the user's e-mail address with a text label:

```
<p><strong>Your E-Mail Address:</strong><br>
<input type=text name=\"email_addr\" size=25 maxlength=100></p>
```

7. Create a set of radio buttons so that the user can select an action of subscribe or unsubscribe. The default should be the subscribe radio button:

```
<p><strong>Action:</strong><br>
<input type=radio name=\"action\" value=\"sub\" checked> subscribe
<input type=radio name=\"action\" value=\"unsub\"> unsubscribe</p>
```

8. Add a submit button and then close the form and string:

```
<p><input type=submit name=\"submit\" value=\"Submit Form\"></p>
</form>";
```

9. Continue the $\texttt{if...else}$ block to check for a value of $\texttt{ds}$ for $\texttt{\$\_POST[op]}$, as well as a value of $\texttt{sub}$ for the $\texttt{\$\_POST[action]}$ variable. This means that the user is attempting to subscribe:

```
} else if (($_POST[op] == "ds") && ($_POST[action] == "sub")) {
```

10. But what if someone clicks on the button and doesn't enter an e-mail address? Add an $\texttt{if}$ block that checks for a value in $\texttt{\$\_POST[email\_addr]}$. If a value is not found, redirect the user to the original form:

```
if ($_POST[email_addr] == "") {
    header("Location: http://127.0.0.1/manage.php");
    exit;
}
```

11. You'll need to check that the user isn't already subscribed, so open a database connection as you have learned:

```
$connection = @mysql_connect("localhost", "spike", "9sj7En4")
    or die(mysql_error());
```

12. Select the database as you have learned:

```
$db = @mysql_select_db($db_name, $connection) or die(mysql_error());
```

13. Create a SQL statement that looks for records matching the user's e-mail address:

```
$check = "select email_addr from $table_name where
    email_addr = '$_POST[email_addr]'";
```

14. Create a variable to hold the result of the `mysql_query()` function, as you have learned:

```
$check_result = @mysql_query($check,$connection) or die(mysql_error());
```

15. Create a variable to count the number of rows in the result set:

```
$check_num = mysql_num_rows($check_result);
```

16. Create an inner `if...else` block that performs an action based on the value of `$check_num`. If `$check_num` is less than 1, no entries in the `subscribers` table have the user's e-mail address, so it's safe to insert one:

```
if ($check_num < 1) {
```

17. Create a SQL statement to insert the e-mail address and the MySQL function `now()`, which inserts the current date (leave a blank entry for the auto-incrementing `id`):

```
$sql = "insert into $table_name values('', '$_POST[email_addr]',
    now())";
```

18. Execute the query, as you have learned:

```
$result = @mysql_query($sql,$connection) or die(mysql_error());
```

19. Create a message string so that the user knows the result:

```
$text_block = "<P>Thanks for signing up!</P>";
```

20. Finish the `if...else` block by creating a message string that tells the user he has already signed up. Then close the inner `if...else` block:

```
} else {
    $text_block = "<P>You're already subscribed!</P>";
}
```

21. Continue the outer `if...else` block to check for a value of `ds` for `$_POST[op]` as well as a value of `unsub` for the `$_POST[action]` variable. This means that the user is attempting to unsubscribe.

```
} else if (($_POST[op] == "ds") && ($_POST[action] == "unsub")) {
```

22. Again, add the validation that checks for a value in `$_POST[email]_addr`. If a value is not found, redirect the user to the original form:

```
if ($_POST[email_addr] == "") {
    header("Location: http://127.0.0.1/manage.php");
    exit;
}
```

23. You'll need to check that the user is in fact subscribed, so open a database connection and select the database:

```
$connection = @mysql_connect("localhost", "spike", "9sj7En4")
    or die(mysql_error());
$db = @mysql_select_db($db_name, $connection) or die(mysql_error());
```

24. Create a SQL statement that looks for records matching the user's e-mail address. Also select the ID field, because you'll use it to unsubscribe if you find a match:

```
$check = "select id, email_addr from $table_name where
    email_addr = '$_POST[email_addr]'";
```

25. Execute the query:

```
$check_result = @mysql_query($check, $connection) or die(mysql_error());
```

26. Create a variable to count the number of rows in the result set:

```
$check_num = mysql_num_rows($check_result);
```

27. Create an inner `if...else` block that performs an action based on the value of `$check_num`. If `$check_num` is less than 1, no entries in the `subscribers` table have the user's e-mail address, so you can't unsubscribe the user.

```
if ($check_num < 1) {
```

28. Create a message string so that the user knows the result:

```
$text_block = "<P>Couldn't find your e-mail on the list!</P>
<P>You haven't been unsubscribed, because the e-mail you entered
    is not in the database.</P>";
```

29. Continue the inner `if...else` block:

```
} else {
```

30. Create a variable to hold the specific value of `id` from the previous result set:

```
$id = @mysql_result($check_result, 0, "id");
```

31. Create a SQL statement that deletes the user's e-mail address from the `subscribers` table:

```
$sql = "delete from $table_name where id = '$_POST[id]'";
```

32. Execute the query:

```
$result = @mysql_query($sql,$connection) or die(mysql_error());
```

33. Create a message string so that the user knows the result:

```
$text_block = "<P>You're unsubscribed!</p>";
```

34. Close the inner `if...else` block, the outer `if...else` block, and the PHP block:

```
    }
}
?>
```

35. Add the following HTML:

```
<HTML>
<HEAD>
<TITLE>Subscribe/Unsubscribe</TITLE>
</HEAD>
<BODY>
<h1>Subscribe/Unsubscribe</h1>
```

36. Display the contents of `$text_block`:

```
<?php echo "$text_block"; ?>
```

37. Add some more HTML so that the document is valid:

```
</BODY>
</HTML>
```

38. Save the file with the name `manage.php` and place this file in the document root of your Web server.

Your entire code should look something like this:

```php
<?
//set up table and database names
$db_name = "testDB";
$table_name = "subscribers";

//determine if they need to see the form or not
if ($_POST[op] != "ds") {
    //create form block
    $text_block = "
    <form method=POST action=\"$_SERVER[PHP_SELF]\">
    <input type=hidden name=op value=ds>
    <p><strong>Your E-Mail Address:</strong><br>
    <input type=text name=\"email_addr\" size=25 maxlength=100></p>
    <p><strong>Action:</strong><br>
    <input type=radio name=\"action\" value=\"sub\" checked> subscribe
    <input type=radio name=\"action\" value=\"unsub\"> unsubscribe</p>
    <p><input type=submit name=\"submit\" value=\"Submit Form\"></p>
    </form>";
} else if (($_POST[op] == "ds") && ($_POST[action] == "sub")) {
    //trying to subscribe; validate email address
    if ($_POST[email_addr] == "") {
        header("Location: http://127.0.0.1/manage.php");
        exit;
    }
```

```php
        //connect to server and select database
        $connection = @mysql_connect("localhost", "spike", "9sj7En4")
            or die(mysql_error());
        $db = @mysql_select_db($db_name, $connection) or die(mysql_error());


        //check that email is not already in list
        $check = "select email_addr from $table_name
        where email_addr = '$_POST[email_addr]'";
        $check_result = @mysql_query($check,$connection) or die(mysql_error());
        $check_num = mysql_num_rows($check_result);


        //get number of results and do action
        if ($check_num < 1) {
            //add record
            $sql = "insert into $table_name
            values('', '$_POST[email_addr]', now())";
            $result = @mysql_query($sql,$connection) or die(mysql_error());
            $text_block = "<P>Thanks for signing up!</P>";
        } else {
            //print failure message
        $text_block = "<P>You're already subscribed!</P>";
        }


} else if (($_POST[op] == "ds") && ($_POST[action] == "unsub")) {
    //trying to unsubscribe; validate email address
    if ($_POST[email_addr] == "") {
        header("Location: http://127.0.0.1/manage.php");
        exit;
    }


    //connect to server and select database
    $connection = @mysql_connect("localhost", "spike", "9sj7En4")
or die(mysql_error());
    $db = @mysql_select_db($db_name, $connection) or die(mysql_error());


    //check that email is in list
    $check = "select id, email_addr from $table_name
    where email_addr = '$_POST[email_addr]'";
    $check_result = @mysql_query($check, $connection) or die(mysql_error());
    $check_num = mysql_num_rows($check_result);


    //get number of results and do action
    if ($check_num < 1) {
        //print failure message
        $text_block = "<P>Couldn't find your e-mail on the list!</P>
        <P>You haven't been unsubscribed, because the e-mail
        you entered is not in the database.</P>";
```

```
        } else {
            //unsubscribe the address
            $id = @mysql_result($check_result, 0, "id");
            $sql = "delete from $table_name where id = '$id'";
            $result = @mysql_query($sql,$connection) or die(mysql_error());
            $text_block = "<P>You're unsubscribed!</p>";
        }
    }
?>
<HTML>
<HEAD>
<TITLE>Subscribe/Unsubscribe</TITLE>
</HEAD>
<BODY>
<h1>Subscribe/Unsubscribe</h1>
<?php echo "$text_block"; ?>
</BODY>
</HTML>
```

In the next section, you'll subscribe and unsubscribe sample users and see how all the address validation works out.

Testing the Subscription Form

Now that you've made it through all those steps in creating the subscription form, it's time to test it!

Figure 23.4 The e-mail management form.

1. Open your Web browser and type `http://127.0.0.1/manage.php`. See Figure 23.4.

You will see a form containing a text field for the person's e-mail address, two radio buttons for either subscribing or unsubscribing, and a button that says Submit Form.

Figure 23.5 E-mail addition confirmation.

2. Type your e-mail address in the Your E-Mail Address field, select the Subscribe radio button, and then submit the form (see Figure 23.5).

You will see a confirmation that your subscription was successful.

Figure 23.6 Notice of previous subscription.

3. Return to the form using your Web browser's Back button and type the same e-mail address in the Your E-Mail Address field.

4. Select the Subscribe radio button (again) and then submit the form (see Figure 23.6).

You will see a message indicating that you've already subscribed.

Figure 23.7 Notice of removal of subscription.

5. Return to the form using your Web browser's Back button and type the same e-mail address in the Your E-Mail Address field. This time, select the Unsubscribe radio button and submit the form (see Figure 23.7).

You will see a confirmation that you have unsubscribed.

Figure 23.8 Error in unsubscribing.

6. Return to the form using your Web browser's Back button and attempt to unsubscribe the same e-mail address (see Figure 23.8).

You will see a confirmation that your e-mail address wasn't in the database, so you haven't been unsubscribed.

Continue adding a few of your own e-mail addresses because in the next section you'll create the form and script to send a newsletter to a list of people, and it would be great to have a real list of people.

Developing the Mailing Mechanism

Now that you have the subscribe/unsubscribe mechanism in place, you can create a very basic form interface to a mailing script. This mailing mechanism will take the contents of your form and send them to every address in your `subscribers` table.

Creating the Newsletter Form

I wasn't kidding when I said you'd create a "simple" form. I just use a text field for the subject of the newsletter and a text area for the newsletter body. You can use as many form fields as you like, as long as you modify the form and script appropriately.

1. Open a new file in your text editor and type the following HTML:

```
<HTML>
<HEAD>
<TITLE>Send a Newsletter</TITLE>
</HEAD>
<BODY>
<h1>Send a Newsletter</h1>
```

2. Begin your form. Assume that the method is POST and the action is a script called `do_send_newsletter.php`:

```
<FORM METHOD="POST" ACTION="do_send_newsletter.php">
```

3. Create an input field for the newsletter subject with a text label:

```
<P><strong>Give it a subject:</strong><br>
<input type="text" name="subject" size=30></p>
```

4. Create a text area for the newsletter body with a text label:

```
<P><strong>Newsletter body:</strong><br>
<textarea name="newsletter" cols=50 rows=10 wrap=virtual></textarea>
```

5. Add a submit button:

```
<p><input type="submit" name="submit" value="Send Newsletter"></p>
```

6. Close your form and add some more HTML so that the document is valid:

```
</FORM>
</BODY>
</HTML>
```

Figure 23.9 The send_newsletter page.

7. Save the file with the name send_newsletter.html and place this file in the document root of your Web server.

8. Open your Web browser and type **http://127.0.0.1/ send_newsletter.html**. See Figure 23.9.

You will see a form containing a text field for the newsletter subject, a text area for the message, and a button that says Send Newsletter.

In the next section, you'll create the back-end script. That script will expect two variables: $_POST[subject] and $_POST[newsletter].

Creating the Script to Mail Your Newsletter

According to the form action in send_newsletter.html, you need a script called do_send_newsletter.php. The goal of this script is to accept the text in $_POST[subject] and $_POST[newsletter] and then send it off in the form of an e-mail to everyone listed in your subscribers table.

1. Open a new file in your text editor and begin a PHP block:

```
<?
```

2. Start an `if...else` block and check that a value has been entered for `$_POST[subject]` and `$_POST[newsletter]`. If either variable is empty, direct the user back to the form:

```
if (($_POST[subject] =="") || ($_POST[newsletter] == "")) {
    header("Location: http://127.0.0.1/send_newsletter.html");
    exit;
```

3. Continue the `if...else` block:

```
} else {
```

4. Create variables to hold the name of the database in which the table resides, as well as the table itself:

```
$db_name = "testDB";
$table_name = "subscribers";
```

5. Connect to the database server and select the database, as you have learned:

```
$connection = @mysql_connect("localhost", "spike", "9sj7En4")
    or die(mysql_error());
$db = @mysql_select_db($db_name, $connection) or die(mysql_error());
```

6. Create a SQL statement that selects all the e-mail addresses in your `subscribers` table:

```
$sql = "select email_addr from $table_name";
```

7. Execute the query:

```
$result = @mysql_query($sql,$connection) or die(mysql_error());
```

8. Create a variable to hold a `From:` mail header.

```
$headers = "From: Your Mailing List <you@yourdomain.com>\n";
```

9. Start the `while` loop. The `while` loop will send an e-mail message to each record in the table and then print a confirmation that the mail was sent:

```
while ($row = mysql_fetch_array($result)) {
```

10. Get the e-mail address for the record:

```
$email_addr = $row['email_addr'];
```

11. Format the call to the `mail()` function. Use the `stripslashes()` function on the value of the `$_POST[subject]` and `$_POST[newsletter]` variables. This will remove any slashes automatically entered in your text by PHP to escape special characters:

```
mail("$email_addr", stripslashes($_POST[subject]),
    stripslashes($_POST[newsletter]), $headers);
```

12. Print a confirmation:

```
echo "newsletter sent to: $email_addr<br>";
```

13. Close the `while` loop, the `if...else` block, and the PHP block:

```
    }
}
?>
```

14. Save the file with the name `do_send_newsletter.php` and place this file in the document root of your Web server.

Your code should look something like this:

```
<?
//check for required fields
if (($_POST[subject] =="") || ($_POST[newsletter] == "")) {
    header("Location: http://127.0.0.1/send_newsletter.html");
    exit;
} else {
    //set up table and database names
     $db_name = "testDB";
    $table_name = "subscribers";

    //connect to server and select database
    $connection = @mysql_connect("localhost", "spike", "9sj7En4")
        or die(mysql_error());
    $db = @mysql_select_db($db_name, $connection) or die(mysql_error());

    //build and issue query
    $sql = "select email_addr from $table_name";
    $result = @mysql_query($sql,$connection) or die(mysql_error());
```

```
        //create a From: mailheaders
        $headers = "From: Your Mailing List <you@yourdomain.com>\n";

    //loop through results and send mail
      while ($row = mysql_fetch_array($result)) {
          $email_addr = $row['email_addr'];
          mail("$email_addr", stripslashes($_POST[subject]),
              stripslashes($_POST[newsletter]), $headers);
          echo "newsletter sent to: $email_addr<br>";
      }
}
?>
```

In the next section, you'll create and send a sample newsletter to your subscribers.

Testing Your Mailing List Mechanism

In this section, you put your script to the test and send a newsletter to all of your subscribers. Be sure your own e-mail address is in the list; otherwise you won't be absolutely sure that the system worked.

Figure 23.10 Send a newsletter form.

1. With your Web browser already open to the form for sending the newsletter, type a subject in the subject field and a chunk of text in the text area to represent the newsletter. See Figure 23.10.

YOUR MILEAGE MAY VARY

The figures show sample text that I typed and e-mail addresses on my sample subscriber list. Your results will differ, although the sequence of events remains the same.

Figure 23.11 Confirmation of newsletter being sent.

2. Submit the form by pressing the Send Newsletter button (see Figure 23.11).

You will see a confirmation of the e-mail addresses to which your newsletter was sent.

3. Check your e-mail if your address is in the `subscribers` table.

You should have a nicely formatted newsletter in your mailbox.

Troubleshooting Your Mailing List Mechanism

If you receive an error such as "Warning: Can't connect," you must make sure you modified the value of SMTP in your `php.ini` file. This topic is covered in Chapter 8 and is a simple fix.

Another common problem when using this type of mailing list mechanism is that the script will eventually time out if your list is long enough. This is one of the reasons not to use this type of mechanism for sending newsletters to large lists of recipients. Because all this script does is execute the `mail()` function numerous times, it does not take into account the queuing factors in real mailing list software, which are designed to ease the burden on your outgoing mail server.

To get around a problem with the script timing out, you can reset the timer within the execution of the script. Essentially, by inserting the following line within your `while` loop, you are setting the timer to 0 before each call to the `mail()` function:

```
set_time_limit(0);
```

Your `while` loop would now look like this:

```
while ($row = mysql_fetch_array($result)) {
    set_time_limit(0);
    $email_addr = $row['email_addr'];
    mail("$email_addr", stripslashes($_POST[$subject]),
        stripslashes($_POST[newsletter]), $headers);
    echo "newsletter sent to: $email_addr<br>";
    }
```

Remember, this does not ease the burden on your outgoing mail server, it just allows the script to continue to run, when it might have timed out before.

In the next chapter, you'll tackle another project. When you create a Web site, you will want to know some numbers regarding visitors—who, what, where, and how. Your next project will be to build a custom reporting mechanism for these sorts of metrics.

24

Creating Custom Logs and Reports

If you're building a Web site for public use, chances are good that you'll want to know which part of your site is most popular, least popular, what types of Web browsers are used, and so on. Although Apache keeps a generic log file of accesses and errors, you can create a few code snippets to store specific information in your MySQL database. In this chapter, you'll learn how to:

- Create a simple access-counting mechanism with MySQL.
- Display the access counts on a page and in a report.
- Track form submissions.
- Create a synopsis report of the form submissions.

A Note About Apache Log Files

The Apache Web server automatically logs specific information regarding user accesses and errors. These log files are found in the `logs` directory. A file called `access.log` handles the accesses, and the `error.log` file handles errors.

The default display for the access log looks something like the following (this was taken from my own access log):

```
127.0.0.1 [22/Feb/2004:05:27:10] "GET /show_createtable.html HTTP/1.1" 304 -
127.0.0.1 [22/Feb/2004:05:27:46] "POST /do_showfielddef.php HTTP/1.1" 200 2402
127.0.0.1 [22/Feb/2004:05:28:49] "POST /do_createtable.php HTTP/1.1" 200 185
127.0.0.1 [22/Feb/2004:05:43:33] "GET /manage.php HTTP/1.1" 200 562
```

This looks rather cryptic, I know. You can set the format in your `httpd.conf` file like so:

```
LogFormat "%h %l %u %t \"%r\" %s %b"
```

In this case, the format maps to the descriptions listed in Table 24.1.

Table 24.1 Apache Log File Settings

Symbol	Description
%h	Remote host name of the machine making the request, or IP if `HostnameLookup = off`
%l	Remote log name (usually empty)
%u	URL path requested by the user
%t	Time of access
"%r"	First line of request, inside quotation marks
%s	Status of the request
%b	Number of bytes sent, excluding headers

LOGGING USER AGENT

You can also log elements such as the user agent (Web browser) within the Apache access log.

Although many log analysis packages are available to purchase or download, the all-encompassing Apache access log might be overkill for simple tasks. This chapter shows you some methods of tracking specific accesses and actions, which have more relevance to you than "all access, all information, all the time."

Simple Access Counting with MySQL

To capture access information for specific subsections of your Web site, or even just the main page, you can create a simple database table and accompanying PHP code snippet to do just that.

Using the now-familiar process of table creation, first you'll create a simple database table to hold all your access records.

Creating the Database Table

In this example, you will log four elements: page name, page description, user agent, and date accessed. First, create the database table.

1. Open your Web browser and type `http://127.0.0.1/show_createtable.html`.

2. In the Table Name field, type `page_track`.

3. In the Number of Fields field, type 5.

4. Click the Go to Step 2 button. You should see a form with five rows, corresponding to the five fields you want to create in the `page_track` table.

Populate the fields in these next steps:

1. In the first row, type `id` for the Field Name, select `int` from the Field Type drop-down menu, and check the Primary Key and Auto-Increment boxes.

2. In the first row, type `page_name` for the Field Name, select `varchar` from the Field Type drop-down menu, and specify a Field Length of 50.

3. In the second row, type `page_desc` for the Field Name and select `text` from the Field Type drop-down menu.

4. In the third row, type `user_agent` for the Field Name and select `text` from the Field Type drop-down menu.

Figure 24.1 The completed database creation form.

5. In the fourth row, type `date_added` for the Field Name and select `date` from the Field Type drop-down menu.

The completed form should look like Figure 24.1.

6. Click the Create Table button to create the `page_track` table.

In the next section, you'll create a code snippet that writes tracking information to the `page_track` table.

Creating the Code Snippet

"Code snippet" is a highly technical term that means "a little bit of code." I'm kidding about the "highly technical" part, but a code snippet is usually something that doesn't qualify as a long script. Rather, it just serves a simple purpose. In this case, your code snippet will write some basic information to the `page_track` table and then merrily finish displaying some rather boring HTML.

1. Open a new file in your text editor and start a PHP block:

```
<?
```

2. Create four variables, corresponding to the four non-ID fields in the `page_track` table, and give them some values:

```
$page_name = "sample 1";
$page_desc = "This is a sample page of no use.";
$user_agent = getenv("HTTP_USER_AGENT");
$date_added = date("Y-m-d");
```

3. Create variables to hold the name of the database in which the table resides, as well as the table itself:

```
$db_name = "testDB";
    $table_name = "page_track";
```

4. Add the connection information as you have been doing:

```
$connection = @mysql_connect("localhost", "spike", "9sj7En4")
    or die(mysql_error());
```

5. Select the database as you have learned:

```
$db = @mysql_select_db($db_name, $connection) or die(mysql_error());
```

6. Create a SQL statement that inserts the values into four fields in the `page_track` table, leaving the ID field blank so that it automatically increments:

```
$sql = "insert into $table_name values
    ('', '$page_name', '$page_desc', '$user_agent', '$date_added')";
```

7. Execute the query and then close the PHP block:

```
$result = @mysql_query($sql,$connection) or die(mysql_error());
?>
```

You've just created the code snippet, which should look something like this:

```
<?
//set up static variables
$page_name = "sample 1";
$page_desc = "This is a sample page of no use.";
$user_agent = getenv("HTTP_USER_AGENT");
$date_added = date("Y-m-d");

//set up table and database names
$db_name = "testDB";
$table_name = "page_track";

//connect to server and select database
$connection = @mysql_connect("localhost", "spike", "9sj7En4")
    or die(mysql_error());
$db = @mysql_select_db($db_name, $connection) or die(mysql_error());

//build and issue query
$sql = "insert into $table_name values
('', '$page_name', '$page_desc', '$user_agent', '$date_added')";
$result = @mysql_query($sql,$connection) or die(mysql_error());
?>
```

Now create a bit of filler HTML, directly after the code snippet:

```
<HTML>
<HEAD>
<TITLE>Sample Page #1</TITLE>
</HEAD>
<BODY>
<h1>Useless Sample Page #1</h1>
<P>This sample page serves no real purpose!</p>
</BODY>
</HTML>
```

Save the file with the name `sample_page1.php` and place this file in the document root of your Web server. To make things a little more interesting in your reports, make another one of these sample files so that you've got something more to count than just this one file. Copy `sample_page1.php` to `sample_page2.php` and change the first two variables in `sample_page2.php` to the following:

```
$page_name = "sample 2";
$page_desc = "Another useless sample page.";
```

Replace the HTML block in `sample_page2.php` with this:

```
<HTML>
<HEAD>
<TITLE>Sample Page #2</TITLE>
</HEAD>
<BODY>
<h1>Useless Sample Page #2</h1>
<P>I can't believe how useless this page is!</p>
</BODY>
</HTML>
```

Figure 24.2 Sample page with heading and text.

Figure 24.3 Second sample page with heading and text.

Now save this file and place it in the document root of your Web server as well.

Next, you'll access these pages a few times to get the internal counting going.

1. Open your Web browser and type **http://127.0.0.1/sample_page1.php**. See Figure 24.2.

You will see the HTML page, with a heading and some text.

2. Open your Web browser and type **http://127.0.0.1/sample_page2.php**. See Figure 24.3.

You will see the HTML page with a heading and some text.

Keep reloading these pages a few times and then move on to the next section where the count will be displayed.

Displaying the Count

Displaying the count on each of these pages is a snap. You just add three lines to your code snippet and one line inside your HTML block.

1. Open `sample_page1.php` in your text editor.

2. Directly before the end of the PHP block, create a SQL statement that gets the number of accesses for this particular page:

```
$count_sql = "select count(page_name) from $table_name
    where page_name = '$page_name'";
```

ORDER OF COUNTING CODE

Place the counting code after the insertion code to be sure that you're counting the current access as well.

---

3. Execute the query:

```
$count_res = @mysql_query($count_sql,$connection) or die(mysql_error());
```

4. Create a variable to hold the specific count within the context of the current result set:

```
$count = @mysql_result($count_res, 0, "count(page_name)");
```

5. In your HTML block, mingle HTML with PHP to print the value of `$count`:

```
<P>Accesses: <? echo "$count"; ?></p>
```

Your new `sample_page1.php` script should look like this:

```
<?
//set up static variables
$page_name = "sample 1";
$page_desc = "This is a sample page of no use.";
$user_agent = getenv("HTTP_USER_AGENT");
$date_added = date("Y-m-d");

//set up table and database names
$db_name = "testDB";
$table_name = "page_track";
```

```
//connect to server and select database
$connection = @mysql_connect("localhost", "spike", "9sj7En4")
    or die(mysql_error());
$db = @mysql_select_db($db_name, $connection) or die(mysql_error());

//build and issue query
$sql = "insert into $table_name values
    ('', '$page_name', '$page_desc', '$user_agent', '$date_added')";
$result = @mysql_query($sql,$connection) or die(mysql_error());

//get count
$count_sql = "select count(page_name) from $table_name
    where page_name = '$page_name'";
$count_res = @mysql_query($count_sql,$connection) or die(mysql_error());
$count = @mysql_result($count_res, 0, "count(page_name)");
?>
<HTML>
<HEAD>
<TITLE>Sample Page #1</TITLE>
</HEAD>
<BODY>
<h1>Useless Sample Page #1</h1>
<P>This sample page serves no real purpose!</p>
<P>Accesses: <? echo "$count"; ?></p>
</BODY>
</HTML>
```

Make the same types of changes to `sample_page2.php` and make sure you save both files.

Figure 24.4 Updated sample page 1.

Next, you access these pages again and see the count display on the page.

1. Open your Web browser and type **http://127.0.0.1/ sample_page1.php**, as shown in Figure 24.4.

You will see the HTML page, with a heading and some text, followed by the access count you've reached. In this example, I've accessed this sample page five times.

Figure 24.5 Updated sample page 2.

2. Open your Web browser and type **http://127.0.0.1/ sample_page2.php**.

You will see the HTML page, with a heading and some text, followed by the access count you've reached. In Figure 24.5, I've accessed this sample page two times.

In the next section, you'll create an access report page, which you can use to check the status of the pages you're tracking in the page_track table.

Creating Your Personal Access Report

You have all this great data in your page_track table, so now it's time to create a simple page that counts it all up for you. There's no need to weed through cryptic Apache access logs or install additional software packages to display statistics for you when it's this simple.

Start by creating a simple count of the total hits to your tracked pages (all-inclusive).

1. Open a new file in your text editor and start a PHP block:

```
<?
```

2. Create variables to hold the name of the database in which the table resides, as well as the table itself:

```
$db_name = "testDB";
$table_name = "page_track";
```

3. Add the connection information as you have been doing:

```
$connection = @mysql_connect("localhost", "spike", "9sj7En4")
    or die(mysql_error());
```

4. Select the database as you have learned:

```
$db = @mysql_select_db($db_name, $connection) or die(mysql_error());
```

5. Create a SQL statement that counts all the entries in the page_track table:

```
$count_sql = "select count(page_name) from $table_name";
```

6. Execute the query:

```
$count_res = @mysql_query($count_sql, $connection) or die(mysql_error());
```

7. Create a variable to hold the specific count within the context of the current result set and then close the PHP block:

```
$all_count = @mysql_result($count_res, 0, "count(page_name)");
?>
```

8. Add this HTML:

```
<HTML>
<HEAD>
<TITLE>My Access Report</TITLE>
</HEAD>
<BODY>
<h1>My Access Report</h1>
```

9. Mingle HTML and PHP to print the name of the table as well as the number of accesses tracked in the table:

```
<P><strong>Total Accesses Tracked in
<? echo "$table_name"; ?>:</strong> <? echo "$all_count"; ?></p>
```

10. Add some more HTML so that the document is valid:

```
</BODY>
</HTML>
```

11. Save the file with the name `access_report.php` and place this file in the document root of your Web server.

Your code should look something like this:

```php
<?
//set up table and database names
$db_name = "testDB";
$table_name = "page_track";

//connect to server and select database
$connection = @mysql_connect("localhost", "spike", "9sj7En4")
    or die(mysql_error());
$db = @mysql_select_db($db_name, $connection) or die(mysql_error());

//issue query and select results
$count_sql = "select count(page_name) from $table_name";
$count_res = @mysql_query($count_sql, $connection) or die(mysql_error());
$all_count = @mysql_result($count_res, 0, "count(page_name)");
?>
<HTML>
<HEAD>
<TITLE>My Access Report</TITLE>
</HEAD>
<BODY>
<h1>My Access Report</h1>
<P><strong>Total Accesses Tracked in <? echo "$table_name";
    ?>:</strong> <? echo "$all_count"; ?></p>
</BODY>
</HTML>
```

Figure 24.6 Access report.

Next, test it! Open your Web browser and type **http://127.0.0.1/access_report.php**. See Figure 24.6.

You will see the HTML page with a heading and some text, followed by the access count you've reached for all pages. In this example, I've accessed the two sample pages a total of four times.

Displaying the User Agents

In this section, you'll make some minor additions to the `access_report.php` script to display and count the different Web browsers used by those accessing your pages.

1. Open `access_report.php` in your text editor.

2. Before the closing PHP tag, create a SQL statement that finds all distinct entries in the `user_agent` field of the `page_track` table, counts these entries, and returns the results in descending order:

```
$user_agent_sql = "select distinct user_agent, count(user_agent) as count
from $table_name group by user_agent order by count desc";
```

3. Execute the query:

```
$user_agent_res = @mysql_query($user_agent_sql, $connection)
    or die(mysql_error());
```

4. You'll create a bulleted list within a `while` block in a moment. Start the bulleted list outside the `while` block:

```
$user_agent_block = "<ul>";
```

5. Start the `while` loop. The `while` loop will create an array called `$row_ua` for each record in the result set (`$user_agent_res`):

```
while ($row_ua = mysql_fetch_array($user_agent_res)) {
```

6. Get the individual elements of the record and give them good names:

```
$user_agent = $row_ua['user_agent'];
$user_agent_count = $row_ua['count'];
```

7. Add to `$user_agent_block` by creating one bulleted item and an additional bulleted list. The bulleted item will show the name of the user agent. Then the second bulleted list will show the number of accesses by that particular user agent. After adding to `$user_agent_block`, close the `while` loop:

```
$user_agent_block .= "
    <li>$user_agent
     <ul>
    <li><em>accesses per browser: $user_agent_count</em>
      </ul>";
}
```

8. Close the bulleted list you created in `$user_agent_block`:

```
$user_agent_block .= "</ul>";
```

9. In the HTML section, add the following and then save the file:

```
<P><strong>Web Browsers Used:</strong>
<? echo "$user_agent_block"; ?>
```

Your new code should look something like this:

```
<?
//set up table and database names
$db_name = "testDB";
$table_name = "page_track";

//connect to server and select database
$connection = @mysql_connect("localhost", "spike", "9sj7En4")
    or die(mysql_error());
$db = @mysql_select_db($db_name, $connection) or die(mysql_error());

//issue query and select results for counts
$count_sql = "select count(page_name) from $table_name";
$count_res = @mysql_query($count_sql, $connection) or die(mysql_error());
$all_count = @mysql_result($count_res, 0, "count(page_name)");

//issue query and select results for user agents
$user_agent_sql = "select distinct user_agent, count(user_agent) as count
from $table_name group by user_agent order by count desc";
$user_agent_res = @mysql_query($user_agent_sql, $connection)
    or die(mysql_error());
```

```
//start user agent display block
$user_agent_block = "<ul>";

//loop through results
while ($row_ua = mysql_fetch_array($user_agent_res)) {
      $user_agent = $row_ua['user_agent'];
      $user_agent_count = $row_ua['count'];
      $user_agent_block .= "
      <li>$user_agent
      <ul>
      <li><em>accesses per browser: $user_agent_count</em>
      </ul>";
}
//finish up the user agent block
$user_agent_block .= "</ul>";
?>
<HTML>
<HEAD>
<TITLE>My Access Report</TITLE>
</HEAD>
<BODY>
<h1>My Access Report</h1>
<P><strong>Total Accesses Tracked in
<? echo "$table_name"; ?>:</strong> <? echo "$all_count"; ?></p>

<P><strong>Web Browsers Used:</strong>
<? echo "$user_agent_block"; ?>

</BODY>
</HTML>
```

Figure 24.7 Access report with user agents.

Let's see what user agents have been accessing your pages. Open your Web browser and type **http://127.0.0.1/ access_report.php**. See Figure 24.7.

You will see the HTML page, with a heading and some text, followed by the access count you've reached for all pages. You will also see a list of user agents and the total accesses for each type. In this example,

I've accessed the two sample pages a total of four times with a single unique Web browser. Try it with a few different browsers, to see the differences.

In the next section, you'll make the final modifications to the `access_report.php` script, displaying the individual page breakdowns.

Displaying Specific Page Breakdowns

In this section, you'll make some minor additions to the `access_report.php` script to provide a breakdown of the specific pages that you're tracking in the `page_track` table.

1. Open `access_report.php` in your text editor.

2. Before the closing PHP tag, create a SQL statement that finds all distinct entries in the `page_name` field of the `page_track` table, counts these entries, and returns the results in descending order:

```
$page_name_sql = "select distinct page_name, page_desc,
    count(page_name) as count from $table_name
    group by page_name order by count desc";
```

3. Execute the query:

```
$page_name_res = @mysql_query($page_name_sql, $connection)
    or die(mysql_error());
```

4. You'll create a bulleted list within a `while` block in a moment. Start the bulleted list outside the `while` block:

```
$page_name_block = "<ul>";
```

5. Start the `while` loop. The `while` loop will create an array called `$row_pn` for each record in the result set (`$page_name_res`):

```
while ($row_pn = mysql_fetch_array($page_name_res)) {
```

6. Get the individual elements of the record and give them good names:

```
$page_name = $row_pn['page_name'];
$page_desc = $row_pn['page_desc'];
$page_count = $row_pn['count'];
```

7. Add to `$page_name_block` by creating one bulleted item and an additional bulleted list. The bulleted item will show the name of the page accessed. Then the second bulleted list will show the number of accesses to that page. After adding to `$page_name_block`, close the `while` loop with this code:

```
$page_name_block .= "
    <li>$page_name (\"$page_desc\")
      <ul>
    <li><em>accesses per page: $page_count</em>
      </ul>";
}
```

8. Close the bulleted list you created in `$page_name_block`:

```
$page_name_block .= "</ul>";
```

9. In the HTML section, add the following code and then save the file:

```
<P><strong>Individual Pages:</strong>
<? echo "$page_name_block"; ?>
```

Your new code should look something like this:

```
<?
//set up table and database names
$db_name = "testDB";
$table_name = "page_track";

//connect to server and select database
$connection = @mysql_connect("localhost", "spike", "9sj7En4")
or die(mysql_error());
$db = @mysql_select_db($db_name, $connection) or die(mysql_error());

//issue query and select results for counts
$count_sql = "select count(page_name) from $table_name";
$count_res = @mysql_query($count_sql, $connection) or die(mysql_error());
$all_count = @mysql_result($count_res, 0, "count(page_name)");

//issue query and select results for user agents
$user_agent_sql = "select distinct user_agent, count(user_agent) as count
from $table_name group by user_agent order by count desc";
$user_agent_res = @mysql_query($user_agent_sql, $connection)
    or die(mysql_error());
```

```php
//start user agent display block
$user_agent_block = "<ul>";


//loop through results
while ($row_ua = mysql_fetch_array($user_agent_res)) {
    $user_agent = $row_ua['user_agent'];
    $user_agent_count = $row_ua['count'];
    $user_agent_block .= "
    <li>$user_agent
    <ul>
    <li><em>accesses per browser: $user_agent_count</em>
    </ul>";
}
//finish up the user agent block
$user_agent_block .= "</ul>";


//issue query and select results for pages
$page_name_sql = "select distinct page_name, page_desc,
count(page_name) as count from $table_name
group by page_name order by count desc";
$page_name_res = @mysql_query($page_name_sql, $connection)
    or die(mysql_error());


//start page name display block
$page_name_block = "<ul>";


//loop through results
while ($row_pn = mysql_fetch_array($page_name_res)) {
    $page_name = $row_pn['page_name'];
    $page_desc = $row_pn['page_desc'];
    $page_count = $row_pn['count'];
    $page_name_block .= "
    <li>$page_name (\"$page_desc\")
    <ul>
    <li><em>accesses per page: $page_count</em>
    </ul>";
}
//finish up the page name block
$page_name_block .= "</ul>";
?>
<HTML>
<HEAD>
<TITLE>My Access Report</TITLE>
</HEAD>
<BODY>
<h1>My Access Report</h1>
<P><strong>Total Accesses Tracked in
<? echo "$table_name"; ?>:</strong> <? echo "$all_count"; ?></p>
```

```
<P><strong>Web Browsers Used:</strong>
<? echo "$user_agent_block"; ?>

<P><strong>Individual Pages:</strong>
<? echo "$page_name_block"; ?>

</BODY>
</HTML>
```

Figure 24.8 The final access report.

It's time to check the final results. Open your Web browser and type `http://127.0.0.1/access_report.php` (see Figure 24.8).

You will see the HTML page with a heading and some text, followed by the access count you've reached for all pages. You will also see a list of user agents and the total accesses for each type. Finally, you'll see a list of all pages accessed, as well as the short description and individual access count for each.

That's a lot easier than wading through Apache access logs, but I wouldn't recommend completely replacing your access logs with a database-driven system. That's a bit too much database-connection overhead, even if MySQL is particularly nice on your system. Instead, target your page tracking to something particularly important to you.

In the next chapter, you'll tackle another project. You are introduced to the wonderful world of XML and how to use XML and PHP together for storage and display of data.

25

Working with XML

This chapter will give you a hands-on introduction to using XML and PHP, but in no way should this be considered a definitive guide on the subject. Use this chapter as a primer for a subject you might decide to explore further on your own. In PHP 6, all things XML-related have been completely rewritten, so that the functionality, efficiency, and overall integration are much more reliable and full featured. In this chapter, you will learn how to:

- Create a basic XML document structure.
- Use XML with PHP.
- Parse and display content from XML files.

What Is XML?

The name XML comes from the full name of the language, Extensible Markup Language. Although "markup" is in its name, do not think of XML as you do HTML, because aside from the fact that both languages are based on tag pairs, there are no similarities. XML is a method of data exchange, in that it holds well-defined content within its boundaries. HTML, on the other hand, couldn't care less what is contained in the content or how it is structured—its only purpose is to display the content to the browser. XML is used to define and carry the content, whereas HTML is used to make it "pretty."

This is not to say that XML data cannot be made pretty, or that you cannot display XML data in your Web browser. In fact, this is exactly what you do using Extensible Style Language (XSL) and Cascading Style Sheets (CSS) to render your content into a format that your Web browser can understand, while still preserving the content categorization. For example, say you have an area on your Web site reserved for recent system messages, and those items each contain the following:

- Title
- Message
- Author
- Date of message

You might want to display the title in bold, the message as a paragraph, the author's name in italics, and the date in a small font. For this, you would use HTML. XML, on the other hand, only cares that there are four distinct content elements. By separating the data and its structure from the presentation elements, you can use the content however you want and are not limited to the particular marked-up style that static HTML has forced on you.

Basic XML Document Structure

Before moving forward into working with XML documents, you need to know exactly how to create them. XML documents contain two major elements: the prolog and the body. The *prolog* contains the XML declaration statement (much like an HTML document type definition statement) and any processing instructions and comments you want to add.

XML SPECIFICATION

For a complete definition of XML documents, read the XML specification at http://www.w3.org/TR/REC-xml (last updated in September 2006).

Using the system message example from the previous section, open a text editor and create a file called `messages.xml`. Type the following:

```
<?xml version="1.0" ?>
<!-- Sample XML document -->
```

Next, the fun begins in the body area of the document, where the content structure is contained. XML is hierarchical, like a book—books have titles and chapters, each of which contains paragraphs, and so forth. There is only one root element in an XML document—using the book example, the element might be called `Book`, and the tags `<Book></Book>` surround all other information.

But I am using the system messages example here, so call the root element `SystemMessage` and add an open tag to your `messages.xml` document:

```
<SystemMessage>
```

Next, add any subsequent elements—called *children*—to your document. Using the system messages example, you need title, body, author, and date information. Call the children elements `MessageTitle`, `MessageBody`, `MessageAuthor`, and `MessageDate`. But what if you want both the name and an e-mail address for the author? Not a problem—you just create another set of child elements within your parent element (which just also happens to be a child element of the root element). For example, just the `<MessageAuthor>` element could look like this:

```
<MessageAuthor>
<MessageAuthorName>Joe SystemGod</MessageAuthorName>
<MessageAuthorEmail>systemgod@someserver.com</MessageAuthorEmail>
</MessageAuthor>
```

All together, your sample `messages.xml` document could look something like this:

```
<?xml version="1.0" ?>
<!--Sample XML document -->
<SystemMessage>
        <MessageTitle>System Down for Maintenance</MessageTitle>
        <MessageBody>Going down for maintenance soon!</MessageBody>
        <MessageAuthor>
<MessageAuthorName>Joe SystemGod</MessageAuthorName>
<MessageAuthorEmail>systemgod@someserver.com</MessageAuthorEmail>
        </MessageAuthor>
        <MessageDate>March 4, 2004</MessageDate>
</SystemMessage>
```

Here are two very important rules to keep in mind for creating valid XML documents:

- XML is case sensitive, so `<Book>` and `<book>` are different elements.

- All XML tags must be properly closed, XML tags must be properly nested, and no overlapping tags are allowed.

Figure 25.1 View of `messages.xml` with all elements open.

Put the `messages.xml` file (or one like it) in the document root of your Web server for use in later examples. As a side note, current versions of some browsers, such as Microsoft Internet Explorer and Netscape, allow you to view your XML document in a tree-like format, using their own internal style sheets. Figure 25.1 shows the original view of the `messages.xml`

Figure 25.2 View of XML file with collapsed tree.

file with all elements opened, whereas Figure 25.2 shows the `messages.xml` file with the `SystemMessage` element collapsed.

Preparing to Use XML with PHP

XML functionality in PHP is based on the `libxml2` library and is enabled by default at the time of PHP configuration and installation—on both Linux/UNIX and Windows platforms.

Figure 25.3 XML entries in PHP.

You can determine whether XML support is enabled in your installation of PHP by looking at the output of the `phpinfo()` function. Figure 25.3 shows some of the XML-related entries you will see in an XML-enabled installation.

A NOTE ON ORDER

You won't see these items listed in this order in your `phpinfo()` output, as there will be several entries in between in the alphabetical display of enabled elements.

After you have confirmed that XML support is enabled within PHP, you can move on to parsing, transforming, and even generating XML on your system. All of the examples used in this chapter are very basic, and again I recommend reading additional books or entries in the PHP manual (http://www.php.net/manual/) if you're interested in working with XML to any great extent.

Parsing XML with PHP

In this section, you'll see a few examples of how PHP can parse a valid XML document using the `messages.xml` file created earlier in this chapter. These basic scripts show you the stepwise methods used to parse XML files with PHP; as with everything in this book, it's all about gaining a foundation for learning.

The first example script will simply load the `messages.xml` file into the XML parser and then have the parser display back the distinct elements it finds.

1. Open a new file in your text editor and start a PHP block:

```
<?
```

2. Use the `simplexml_load_file()` function to load contents of the `messages.xml` file into an object called `$xml`:

```
$xml = simplexml_load_file('messages.xml');
```

WRITING YOUR OWN OBJECTS

Objects are introduced in Appendix C, "Writing Your Own Functions," but for now think of an object as a big container, go with the flow, and grasp the overall concept of what's occurring.

---

3. Use the `var_dump()` function to print all the element names in the object and their values, and then close the PHP block:

```
var_dump($xml);
    ?>
```

4. Save the file as `xmlload.php` and place it in the document root of your Web server with the `messages.xml` file.

Figure 25.4 The XML object dumped to the screen.

When you access this file with your browser, you will see something like Figure 25.4.

This rather unattractive output shows that the XML parser read the file, identified elements such as `MessageTitle` and so forth, and read the values of these elements. In the next section, you'll see how to map XML elements to specific types of HTML markup, eventually displaying the information in presentation form.

Parse and Display Content from XML Files

In this section, you'll create a script that will map HTML markup to XML elements, eventually displaying what you'd normally see in a Web browser. This example uses an XML file called `books.xml`, which stores a list of books and publication information. In this example, the list is of three of my books, and the elements are the following:

- `BookStore`
- `Book`
- `BookTitle`
- `BookAuthor`

- `BookPublisher`
- `BookISBN`
- `BookPrice`

Before you move on to the coding aspect, create a `books.xml` file and put the following into it (or any books of your choice; just follow the same structure):

```xml
<?xml version="1.0" ?>
<BookStore>
    <Book>
    <BookTitle>PHP5 Fast &amp; Easy Web Development </BookTitle>
    <BookAuthor>Julie Meloni</BookAuthor>
    <BookPublisher>Premier Press</BookPublisher>
    <BookISBN>1592004733</BookISBN>
    <BookPrice>29.99</BookPrice>
    </Book>
    <Book>
    <BookTitle>PHP Essentials, 2nd edition</BookTitle>
    <BookAuthor>Julie Meloni</BookAuthor>
    <BookPublisher>Premier Press</BookPublisher>
    <BookISBN>1931841349</BookISBN>
    <BookPrice>39.99</BookPrice>
    </Book>
    <Book>
    <BookTitle>PHP Fast &amp; Easy Web Development, 2nd edition</BookTitle>
    <BookAuthor>Julie Meloni</BookAuthor>
    <BookPublisher>Premier Press</BookPublisher>
    <BookISBN>193184187X</BookISBN>
    <BookPrice>29.99</BookPrice>
    </Book>
</BookStore>
```

The goal of the XML parsing script is to display each XML element in a consistent HTML markup. During the process by which you loop through the elements, you will wrap HTML around their values—much like you do when looping through a MySQL result set from a database query.

1. Open a new file in your text editor and start a PHP block:

```
<?
```

2. Use the `simplexml_load_file()` function to load contents of the `books.xml` file into an object called `$xml`:

```
$xml = simplexml_load_file('books.xml');
```

3. Begin a `for` loop that looks for each `Book` element in the just-parsed XML file and allows it to be accessible via `$Book`:

```
foreach($xml->Book as $Book) {
```

4. Start to `echo` the output from the `for` loop:

```
echo "
```

5. Output the book's title, wrapping it in HTML:

```
<p><strong>".$Book->BookTitle."</strong><br>
```

6. Output the book's author information, wrapping it in HTML:

```
<em>by ".$Book->BookAuthor."</em><br>
```

7. Output the book's publisher information, wrapping it in HTML:

```
(Published by ".$Book->BookPublisher.",
```

8. Output the book's ISBN, wrapping it in HTML:

```
ISBN: ".$Book->BookISBN.")<br>
```

9. Output the book's price, wrapping it in HTML:

```
<font color=red>price:</font> \$".$Book->BookPrice."</p>
```

10. Finish the `for` loop by adding a separator and closing the braces and then the PHP block:

```
<hr noshade>";
}
?>
```

Save this file as `xmlparse.php` and place it in the document root of your Web server. The entire script should look something like this:

```
<?
$xml = simplexml_load_file("books.xml");
foreach($xml->Book as $Book) {
    echo "
    <p><strong>".$Book->BookTitle."</strong><br>
    <em>by ".$Book->BookAuthor."</em><br>
    (Published by ".$Book->BookPublisher.",
    ISBN: ".$Book->BookISBN.")<br>
    <font color=red>price:</font> \$".$Book->BookPrice."</p>
    <hr noshade>";
}
?>
```

Figure 25.5 Formatted XML display.

When you access this file with your browser, you will see something like Figure 25.5.

The `xmlparse.php` script provides a basic example of reading an XML document and working with its content. To take this concept further, have a look at the examples in the PHP manual:

- DOM XML functions are documented at http://www.php.net/domxml.
- SimpleXML functions are documented at http://www.php.net/simplexml.

Although this chapter ends the lessons and projects, this book also has six appendixes full of useful information. General PHP reference items can be found in the first two appendixes, and a lesson on functions is in Appendix C. Appendix D contains a wealth of information about new features in PHP 6.0, including writing your own classes and objects. Database normalization and a basic SQL reference can be found in Appendix E, "Database Normalization and SQL Reference," and a new element in PHP6—SQLite—is covered in Appendix F, "Using SQLite." These appendixes wrap up with Appendix G, "Getting Help," which points you in the right direction for additional resources and tutorials.

PART VIII

Appendixes

A

Additional Configuration Options

The installation instructions at the beginning of this book detailed a simple configuration of PHP. If you feel like venturing out on your own by adding additional extensions (on Windows) or recompiling PHP (on Linux), this appendix gives you a brief rundown of some of your options. PHP can be as powerful or as streamlined as you want it to be, but a general rule of thumb is only to add functionality that you really need. For example, if you have no plans for connecting to an Oracle database, you do not need to enable support for the Oracle functions. But PHP is very extendable, meaning you do have the capability to add functionality whenever you want—such as if your company decides to buy an Oracle license!

Windows Extensions

Basic functionality is already built into PHP binary distributions for Windows, including:

- Regular expression support
- Dynamic library support
- Internal sendmail support
- Perl-compatible regular expression support
- ODBC support
- Session support
- XML support
- MySQL support

and much more!

To get additional functionality, you must use additional extensions (`.dll` files), over 40 of which are included with the distribution. Some of the more popular extensions are listed in Table A.1.

To turn an extension "on," you must modify your `php.ini` file.

1. Open `php.ini` in a text editor and find the following lines:

```
; Directory in which the loadable extensions (modules) reside.
extension_dir = ./
```

2. Change the second line so that it points to the directory containing your extensions, such as:

```
extension_dir = /php/extensions
```

Table A.1 Windows Extensions

Filename	Description
php_bz2.dll	Enables BZIP functions
php_cpdf.dll	Enables ClibPDF functions
php_curl.dll	Enables CURL-related functions
php_dba.dll	Enables Database Abstraction Layer functions
php_dbase.dll	Enables database functions
php_fdf.dll	Enables Forms Data Format functions
php_gd2.dll	Enables GD library image functions
php_gettext.dll	Enables GetText functions
php_ifx.dll	Enables Informix functions
php_imap.dll	Enables IMAP, POP3, and NNTP functionality.
php_interbase.dll	Enables Interbase (Borland database) functionality
php_ldap.dll	Enables LDAP functions
php_mcrypt.dll	Enables Mcrypt Encryption functions
php_mhash.dll	Enables mhash functions
php_mime_magic.dll	Enables MIME functions.
php_ming.dll	Enables Ming-related Macromedia Flash functions
php_msql.dll	Enables MSQL functionality
php_mssql.dll	Enables Microsoft SQLServer functions
php_mysql.dll	Enables MySQL functions
php_oci8.dll	Enables Oracle 8+ functions
php_openssl.dll	Enables OpenSSL functions
php_pgsql.dll	Enables PostgreSQL functions
php_sybase_ct.dll	Enables Sybase functions
php_xsl.dll	Enables XSL functionality

3. Next, find a section that starts like this:

```
; Windows Extensions
; Note that ODBC support is built in, so no dll is needed for it.
; Note that many DLL files are located in the extensions/ (PHP 4) ext/
(PHP 5)
; extension folders as well as the separate PECL DLL download (PHP 5).
; Be sure to appropriately set the extension_dir directive.
```

4. For each extension you want to use, take away the semicolon before the name if the file is in the list.

5. If the file is not in the list, add it:

```
extension=[your_extension_name].dll
```

6. After changing anything in the `php.ini` file, restart the Web server and then check the output of `phpinfo()` to verify your changes.

For more information on the Windows configuration options in PHP, please see the PHP manual's section on installation and configuration.

Linux Configuration Options

Here is the configuration line used in Chapter 3 to build PHP:

```
./configure --with-mysql/
--with-apxs2=/usr/local/apache2/bin/apxs
```

This line tells PHP to include support for MySQL and to build as a dynamic module. Many other extensions and other configurations are available to you, many of which you'll never use (I know I don't). Table A.2 lists some more popular extensions in case you want to fiddle with your installation. However, for a complete list of extensions and configuration options, you can use the following command at your shell prompt when in the PHP source directory:

```
./configure --help
```

This will list all available configuration options.

Remember, because PHP is an Apache dynamic module, you don't have to recompile Apache when making changes to PHP.

For more information on Linux/UNIX configuration options in PHP, please see the PHP manual's section on installation and configuration.

Table A.2 Some Available Extensions

Extension	Description
`--disable-all`	Disable all extensions enabled by default.
`--disable-libxml`	Disable new LIBXML support.
`--with-openssl[=DIR]`	Include OpenSSL support (requires OpenSSL >= 0.9.6).
`--with-zlib[=DIR]`	Include ZLIB support (requires `zlib` >= 1.0.9).
`--enable-bcmath`	Enable bc style precision math functions.
`--with-curl[=DIR]`	Include CURL support.
`--enable-dbase`	Enable the bundled dbase library.
`--disable-dom`	Disable new DOM support.
`--enable-ftp`	Enable FTP support.
`--with-gd[=DIR]`	Include GD support where `DIR` is GD install prefix.
`--with-jpeg-dir[=DIR]`	GD: Set the path to `libjpeg` install prefix.
`--with-png-dir[=DIR]`	GD: Set the path to `libpng` install prefix.
`--with-zlib-dir[=DIR]`	GD: Set the path to `libz` install prefix.
`--with-xpm-dir[=DIR]`	GD: Set the path to `libXpm` install prefix.
`--with-ttf[=DIR]`	GD: Include FreeType 1.x support.
`--with-freetype-dir[=DIR]`	GD: Set the path to FreeType 2 install prefix.
`--with-informix[=DIR]`	Include Informix support.
`--with-ldap[=DIR]`	Include LDAP support.
`--enable-mbstring`	Enable multibyte string support.

Table A.2 Some Available Extensions (continued)

Extension	Description
`--with-mcrypt[=DIR]`	Include mcrypt support.
`--with-mhash[=DIR]`	Include mhash support.
`--with-mssql[=DIR]`	Include MSSQL-DB support. DIR is the FreeTDS home directory.
`--with-mysql[=DIR]`	Include MySQL support. DIR is the MySQL base directory.
`--with-oci8[=DIR]`	Include Oracle-oci8 support. Default DIR is ORACLE_HOME.
`--with-ibm-db2[=DIR]`	Include IBM DB2 support. DIR is the DB2 base.
`--with-custom-odbc[=DIR]`	Include a user-defined ODBC support. DIR is the ODBC base directory.
`--with-iodbc[=DIR]`	Include iODBC support. DIR is the iODBC base directory.
`--disable-posix`	Disable POSIX-like functions.
`--disable-session`	Disable session support.
`--without-sqlite`	Do not include SQLite support.
`--with-sybase[=DIR]`	Include Sybase-DB support. DIR is the Sybase home directory.

B

Basic PHP Language Reference

This appendix is nowhere near as comprehensive as the PHP manual (found at http://www.php.net/manual/index.php), which contains descriptions of every PHP function that exists, plus user-submitted comments and code samples. Instead, this appendix serves as a basic, or "essential" reference—it contains the elements of PHP that (in my opinion) you can't live without. The PHP development team and all of the documentation contributors have done a wonderful job with the entire PHP manual, and there's no need to reinvent the wheel. However, because this appendix touches on only a small percentage of all there is to know about PHP, check the PHP manual before asking a question on one of the PHP mailing lists.

PLACEHOLDERS

In all of these examples, when something like string or int appears in a function, it is a placeholder for your own string or integer.

PHP Start and End Tags

To combine PHP code with HTML, the PHP code must be *escaped*, or set apart, from the HTML. The PHP engine will consider anything within the tag pairs shown in Table B.1 as PHP code.

Table B.1 Basic PHP Start and End Tags

Opening Tag	Closing Tag
`<?php`	`?>`
`<?`	`?>`
`<script language="php">`	`</script>`

Variables

You create variables to represent data. For instance, the following variable holds a value for sales tax:

```
$sales_tax = 0.0875;
```

This variable holds a SQL statement:

```
$sql = "SELECT * FROM MY_TABLE";
```

You can refer to the value of other variables when determining the value of a new variable:

```
$tax_total = $sales_tax * $sub_total;
```

The following are true of variable names:

- They begin with a dollar sign ($).
- They cannot begin with a numeric character.
- They can contain numbers and the underscore character (_).
- They are case sensitive.

Here are some common variable types:

- floats
- integers
- strings

These types are determined by PHP, based on the context in which they appear.

Floats

Each of the following variables is a float, or floating-point number. Floats are also known as "numbers with decimal points."

```
$a = 1.552;
$b = 0.964;
$sales_tax = 0.875;
```

Integers

Integers are positive or negative whole numbers, zero, or "numbers without decimal points." Each of the following variables is an integer:

```
$a = 15;
$b = -521;
```

Strings

A series of characters grouped within double quotation marks is considered a string:

```
$a = "I am a string.";
$b = "<P>This book is <strong>cool</strong>!";
```

You can also reference other variables within your string, which will be replaced when your script is executed. For example:

```
$num = 57; // an integer
$my_string = "I read this book $num times!"; // a string
```

When you run the script, $my_string becomes "I read this book 57 times!"

A note for PHP 6.0 users: If you are accustomed to using the old-style string indexing format using the { and } characters, you will need to stop. The old style has been deprecated, and you will now need to use the [and] characters, bringing PHP more into line with other modern programming languages.

Variables from HTML Forms

Depending on the method of your HTML form (GET or POST), the variables will be part of the $_POST or $ _GET superglobal associative array. The name of the input field will become the name of the variable. For example, when a form is sent using the POST method, the following input field produces the variable $_POST[first_name]:

```
<input type="text" name="first_name" size="20">
```

If the method of this form were GET, this variable would be $_GET[first_name].

Variables from Cookies

Like variables from forms, variables from cookies are kept in a superglobal associative array called $_COOKIE. If you set a cookie called user with a value of Joe Smith, like so:

```
SetCookie ("user", "Joe Smith", time()+3600);
```

a variable called user is placed in $_COOKIE, with a value of Joe Smith. You then refer to $_COOKIE[user] to get that value.

Environment Variables

When a Web browser makes a request of a Web server, it sends along with the request a list of extra variables called *environment variables*. They can be very useful for displaying dynamic content or authorizing users.

By default, environment variables are available to PHP scripts as $VAR_NAME. However, to be absolutely sure that you're reading the correct value, you can use the getenv() function to assign a value to a variable of your choice. The following are some common environment variables.

REMOTE_ADDR gets the IP address of the machine making the request. For example:

```
$remote_address = getenv("REMOTE_ADDR");
echo "Your IP address is $remote_address.";
```

HTTP_USER_AGENT gets the browser type, browser version, language encoding, and platform. For example:

```
$browser_type = getenv("HTTP_USER_AGENT");
echo "You are using $browser_type.";
```

For a list of HTTP environment variables and their descriptions, visit http://hoohoo.ncsa.uiuc.edu/cgi/env.html.

A note for PHP 6.0 users: The HTTP_*_VARS set of variables, which was once used to get information from the browser cookies, is no longer available as of this version. This set of variables had been deprecated for some time and finally has been removed.

Arrays

Simply put, arrays are sets of variables that are contained as a group. In the following example, $fave_colors is an array that contains strings representing array elements. In this case, the array elements (0 to 3) are names of colors.

```
$fave_colors[0] = "red";
$fave_colors[1] = "blue";
$fave_colors[2] = "black";
$fave_colors[3] = "white";
```

Array elements are counted with 0 as the first position in the numerical index.

Operators

An operator is a symbol that represents a specific action. For example, the + arithmetic operator adds two values, and the = assignment operator assigns a value to a variable.

Arithmetic Operators

Arithmetic operators bear a striking resemblance to simple math, as shown in Table B.2.

Table B.2 Arithmetic Operators

Operator	Example	Action
+	$b = $a + 3;	Adds values together
-	$b = $a - 3;	Subtracts values
*	$b = $a * 3;	Multiplies values
/	$b = $a / 3;	Divides values
%	$b = $a % 3;	Returns the modulus, or remainder

Assignment Operators

The = is the basic assignment operator:

```
$a = 124; // the value of $a is 124
```

Other assignment operators are shown in Table B.3.

Comparison Operators

It should come as no surprise that comparison operators compare two values. A value of true or false is returned by the comparison. The comparison operators are shown in Table B.4.

Table B.3 Assignment Operators

Operator	Example	Action
+=	`$a += 3;`	Changes the value of a variable to the current value plus the value on the right side
-=	`$a -= 3`	Changes the value of the variable to the current value minus the value on the right side
.=	`$a .= "string";`	Concatenates (adds on to) the value on the right side with the current value

Table B.4 Comparison Operators

Operator	Definition
==	Equal to
!=	Not equal to
>	Greater than
<	Less than
>=	Greater than or equal to
<=	Less than or equal to

Increment/Decrement Operators

The increment/decrement operators do just what their name implies: add or subtract from a variable (see Table B.5).

Logical Operators

Logical operators allow your script to determine the status of conditions and, in the context of your if...else or while statements, execute certain code based on which conditions are true and which are false (see Table B.6).

Table B.5 Increment/Decrement Operators

Operator	Usage	Definition
++$a	Pre-increment	Increments by 1 and returns $a
$a++	Post-increment	Returns $a and then increments $a by 1
--$a	Pre-decrement	Decrements by 1 and returns $a
$a--	Post-decrement	Returns $a and then decrements $a by 1

Table B.6 Logical Operators

Operator	Example	Result
!	!$a	TRUE if $a is not true
&&	$a && $b	TRUE if both $a and $b are true
||	$a || $b	TRUE if either $a or $b is true

Control Structures

Programs are essentially a series of statements. Control structures, as their name implies, control how those statements are executed. Control structures are usually built around a series of conditions, such as "If the sky is blue, go outside and play." In this example, the condition is "If the sky is blue" and the statement is "go outside and play."

Control structures utilize curly braces ({}) to separate the groups of statements from the remainder of the program. Examples of common control structures follow; memorizing these will make your life much easier.

if...else if...else

The if...else if...else construct executes a statement based on the value of the expression being tested. In the following sample if statement, the expression being tested is "$a is equal to 10."

```
if ($a == "10") {
    // execute some code
}
```

After $a is evaluated, if it is found to have a value of 10 (that is, if the condition is true), the code inside the curly braces will execute. If $a is found to be something other than 10 (if the condition is false), the code will be ignored, and the program will continue.

To offer an alternative series of statements, should $a not have a value of 10, add an else statement to the structure to execute a section of code when the condition is false:

```
if ($a == "10") {
    echo "a equals 10";
} else {
    echo "a does not equal 10";
}
```

The else if (or one word: elseif) statement can be added to the structure to evaluate an alternative expression before heading to the final else statement. For example, the following structure first evaluates whether $a is equal to 10. If that condition is false, the else if statement is evaluated. If it is found to be true, the code within its curly braces executes. Otherwise, the program continues to the final else statement:

```
if ($a == "10") {
    echo "a equals 10";
} else if ($b == "8") {
    echo "b equals 8";
} else {
    echo "a does not equal 10 and b does not equal 8.";
}
```

You can use if statements alone or as part of an if...else or if...else if...else statement. Whichever you choose, you will find this structure to be an invaluable element in your programs!

while

Unlike the if...else if...else structure, in which each expression is evaluated once and an action is performed based on its value of true or false, the while statement continues to loop until an expression is false. In other words, the while loop continues while the expression is true.

For example, in the following while loop, the value of $a is printed on the screen and is incremented by 1 as long as the value of $a is less than or equal to 3:

```
$a = 0 // set a starting point
while ($a <= "3") {
    echo "a equals $a<br>";
    $a++;
}
```

for

Like while loops, for loops evaluate the set of conditional expressions at the beginning of each loop. Here is the syntax of the for loop:

```
for (expr1; expr2; expr3) {
    // code to execute
}
```

At the beginning of each loop, the first expression is evaluated, followed by the second expression. If the second expression is true, the loop continues by executing the code and then evaluating the third expression. If the second expression is false, the loop does not continue, and the third expression is never evaluated.

Take the counting example used in the while loop and rewrite it using a for loop:

```
for ($a = 0; $a <= "3"; $a++) {
    echo "a equals $a<br>";
}
```

foreach

Like the `for` loop, `foreach` loops permit you to iterate over an array, processing each element in the array. Here is the syntax of the `foreach` loop:

```
foreach (array as variable) {
    // code to execute
}
```

Each element in the array is processed within the statements in the "code to execute" block. For example, to print out all elements of a block in your Web page, you might do something like this:

```
arr = array("one", "two", "three");
foreach ( $arr as $v )
{
    echo "Value: $v\n";
}
```

In addition to variables, you can also iterate over objects (that is, classes). Each element of the class will be printed out as a variable. You can see an example of this when we talk about classes.

Built-In Functions

All of the following functions are part of the numerous functions that make up the PHP language. These really are just a small number of the PHP functions; they are the ones I use on a regular basis. Depending on the types of things you'll be doing with PHP, you might not need more functions, but please visit the PHP manual at http://www.php.net/manual/ and familiarize yourself with what is available.

Array Functions

Numerous PHP functions are available for use with arrays. Only a few are noted here—those that I find absolutely essential, and those that form a foundation of knowledge for working with arrays.

array()

The `array()` function allows you to manually assign values to an array. Here is the syntax of the `array()` function:

```
$array_name = array("val1", "val2", "val3", ...);
```

array_push()

The `array_push()` function allows you to add one or more elements to the end of an existing array. Its syntax is this:

```
array_push($array_name, "element 1", "element 2", ...);
```

array_pop()

The `array_pop()` function allows you to take (pop) off the last element of an existing array. Its syntax is this:

```
array_pop($array_name);
```

array_unshift()

The `array_unshift()` function allows you to add elements to the beginning of an existing array. Its syntax is this:

```
array_unshift($array_name, "element 1", "element 2", ...);
```

array_shift()

The `array_shift()` function allows you to take (pop) off the first element of an existing array. Its syntax is this:

```
array_shift($array_name);
```

array_merge()

The `array_merge()` function allows you to combine two or more existing arrays. Its syntax is this:

```
array_merge($array1, $array2, ...);
```

array_keys()

The `array_keys()` function returns an array of all the key names in an existing array. Its syntax is this:

```
array_keys($array_name);
```

array_values()

The `array_values()` function returns an array of all the values in an existing array. Its syntax is this:

```
array_values($array_name);
```

count()

The `count()` function counts the number of elements in a variable. It's normally used to count the number of elements in an array because any variable that is not an array has only one element—itself.

In the following example, `$a` is assigned a value equal to the number of elements in the `$colors` array:

```
$a = count($colors);
```

If `$colors` contains the values `blue`, `black`, `red`, and `green`, `$a` will be assigned a value of `4`.

each() and list()

The each() and list() functions usually appear together in the context of stepping through an array and returning its keys and values. Here is the syntax for these functions:

```
each(arrayname);
list(val1, val2, val3, ...);
```

For example, when you submit an HTML form via the GET method, each key/value pair is placed in the global variable $_GET. If your form input fields are named first_name and last_name and the user enters values of Joe and Smith, the key/value pairs are first_name/Joe and last_name/Smith. In the $_GET array, these variables are represented as the following:

```
$_GET["first_name"] // value is "Joe"
$_GET["last_name"] // value is "Smith"
```

You can use the each() and list() functions to step through the array in this fashion, printing the key and value for each element in the array:

```
while (list($key, $val) = each($_GET)) {
 echo "$key has a value of $val<br>";
}
```

reset()

The reset() function rewinds the pointer to the beginning of the array. Its syntax is this:

```
reset($array_name);
```

shuffle()

The shuffle() function randomizes the elements of a given array. Its syntax is this:

```
shuffle($array_name);
```

sizeof()

The sizeof() function counts the number of elements in an array. In the following example, $a is assigned a value equal to the number of elements in the $colors array:

```
$a = sizeof($colors);
```

If $colors contains the values blue, black, red, and green, $a is assigned a value of 4.

Database Connectivity Functions for MySQL

Numerous PHP functions exist for connecting to and querying a MySQL server. Following are some basic functions and their syntax. See the PHP manual at http://www.php.net/manual/ for a complete listing of MySQL functions—there are plenty!

mysql_connect()

This function opens a connection to MySQL. It requires a server name, username, and password.

```
$connection = mysql_connect("servername","username","password");
```

mysql_select_db()

This function selects a database on the MySQL server for use by subsequent queries. It requires a valid established connection.

```
$db = mysql_select_db("myDB", $connection);
```

mysql_query()

This function issues the SQL statement. It requires an open connection to the database.

```
$sql_result = mysql_query("SELECT * FROM SOMETABLE",$connection);
```

mysql_error()

This function returns a meaningful error message when something goes wrong with your connection or query. It's normally used in the context of the `die()` function, like this:

```
$sql_result = mysql_query("SELECT * FROM SOMETABLE",$connection)
    or die(mysql_error());
```

mysql_fetch_array()

This function automatically places the SQL statement result row into an array.

```
$row = mysql_fetch_array($sql_result);
```

mysql_num_rows()

This function returns the number of rows in a result set.

```
$num = mysql_num_rows($sql_result);
```

Date and Time Functions

The basic PHP date and time functions let you easily format timestamps for use in database queries and calendar functions, as well as for simply printing the date on an order form receipt.

date()

The `date()` function returns the current server timestamp, formatted according to a given set of parameters. Its syntax is this:

```
date(format, [timestamp]);
```

If the `timestamp` parameter is not provided, the current timestamp is assumed. Table B.7 shows the available formats.

Table B.7 `date()` Function Formats

Character	Meaning
a	Prints "am" or "pm"
A	Prints "AM" or "PM"
h	Hour in 12-hour format (01 to 12)
H	Hour in 24-hour format (00 to 23)
g	Hour in 12-hour format without a leading zero (1 to 12)
G	Hour in 24-hour format without a leading zero (0 to 23)
i	Minutes (00 to 59)
s	Seconds (00 to 59)
Z	Time zone offset in seconds (–43200 to 43200)
U	Seconds since the Epoch (January 1, 1970 00:00:00 GMT)
d	Day of the month in two digits (01 to 31)
j	Day of the month in two digits without a leading zero (1 to 31)
D	Day of the week in text (Mon to Sun)
l	Day of the week in long text (Monday to Sunday)
w	Day of the week in numeric, Sunday to Saturday (0 to 6)
F	Month in long text (January to December)
m	Month in two digits (01 to 12)
n	Month in two digits without a leading zero (1 to 12)
M	Month in three-letter text (Jan to Dec)
Y	Year in four digits (2000)
y	Year in two digits (00)
z	Day of the year (0 to 365)
t	Number of days in the given month (28 to 31)
S	English ordinal suffix (th, nd, st)

checkdate()

The `checkdate()` function validates a given date. Successful validation means that the year is between 0 and 32767, the month is between 1 and 12, and the proper number of days is in each month (leap years are accounted for). Its syntax is this:

```
checkdate(month, day, year);
```

mktime()

The `mktime()` function returns the UNIX timestamp as a long integer (in the format of seconds since the Epoch, or January 1, 1970) for a given date. Thus, the primary use of `mktime()` is to format dates in preparation for mathematical functions and date validation. Its syntax is this:

```
mktime(hour, minute, second, month, day, year);
```

time() and *microtime()*

The `time()` function returns the current system time, measured in seconds since the Epoch. The syntax of `time()` is simply this:

```
time();
```

You could get a result such as 958950466.

Using `microtime()` adds a count of microseconds, so instead of just receiving a result like 958950466, you would get a result like 0.93121600 958950466, at the exact moment you asked for the time since the Epoch (this includes both seconds and microseconds).

File System Functions

The built-in file system functions can be very powerful tools—or weapons, if used incorrectly. Be very careful when using file system functions, especially if you have PHP configured to run as root or some other system-wide user. For example, using a PHP script to issue an `rm -R` command while at the root level of your directory structure would be a very bad thing.

chmod(), chgrp(), and chown()

Like the shell commands of the same name, the chmod(), chgrp(), and chown() functions modify the permissions, group, and owner of a directory or file. Here is the syntax of these functions:

```
chmod("filename", mode);
chmgrp("filename", newgroup);
chown("filename", newowner);
```

In order to change permissions, groups, and owners, the PHP user must be the owner of the file, or the permissions must already be set to allow such changes by that user.

copy()

The copy() function works much like the cp shell command: It needs a filename and a destination in order to copy a file. The syntax of copy() is this:

```
copy("source filename", "destination");
```

The PHP user must have permission to write into the destination directory, or the copy() function will fail.

fopen()

The fopen() function opens a specified file or URL for reading or writing. The syntax of fopen() is this:

```
fopen("filename", "mode")
```

To open a URL, use http:// or ftp:// at the beginning of the filename string. You can open URLs only for reading, not writing.

If the filename begins with anything else, the file is opened from the file system, and a file pointer to the opened file is returned. Otherwise, the file is assumed to reside on the local file system.

The specified mode determines whether the file is opened for reading, writing, or both. Table B.8 lists the valid modes.

Table B.8 *fopen() Function Modes*

Mode	Description
r	Read-only. The file pointer is at the beginning of the file.
r+	Reading and writing. The file pointer is at the beginning of the file.
w	Write-only. The file pointer is at the beginning of the file, and the file is truncated to zero length. If the file does not exist, attempt to create it.
w+	Reading and writing. The file pointer is at the beginning of the file, and the file is truncated to zero length. If the file does not exist, attempt to create it.
a	Write-only. The file pointer is at the end of the file (it appends content to the file). If the file does not exist, attempt to create it.
a+	Reading and writing. The file pointer is at the end of the file (it appends content to the file). If the file does not exist, attempt to create it.
x	Create and open a file for writing only. The file pointer is at the beginning of the file. Will fail if the file already exists.
x+	Create and open a file for reading and writing. The file pointer is at the beginning of the file. Will fail if the file already exists.

fread()

Use the fread() function to read a specified number of bytes from an open file pointer. Its syntax is this:

```
fread(filepointer, length);
```

fputs()

The fputs() function writes to an open file pointer. Its syntax is this:

```
fputs(filepointer, content, [length]);
```

The file pointer must be open in order to write to the file. The `length` parameter is optional. If it isn't specified, all specified content is written to the file.

fclose()

Use the `fclose()` function to close an open file pointer. Its syntax is this:

```
fclose(filepointer);
```

mkdir()

Like the `mkdir` shell command, the `mkdir()` function creates a new directory in the file system. Its syntax is this:

```
mkdir("pathname", mode);
```

The PHP user must have write permission in the specified directory.

rename()

As its name suggests, the `rename()` function attempts to give a new name to an existing file. Its syntax is this:

```
rename("oldname", "newname");
```

The PHP user must have permission to modify the file.

rmdir()

Like the `rmdir` shell command, the `rmdir()` function removes a directory from the file system. Its syntax is this:

```
rmdir("pathname");
```

The PHP user must have write permission in the specified directory.

symlink()

The `symlink()` function creates a symbolic link from an existing file or directory on the file system to a specified link name. Its syntax is this:

```
symlink("targetname", "linkname");
```

The PHP user must have write permission in the specified directory.

unlink()

The `unlink()` function deletes a file from the file system. Its syntax is this:

```
unlink("filename");
```

The PHP user must have write permission for this file.

HTTP Functions

The built-in functions for sending specific HTTP headers and cookie data are crucial aspects of developing large Web-based applications in PHP. Luckily, the syntax for these functions is quite easy to understand and implement.

header()

The `header()` function outputs an HTTP header string, such as a location redirection. This output must occur before any other data is sent to the browser, including HTML tags.

HEADERS

This information bears repeating: Do not attempt to send information of any sort to the browser before sending a `header()`. You can perform any sort of database manipulations or other calculations before the `header()`, but you cannot print anything to the screen—not even a newline character.

For example, to use the `header()` function to redirect a user to a new location, use this code:

```
header("Location: http://www.newlocation.com");
exit;
```

HEADERS AND EXITS

Follow a `header()` statement with the `exit` command. This ensures that the code does not continue to execute.

---

setcookie()

The `setcookie()` function sends a cookie to the user. Cookies must be sent before any other header information is sent to the Web browser. The syntax for `setcookie()` is this:

```
setcookie("name", "value", "expire", "path", "domain", "secure");
```

For example, you would use the following code to send a cookie called `username` with a value of `joe` that is valid for one hour within all directories on the `testcompany.com` domain:

```
setcookie("username","joe", time()+3600, "/", ".testcompany.com");
```

`mail()` Function

The PHP `mail` function makes the interface between your HTML forms and your server's outgoing mail program a snap!

If your server has access to sendmail or an external SMTP server, the `mail()` function sends mail to a specified recipient. Its syntax is this:

```
mail("recipient", "subject", "message", "mail headers");
```

For example, the following code sends mail to julie@thickbook.com, with a subject of "I'm sending mail!" and a message body saying "PHP is cool!" The From line is part of the additional mail headers.

```
mail("julie@thickbook.com", "I'm sending mail!",
    "PHP is cool!", "From: youremail@yourdomain.com\n");
```

Mathematical Functions

Because I have very little aptitude for mathematics, I find PHP's built-in mathematical functions to be of the utmost importance. In addition to all the functions, the value of pi (3.14159265358979323846) is already defined as a constant in PHP (M_PI).

ceil()

The ceil() function rounds a fraction up to the next higher integer. Its syntax is this:

```
ceil(number);
```

decbin() and bindec()

The decbin() and bindec() functions convert decimal numbers to binary numbers and binary numbers to decimal numbers, respectively. The syntax of these functions is this:

```
decbin(number);
bindec(number);
```

dechex() and hexdec()

The dechex() and hexdec() functions convert decimal numbers to hexadecimal numbers and hexadecimal numbers to decimal numbers, respectively. The syntax of these functions is this:

```
dechex(number);
hexdec(number);
```

decoct() and octdec()

The decoct() and octdec() functions convert decimal numbers to octal numbers and octal numbers to decimal numbers, respectively. The syntax of these functions is this:

```
decoct(number);
octdec(number);
```

floor()

The floor() function rounds a fraction down to the next lower integer. Its syntax is this:

```
floor(number);
```

number_format()

The number_format() function returns the formatted version of a specified number. Its syntax is this:

```
number_format("number", "decimals", "dec_point", "thousands_sep");
```

For example, to return a formatted version of the number 12156688 with two decimal places and a comma separating each group of thousands, use this:

```
echo number_format("12156688","2",".",",");
```

The result is 12,156,688.00.

If only a number is provided, the default formatting does not use a decimal point and puts a comma between every group of thousands.

pow()

The pow() function returns the value of a given number raised to the power of a given exponent. Its syntax is this:

```
pow(number, exponent);
```

rand()

The rand() function generates a random value from a specific range of numbers. Its syntax is this:

```
rand(min, max);
```

round()

The round() function rounds a fraction to the next higher or next lower integer. Its syntax is this:

```
round(number);
```

sqrt()

The sqrt() function returns the square root of a given number. Its syntax is this:

```
sqrt(number);
```

srand()

The srand() function provides the random number generator with a set of possible values. Its syntax is this:

```
srand(seed);
```

A common practice is to seed the random number generator by using a number of microseconds:

```
srand((double)microtime()*1000000);
```

Miscellaneous Functions

The die() and exit functions provide useful control over the execution of your script, offering an "escape route" for programming errors. Other functions have found their way into this "miscellaneous" category.

die()

The die() function outputs a given message and terminates the script when a returned value is false. Its syntax is this:

```
die("message");
```

For example, you would use the following code to print a message and stop the execution of your script upon failure to connect to your database:

```
$connection = mysql_connect("servername", "username", "password")
    or die ("Can't connect to database.");
```

exit

The exit statement terminates the execution of the current script at the point where the exit statement is made.

sleep() and usleep()

The sleep() and usleep() functions put a pause, or a delay, at a given point in the execution of your PHP code. The syntax of these functions is this:

```
sleep(seconds);
usleep(microseconds);
```

The only difference between sleep() and usleep() is that the given wait period for sleep() is in seconds, and the wait period for usleep() is in microseconds.

uniqid()

The uniqid() function generates a unique identifier with a prefix if you want one. Its syntax is this:

```
uniqid("prefix");
```

That's boring, though. Suppose you want a unique ID with a prefix of phpuser. You would use this:

```
$id = uniqid("phpuser");
echo "$id";
```

and you would get something like phpuser38b320a6b5482.

But if you use something really cool like this:

```
$id = md5(uniqid(rand()));
echo "$id";
```

you would get an ID like 999d8971461bedfc7caadcab33e65866.

Program Execution Functions

You can use PHP's built-in program execution functions to use programs residing on your system, such as encryption programs, third-party image manipulation programs, and so forth. For all program execution functions, the PHP user must have permission to execute the given program.

exec ( )

The exec() function executes an external program. Its syntax is this:

```
exec(command, [array], [return_var]);
```

If an array is specified, the output of the exec() function will append to the array. If return_var is specified, it will be assigned a value of the program's return status.

For example, you would use the following code to ping a server five times and print the output:

```
$command = "ping -c5 www.thickbook.com";
exec($command, $result, $rval);
for ($i = 0; $i < sizeof($result); $i++) {
    echo "$result[$i]<br>";
}
```

passthru()

Like the `exec()` function, the `passthru()` function executes an external program. The difference between the two is that `passthru()` returns the raw output of the action. The syntax of `passthru()` is this:

```
passthru(command, return_var);
```

If `return_var` is specified, it will be assigned a value of the program's return status.

system()

The `system()` function executes an external program and displays output as the command is being executed. Its syntax is this:

```
system(command, [return_var]);
```

If `return_var` is specified, it will be assigned a value of the program's return status.

For example, you would use the following code to ping a server five times and print the raw output:

```
$command = "ping -c5 www.thickbook.com";
system($command);
```

Regular Expression Functions

Regular expressions are ways in which you can do "pattern matching" on text. For example, you might want to find out whether a string is made up of all numbers or all letters or contains punctuation marks. PHP contains a rich set of regular expression tools for doing just this.

ereg_replace() and eregi_replace()

The `ereg_replace()` and `eregi_replace()` functions replace instances of a pattern within a string and return the new string. The `ereg_replace()` function performs a case-sensitive match, and `eregi_replace()` performs a case-insensitive match. Here is the syntax for both functions:

```
ereg_replace(pattern, replacement, string);
eregi_replace(pattern, replacement, string);
```

For example, you would use the following code to replace ASP with PHP in the string I really love programming in ASP!

```
$old_string = "I really love programming in ASP!";
$new_string = ereg_replace("ASP", "PHP", $old_string);
echo "$new_string";
```

If ASP is mixed case, such as aSp, use the eregi_replace() function:

```
$old_string = "I really love programming in aSp!";
$new_string = eregi_replace("ASP", "PHP", $old_string);
echo "$new_string";
```

split()

The split() function splits a string into an array using a certain separator (comma, colon, semicolon, and so on). Its syntax is this:

```
split(pattern, string, [limit]);
```

The limit is optional. If a limit is specified, the split() function stops at the named position—for example, at the tenth value in a comma-delimited list.

Session-Handling Functions

Session handling is a way of holding on to data as a user navigates your Web site. Data can be variables or entire objects. These simple functions are just a few of the session-related functions in PHP; see the PHP manual at http://www.php.net/manual/ for more.

session_start()

The session_start() function starts a session if one has not already been started, or it resumes a session if the session ID is present for the user. This function takes no arguments and is called simply by placing the following at the beginning of your code:

```
session_start();
```

session_destroy()

The session_destroy() function effectively destroys all the variables and values registered for the current session. This function takes no arguments and is called simply by placing the following in your code:

```
session_destroy();
```

String Functions

This section only scratches the surface of PHP's built-in string manipulation functions, but if you understand these common functions, your programming life will be quite a bit easier!

addslashes() and *stripslashes()*

The addslashes() and stripslashes() functions are very important when inserting and retrieving data from a database. Often, text inserted into a database will contain special characters (single quotes, double quotes, backslashes, NULL) that must be escaped before being inserted. The addslashes() function does just that, using this syntax:

```
addslashes(string);
```

Similarly, the stripslashes() function returns a string with the slashes taken away, using this syntax:

```
stripslashes(string);
```

chop(), *ltrim()*, and *trim()*

All three of these functions remove errant white space from a string. The chop() function removes white space from the end of a string, and ltrim() removes white space from the beginning of a string. The trim() function removes both leading and trailing white space from a string. Here is the syntax of these functions:

```
chop(string);
ltrim(string);
trim(string);
```

echo()

The echo() function returns output. The syntax of echo() is this:

```
echo (parameter1, parameter 2, ...)
```

For example:

```
echo "I'm using PHP!";    // output is: I'm using PHP!
echo 2+6;                 // output is: 8
```

The parentheses are not required when using echo.

explode() and implode()

The explode() function splits a string using a given separator and returns the values in an array. The syntax of explode() is this:

```
explode("separator", "string");
```

For example, the following code takes a string called $color_list, containing a comma-separated list of colors, and places each color into an array called $my_colors:

```
$color_list = "blue,black,red,green,yellow,orange";
$mycolors = explode(",", $color_list);
```

Conversely, the implode() function takes an array and makes it into a string, using a given separator. The syntax of implode() is this:

```
implode("separator", "string");
```

For example, the following code takes an array called $color_list and then creates a string called $mycolors, containing the values of the $color_list array, separated by commas:

```
$mycolors = implode(",", $color_list);
```

htmlspecialchars() and *htmlentities()*

The `htmlspecialchars()` and `htmlentities()` functions convert special characters and HTML entities within strings into their acceptable entity representations. The `htmlspecialchars()` function converts only the less-than sign (< becomes <), greater-than sign (> becomes >), double quotes ("" becomes "), and the ampersand (& becomes &).

The `htmlentities()` function converts the characters in the ISO-8859-1 character set to the proper HTML entity. Here is the syntax of these functions:

```
htmlspecialchars(string);
htmlentities(string);
```

nl2br()

The `nl2br()` function replaces all ASCII newlines with the HTML line break (<BR>). The syntax of the `nl2br()` function is this:

```
nl2br(string);
```

sprintf()

The `sprintf()` function returns a string that has been formatted according to a set of directives, as listed in Table B.9. The syntax of `sprintf()` is this:

```
sprintf(directives, string);
```

For example, to turn the number 5 into $5.00 (five dollars), use:

```
$newnumber = sprintf("%0.02f", 5);
```

strlen()

The `strlen()` function returns the length of a given string. Its syntax is this:

```
strlen(string);
```

Table B.9 `sprintf()` Function Formatting Directives

Directive	Result
%	Adds a percent sign
b	Considers the string an integer and formats it as a binary number
c	Considers the string an integer and formats it with that ASCII value
d	Considers the string an integer and formats it as a decimal number
f	Considers the string a double and formats it as a floating-point number
o	Considers the string an integer and formats it as an octal number
s	Considers and formats the string as a string
x	Considers the string an integer and formats it as a hexadecimal number (lowercase letters)
X	Considers the string an integer and formats it as a hexadecimal number (uppercase letters)

strtolower()

The `strtolower()` function returns a given string with all alphabetic characters in lowercase. Its syntax is this:

```
strtolower(str);
```

strtoupper()

The `strtoupper()` function returns a given string with all alphabetic characters in uppercase. Its syntax is this:

```
strtoupper (str);
```

substr()

The `substr()` function returns a portion of a string, given a starting position and optional ultimate length. Its syntax is this:

```
substr(string, start, [length]);
```

If the start position is a positive number, the starting position is counted from the beginning of the string. If the start position is negative, the starting position is counted from the end of the string.

Similarly, if the optional `length` parameter is used and is a positive number, the length is counted from the beginning of the string. If the `length` parameter is used and is a negative number, the length is counted from the end of the string.

For example:

```
$new_string = substr("PHP is great!", 1);      // returns "HP is great!"
$new_string = substr("PHP is great!", 0, 7);   // returns "PHP is "
$new_string = substr("PHP is great!", -1);     // returns "!"
$new_string = substr("PHP is great!", -6, 5);  // returns "great"
```

ucfirst()

The `ucfirst()` function changes the first alphabetic character in a string to an uppercase character. Its syntax is this:

```
ucfirst(string);
```

ucwords()

The `ucwords()` function changes the first letter of each word in a string to uppercase. Its syntax is this:

```
ucwords(string);
```

Variable Functions

The two basic variable functions, `isset()` and `unset()`, help you manage your variables within the scope of an application.

The `isset()` function determines whether a variable exists. The `unset()` function explicitly destroys the named variable. Here is the syntax of each:

```
isset(var);
unset(var);
```

The `isset()` function returns true if the variable exists and false if it does not.

Other Changes for PHP 6.0

As a final note, there have been a few additional changes for PHP version 6.0 that do not fit in anywhere else in this book, so they are listed here.

Addition of 64-Bit Integers

PHP 6.0 now supports 64-bit integers on platforms that have the capability for such things. They look just like normal integers but will permit 64-bit math.

register_global and safe_mode Option Removed

In previous versions of PHP, global variables were automatically added to your scripts by the interpreter. This capability was defaulted to "off" in PHP 4.2 and has been removed entirely in 6.0.

The safe_mode option, which disabled all sorts of functions in the environment, was also defaulted to "off" and has been removed in this version.

Dynamic Functions No Longer Callable with Static Syntax

In previous versions of PHP, you could call a dynamic function using either dynamic syntax or using standard, static syntax. As of version 6.0, it will no longer be possible to call them other than using dynamic syntax. This will cut down on errors in programming by users who are unsure of what type of function they are calling.

C

Writing Your Own Functions

As you become more comfortable with writing code, you might realize that many times you will write the same bits of code over and over again. A prime example of this is the database connection code used throughout this book. How many times did you think to yourself, "This is really repetitive!" Quite often, I'm sure. This is where writing your own functions comes in to play.

When you program in PHP, you will use predefined functions to achieve certain results. For example, the `mail()` function is a predefined function that sends mail. The `mysql_connect()` function is a predefined function that connects to a MySQL database. The code that makes up these functions is built into the PHP scripting engine, so you never see it. However, you can write your own functions and use them in your scripts, even storing your own functions in external files for use only when you need them.

The Structure of Functions

Functions have a very specific structure, as you can see in the following code, where [function name] and [arguments] should be replaced with your own function name and any arguments you might want to use.

```
function [function_name] ([arguments]) {
    // code
}
```

When you create a function, you precede the name of the function with the keyword function. After that and the name of your function comes the list of arguments inside a set of parentheses. The arguments—which are optional because you don't have to pass any arguments to a function if you don't want to—are separated by commas and hold values that your function needs in order to complete its task or tasks. Essentially, an argument allows you to create a "template" in your function, to be used with all sorts of different kinds of data.

After the arguments, you open a set of curly braces, type all of your code, and finally close the set of braces. For example, the following function (called multiplier) takes an argument called $num and multiplies the value by 5.

```
function multiplier ($num) {
    $answer = $num * 5;
}
```

Say you have already determined that $num equals 8, and that's what you're passing to the multiplier function. Using your own math skills, you know that $answer will equal 40. To get that number back to your script, outside of the function, you must *return* the value.

Returning Values from Functions

The basic method for returning values from your functions is to use the return statement. Usually, this statement comes at the end of the function, like so:

```
function multiplier ($num) {
    $answer = $num * 5;
    return $answer;
}
```

RETURN STATEMENTS IN PHP

A `return` statement can be anywhere in a function, but when used, it ends the execution of the function. This means that the code that is executed is the line of your script from which the `return` statement was called.

When you use a `return` statement, you can then call the function in your code like so:

```
echo multiplier(8);
```

This use would result in the following on your screen:

```
40
```

Because you are passing 8 as the `$num` argument to the `multiplier()` function, `$answer` becomes 40. Because `$answer` is being returned as the result of the function's actions, and you are using `echo` followed by the function call, you're telling PHP to print the result of the code within the function. In this case, that result is the number 40.

RETURNING MULTIPLE VALUES

You can also use the `return` statement to get multiple values, but only if they are part of an array or an object.

Using a `return` statement to pass results from your functions to your main script is a simple and safe method and one of the most common. If you do not use a `return` statement, you must declare as global any variables you want to pass back to your main script. For example:

```
function multiplier($num) {
    global $answer;
    $answer = $num * 5;
}
```

In this case, you call the `multiplier()` function and then use the name of the variable in the `echo` statement, because it's not returned directly from your function. For example, using the modified function, the following code will print the number 40 to your screen:

```
multiplier(5);
echo $answer;
```

If you had not declared `$answer` as a global variable, the result would have been a blank screen.

GLOBAL VARIABLES

Use some thought to determine which variables you really want to become globally available to your scripts. Each time you declare something as global, you must employ additional programming constraints in order to maintain the integrity of the data. In other words, you have to be careful and watch what you do. If you have declared a variable as global but use a variable of the same name in another part of your script, you will overwrite one or the other. A good rule of thumb is to keep a handle on your global variables and keep them local to the procedures that directly use them.

One of the most useful points about functions is that they can return data that you can use in your own applications. Suppose, for example, that you wanted to write a function that computed the square of a number that was passed in. The square of a number, of course, is simply the number multiplied by itself. You might write such a function like this:

```
function square($num) {
    return $num * $num;
}
```

Notice that the function multiplies the `$num` parameter by itself and returns the value all in one line. There is no need in PHP to use intermediate variables to hold values if you don't want to. However, once we have the value, we can then return it to the user. This value might be stored in a variable in the calling program, like this:

```
$sq_num = square(5);
```

This line of code passes the constant value 5 to the function, and stores the result (25) in the variable $sq_num.

Using Functions in Your Code

So far, you've learned the basic structure of a user-defined function but not how it fits within your own scripts. In the case of the `multiplier()` function, it does seem awfully time consuming to create a script like the following, just to print a number on the screen:

```
<?
function multiplier($num) {
    $answer = $num * 5;
    return $answer;
}
echo multiplier(5);
?>
```

Instead, imagine a function called `db_connect()`, which contains your database connection and selection code:

```
function db_connect() {
    $connection = @mysql_connect("localhost", "spike", "9sj7En4")
        or die(mysql_error());
    $db = @mysql_select_db($db_name, $connection)
        or die(mysql_error());
}
```

Instead of typing those two lines over and over in every script, imagine simply typing:

```
db_connect();
```

If your host name, username, password, or database name changes, you have to change this information in only one place—the `db_connect()` function code. Now the only trick is where to put this function. Obviously, if you are creating a function in order to reuse the code within it, you don't want the function to be part of the script. Instead, you place the function in a file of its own (or a file containing other functions) and use `include()` or `require()` to pull the information into your script as appropriate.

DESIGNING FUNCTIONS FOR REUSE

Obviously, it makes very little sense to write a function like this and not have it accept arguments that would be used to connect to the database. If you were really writing a function called `db_connect`, you would likely write it like this:

```
function db_connect($machine, $user, $pwd ) {
    $connection = @mysql_connect($machine, $user, $pwd)
        or die(mysql_error());
    $db = @mysql_select_db($db_name, $connection)
        or die(mysql_error());
    return $db;
}
```

This would allow you to reuse the function anywhere in a script that needed access to a MySQL database.

Using `include()` and `require()`

The `include()` and `require()` functions do essentially the same thing: When called, the code in the included file becomes part of the script calling it. From that point forward, anything in the included file can be used in the script calling it.

The difference between `include()` and `require()` pops up when the file to be included cannot be opened. This can occur because of incorrect permissions, or perhaps the file isn't in the location specified. When a failure occurs using `include()`, you get a warning, but the code continues to execute as best it can, which is to say not very well if it needs a function that's in some other file! When `require()` cannot find or open the file, you will get a fatal error, and PHP will stop processing the code all together.

Included files look just like any other PHP files, starting with an opening PHP tag and ending with a closing PHP tag. For example, suppose that you have a file called myfunctions.php, containing the following code:

```
<?
/* The multiplier() function multiplies a number by 5 and returns it */
function multiplier($num) {
     $answer = $num * 5;
return $answer;
}

/* The db_connect() function connects to my database. */
function db_connect() {
     $connection = @mysql_connect("localhost", "spike", "9sj7En4")
     or die(mysql_error());
     $db = @mysql_select_db($db_name, $connection)
     or die(mysql_error());
}
?>
```

Then, in your actual PHP script, which needs to connect to a database, you would have the following:

```
<?
//include the file that has the function you need
include("/path/to/myfunctions.php");

//call a function
db_connect();

//now you can do things like issue queries and get results
?>
```

Obviously, this is a very simple example of using included files as function libraries, but you probably can already see the benefits. Anywhere you have repetitive code, think about using your own function to replace it. You can have multiple files full of function libraries named appropriately for their tasks. You can easily optimize your code when you go through the exercise of determining where functions can be used. Try it yourself—there is plenty of repetitive code used in this book that you can quickly turn into your own tightly wound application!

D

Writing Your Own Classes and Objects

Once you have worked with functions for a while, you may notice that you tend to have sets of them that fall within a specific grouping. For example, you might have a set of functions that work with a database. Quite often, you will find yourself passing the same bits of data (say, the database "handle") to each of the functions. Wouldn't it be nice to be able to just create the handle once and have the functions remember it? This sort of thing is accomplished in PHP with classes and objects.

Working with Objects

Occasionally in this book, I've mentioned "object-oriented programming" in reference to a more complex type of programming, beyond the procedural scripts on which this book is based. An object is sort of a theoretical box of things—variables, functions, and so forth—that exists in a templated structure called a *class*. Although it's easy to visualize a simple variable, such as $color, with a value of red, or an array called $rainbow with three or four elements inside it, some people have a difficult time visualizing objects.

For now, try to think of an object like a little box, with inputs and outputs on either side. The input mechanisms are called *methods*, and methods have *properties*. Throughout this section, you'll take a look at how classes, methods, and properties all work together to produce various outputs. This will give you a good picture of what object-oriented programming is all about, should you want to go that route when building your applications. To learn plenty more on the topic, check the PHP manual chapter called "Classes and Objects" at http://www.php.net/manual/en/language.oop.php.

An object has a structure, called a class. In a class, a set of characteristics is defined. For example, say that you have created a house class. In the house class, you might have architectural type, square footage, and color characteristics. Each house object uses all of the characteristics, but they are initialized to different values, such as ranch, 1500, and white aluminum siding, or condominium, 786, and tan stucco.

You can think of a class as a very small script of its own that you can call from the outside world. For example, you might have a script that deals with a specific database and a specific table within that database. You could "encapsulate" (an object-oriented programming term) the functionality of dealing with that table in a single class in PHP.

Because classes are so tightly structured but yet self-contained and independent of one another, they can be reused from one application to another. For example, suppose that you write some text-formatting classes on one project and decide you can use that class in another project. Because a class is just a set of characteristics, you can pick up the code and use it in the second project, reaching into it with methods specific to the second application but using the inner workings of the existing code to achieve new results.

Creating an Object

Creating an object is quite simple; you simply declare it to be in existence:

```
class myClass {
     //code will go here
}
```

Now that you have a class, you can create a new instance of an object:

```
$object1 = new myClass();
```

The following code snippet shows you that your object exists:

```
<?php
class myClass {
     //code will go here
}
$object1 = new myClass();
echo "\$object1 is an ".gettype($object1);
?>
```

If you save this code as `objtest.php`, place it in your document root, and access it with your Web browser, you will see the following on your screen:

```
$object1 is an object
```

Next, you will learn about object properties and methods.

Properties of Objects

The variables declared inside an object are called *properties*. It is standard practice to declare your variables at the top of the class. These properties can be values, arrays, or even other objects. The following snippet uses simple scalar variables inside the class, prefaced with the `var` keyword:

```
class myHouse {
     var $type = "condo";
     var $sqfootage = "786";
     var $color = "tan stucco";
}
```

Now, when you create a myHouse object, it will always have these three properties, which you can reference. The following shows how this works:

```
<?
class myHouse {
     var $type = "condo";
     var $sqfootage = "786";
     var $color = "tan stucco";
}
$house = new myHouse();
echo "I live in a ".$house -> color." ".$house -> sqfootage."
square foot ".$house -> type;
?>
```

If you save this code as myHouse.php, place it in your document root, and access it with your Web browser, you will see the following on your screen:

```
I live in a tan stucco 786 square foot condo
```

Object Methods

Methods add functionality to your objects; instead of simply containing properties, the objects will actually do something useful. For example, the following class outputs a string:

```
<?
class anotherClass {
     function sayHello() {
          echo "HELLO!";
     }
}
$object1 = new anotherClass();
$object1 -> sayHello();
?>
```

If you save a file containing this code in your document root and access it with your Web browser, you will see the following on your screen:

```
HELLO!
```

So a method looks and acts like a normal function but is defined within the framework of a class. The -> operator is used to call the object method in the context of your script. Had there been any variables stored in the object, the method would have been capable of accessing them for its own purposes. For example:

```
<?
class anotherClass {
     var $name = "Joe";
     function sayHello() {
          echo "HELLO! My name is ".$this->name;
     }
}
$object1 = new anotherClass();
$object1 -> sayHello();
?>
```

If you save this code and place it in your document root and then access it with your Web browser, you will see the following on your screen:

```
HELLO! My name is Joe
```

The special variable $this is used to refer to the currently instantiated object. Anytime an object refers to itself, you must use the $this variable. Using the $this variable in conjunction with the -> operator enables you to access any property or method in a class, within the class itself.

Constructors

A constructor is simply a function that lives within a class and, given the same name as the class, is automatically called when a new instance of the class is created using new *classname*. Using constructors enables you to provide arguments to your class, to be processed immediately when it is first called. As of PHP 5.0 and beyond, constructors can be written by the developer, using the _construct keyword:

```
class MyClass  {
    function __construct() {
        print "Creating MyClassn";
    }
}

$my_obj = new MyClass();
```

If you run the above bit of code in your own script, you will see the `print` statement executed, even though it doesn't look like the `my_obj` object ever explicitly called the `_construct` method. This is because the interpreter looks for a method called `_construct` in the class definition and calls it automatically if it is found.

Destructors

A destructor is a function that lives within a class and, when an object of that class goes out of scope, is automatically called as the last thing done in the object. Using destructors in your class allows you to keep track of when objects come into and go out of scope and clean up any kinds of things that need to be done when the object terminates. For example, you might want to write a log file that keeps track of when an object comes into and goes out of existence. This would be done by overriding the constructor and destructor for the class:

```
class MyClass  {
    function __construct() {
        print "Creating MyClassn";
        $this->name = "My Class";
    }
    function __destruct() {
        print "Destroying " . $this->name . "\n";
    }
}
```

In this code, the initial construction prints out a message and then prints out a second message when the object goes out of scope. Try it in your own script, and you will see two messages when you create an object.

Class Constants

Sometimes it is nice to be able to define constants by name in your class, so that others can refer to them without using magic numbers or magic strings. For example, suppose that you wanted to create a class that modeled a traffic light. You might create constants for the colors of the lights, since they could vary by jurisdiction. Then you could refer to those constants, either internally or externally:

```
class TrafficLight  {
    const red = "Red";
    const green = "Green";
    const amber = "Yellow";
```

```
        function __construct() {
            print "Creating MyClassn";
            $this->name = "My Class";
        }
        function __destruct() {
            print "Destroying " . $this->name . "\n";
        }
        function Stop() {
                echo "setting status to";
                echo self::red;
        }
    }

    $my_obj = new TrafficLight();
    $my_obj->Stop()
```

Object Inheritance

Having learned the very basics of objects, properties, and methods, you can start to look at object inheritance. Inheritance with regard to classes is just what it sounds like: One class inherits the functionality from its parent class. An example is shown here:

```
<?
class myClass {
    var $name = "Joe";
    function myClass($n) {
        $this->name = $n;
    }
    function sayHello() {
        echo "HELLO! My name is ".$this->name;
    }
}
class childClass extends myClass {
//code goes here
}
$object1 = new childClass("Child of Joe");
$object1 -> sayHello();
?>
```

If you save this code, place it in your document root, and access it with your Web browser, you will see the following on your screen:

```
HELLO! My name is Child of Joe
```

These lines make up the constructor:

```
function myClass($n) {
    $this->name = $n;
}
```

This function is named the same as the class in which it is contained: `myClass`. You then see that the `childClass` is defined but contains no code. In this example, it's meant to demonstrate only inheritance from the parent class. The inheritance occurs through the use of the `extends` clause, as in:

```
class childClass extends myClass {
```

The second class inherits the elements of the first class because this clause is used. Like most elements of object-oriented programming, inheritance is useful when attempting to make your code flexible. Suppose that you created a text-formatting class that organized and stored data, formatted it in HTML, and output the result to a browser—your own personal masterpiece. Now suppose you had a client who wanted to use that concept, but instead of formatting the content into HTML and sending it to a browser, he wanted to format it for plain text and save it to a text file. No problem—you just add a few methods and properties, and away you go. Finally, the client comes back and says that he really wants the data to be formatted and sent as an e-mail—and then, what the heck, why not create XML-formatted files as well?

If you separate the compilation and storage classes from the formatting classes—one for each of the various delivery methods (HTML, text, e-mail, and XML)—you essentially have a parent-child relationship. Consider the parent class the one that holds the compilation and storage methods. The formatting classes are the children—they inherit the information from the parent, and they output the result based on their own functionality.

Namespaces

With PHP 6.0, the language finally supports something that other languages have had for some time, the idea of namespaces. The basic idea behind a namespace is simple: Lots of people name their functions and classes the same thing. After all, you might have a table class that models a real-world table, or a database table, or simply a row and column table in a spreadsheet. Each of the classes might be called `table`. If I now create my own script and try to do this:

```
$my_table = new table();
```

which one of the `table` objects is the PHP interpreter going to create? Since you can't tell, the interpreter can't tell, either. For this reason, the designers of PHP 6.0 added the ability to "qualify" a class by enclosing it in a namespace. Think of a namespace as the file in which the class exists, if that makes it easier. The basic syntax of a namespace is this:

```
namespace <name> {
    class foo {
        // Code goes here
    } // End of class foo
} End of namespace <name>
```

In this example, you will see that the namespace wraps around our class. Let's say that the namespace in this example (the `<name>` parameter) is `meloni`. Then the entire block would look like this:

```
namespace meloni {
    class foo {
        // Code goes here
    } // End of class foo
} End of namespace meloni
```

If you wanted to create a class of the name `foo` in our script, you would need to "qualify" the name using the full namespace and class names:

```
$my_foo = new meloni::foo();
```

In no way do these brief pages cover all the aspects of object-oriented programming—universities teach entire series of courses devoted to this topic. However, you did learn how to create classes and instantiate objects from them, how to create and access the properties and methods of a class, how to build new classes, and how to inherit features from parent classes. You should now be able to pick up a book on object-oriented programming and not feel completely lost.

E

Database Normalization and SQL Reference

The database tables used in this book were designed for simplicity's sake to help you understand the basic interaction between PHP and MySQL. These are not "normalized" databases. "Normalization" is a word you'll hear a lot when you begin to create detailed database-driven applications, and it requires a different type of thought process—thinking in relational terms before seeing the relationships in front of you. In this appendix, you'll learn the basics of database normalization, along with some key elements of the SQL language.

Understanding Database Normalization

Database normalization is essentially a set of rules that allows you to organize your database in such a way that your tables are related where appropriate, and they are flexible for future growth and relationships. The sets of rules used in normalization are called *normal forms*. If your database design follows the first set of rules, it's considered in the *first normal form*. If the first three sets of rules of normalization are followed, your database is said to be in the *third normal form*. This appendix goes through the normal forms using the concept of students and courses in a school and shows you how to normalize the `my_contacts` table used previously in the book.

Applying the Normal Forms

Before explaining the first normal form, let's start with something that needs to be normalized. In the case of a database, a *flat table* is a prime example of something needing to be normalized. A flat table is like a spreadsheet with many columns of data. In a flat table, there are no relationships between multiple tables, as all the data you could possibly want is right there in that single flat table. This scenario is not the most efficient design and will consume more physical space on your hard drive than a set of normalized database tables.

Suppose that you have a table that holds student and course information for a school. You might have the following fields in your flat table, as shown in Table E.1.

Table E.1 The Student and Courses Table

Field Name	Description
StudentName	Name of the student
CourseID1	ID of the first course taken by the student
CourseDescription1	Description of the first course taken by the student
CourseInstructor1	Instructor of the first course taken by the student
CourseID2	ID of the second course taken by the student
CourseDescription2	Description of the second course taken by the student
CourseInstructor2	Instructor of the second course taken by the student

You might then repeat `CourseID`, `CourseDescription`, and `CourseInstructor` columns many more times to account for all the classes a student can take during his academic career. Although redundant, this is the method used when creating a single flat table to store information. Eliminating this redundancy is the first step in database normalization, so next you'll take this flat table to first normal form. If your table remained in its flat format, you could have a lot of unclaimed space and a lot of space being used unnecessarily—not an efficient table design!

Taking a Table to First Normal Form

The main rules for the first normal form are as follows:

- To eliminate repeating information.
- To create separate tables for related data.

Looking at the flat table design, with its many repeated sets of fields for students and courses, you can identify students and courses as its two distinct topics. Taking your student and courses flat table to the first normal form would mean that you would create two tables: one for students (call it `students`) and one for students plus courses (call it `students_courses`). You can see the new table designs in Tables E.2 and E.3.

Your two new tables now represent a one-to-many relationship of one student to many courses. Students can take as many courses as they want and are not limited to the number of `CourseID`/`CourseDescription`/`CourseInstructor` groupings that exist in the flat table. This is a definite improvement, of course, since students could easily want to take multiple courses. However, there is a bit of extra data there. After all, why are we duplicating all of the course information for each student in the class?

Table E.2 The `students` Table

Field Name	Description
`StudentID`	A unique ID for the student. This new field is now a primary key.
`StudentName`	Name of the student.

Table E.3 The `students_courses` Table

Field Name	Description
StudentID	Unique ID of the student, matching an entry in the `students` table.
CourseID	ID of the course being taken by the student.
CourseDescription	Description of the course taken by the student.
CourseInstructor	Instructor of the course taken by the student.

You still have some work to do, and the next step is to put these tables into second normal form.

Taking Tables to Second Normal Form

The basic rule for the second normal form is this:

● No non-key attributes depend on a portion of the primary key.

In plain English, this means that if fields in your table are not entirely related to a primary key, you have to keep working on them. In the students and courses example, it means breaking out the courses into their own table so that the original flat table is now just a table full of unique students.

`CourseID`, `CourseDesc`, and `CourseInstructor` can become a table called `courses` with a primary key of `CourseID`. The `students_courses` table should then just contain two fields: `StudentID` and `CourseID`. You can see the new table designs in Tables E.4 and E.5.

Table E.4 The `courses` Table

Field Name	Description
CourseID	Unique ID of a course
CourseDescription	Description of the course
CourseInstructor	Instructor of the course

Table E.5 The New students_courses Table

Field Name	Description
StudentID	Unique ID of the student, matching an entry in the students table.
CourseID	Unique ID of the course being taken, matching an entry in the courses table.

This, obviously, is a vast improvement. Now, we can meddle with a course description, for example, without having to change every student record in the database. This, of course, is the reason that you are trying to put the database into more "normal" forms, not only to save space, but to limit the impact of changes across the database. The more you can spread out the data, the fewer number of records you need to change to affect one area of the data.

Believe it or not, you can go even further with this example, to the third normal form.

Taking Tables to Third Normal Form

The rule for the third normal form is:

- No attributes depend on other non-key attributes.

This rule simply means that you need to look at your tables and determine whether more fields exist that can be broken down further and that aren't dependent on a key. Think about removing repeated data, and you'll find your answer—instructors. Usually, an instructor will teach more than one class. However, the CourseInstructor field in the courses table is not a key of any sort. So if you break out this information and create a separate table purely for the sake of efficiency and maintenance, that's the third normal form. Take a look at the new courses table and the instructors table in Tables E.6 and E.7.

The third normal form is usually adequate for removing redundancy and allowing for flexibility and growth. Next, you will normalize the my_contacts table, used previously in this book.

Table E.6 The courses Table

Field Name	Description
CourseID	Unique ID of a course
CourseDescription	Description of the course
CourseInstructorID	ID of the instructor, matching an entry in the instructors table

Table E.7 The instructors Table

Field Name	Description
InstructorID	Unique ID of an instructor
InstructorName	Name of the instructor
InstructorNotes	Any notes regarding the instructor

Normalizing the my_contacts Table

In the original my_contacts table, there's not a lot of repeating information, but there easily could be if you expanded it to be an actual address book. In an address book, people usually have contact information for home and work, or multiple phone methods (land line, cell phone, and so on), and even multiple e-mail addresses. It would make much more sense to break all of those elements into separate tables and attach the information to people through a primary key. Table E.8 shows the original my_contacts table as reference.

Now identify the different areas for which different tables will exist: Address, phone, and e-mail are adequate for this example. Tables E.9, E.10, and E.11 show the fields for these new tables.

These new tables all contain the contact_id key, which corresponds to an entry in the new master contact table. The basic my_contacts table, used as the master contact table, should now look something like Table E.12.

Table E.8 The Original `my_contacts` Table

Field Name	Description
id	Creates a unique ID number for the entry
f_name	The person's first name
l_name	The person's last name
address1	First line of the address
address2	Second line of the address
address3	Third line of the address
postcode	ZIP or postal code
country	Country in which the person resides
prim_tel	Primary telephone number
sec_tel	Secondary telephone number
email	E-mail address
birthday	The person's birthday

Table E.9 Fields for the `address` Table

Field Name	Description
id	Creates a unique ID number for the address entry
contact_id	ID corresponding to a person in the master contact table
address1	First line of the address
address2	Second line of the address
address3	Third line of the address
postcode	ZIP or postal code
address_type	Type of address, such as home, work, or other

Table E.10 Fields for the `phone` Table

Field Name	Description
id	Creates a unique ID number for the phone entry
contact_id	ID corresponding to a person in the master contact table
phone_number	Phone number
phone_type	Type of phone number, such as home, work, cell, or fax

Table E.11 Fields for the `email` Table

Field Name	Description
id	Creates a unique ID number for the e-mail entry
contact_id	ID corresponding to a person in the master contact table
country	Country in which the person resides
email	E-mail address
email_type	Type of e-mail address, such as home or work

Table E.12 The New `my_contacts` Table

Field Name	Description
id	Creates a unique ID number for the entry
f_name	Person's first name
l_name	Person's last name
birthday	Person's birthday

With these new tables in place, you will have a much more flexible (and normalized!) set of tables for maintaining contact information.

Other Normal Forms

In addition to the basic three normal forms, there are quite a few others that you might hear about when discussing database normalization. This doesn't mean you really need to know how to apply them, but it can be useful to understand the terminology that DBA folks might throw at you when you are in a meeting.

A table is in Boyce-Codd normal form (BCNF) if and only if, for every one of its non-trivial functional dependencies X _ Y, X is a superkey—that is, X is either a candidate key or a superset thereof.

Basically, Boyce-Codd says that no attribute that determines a key can be anything other than a candidate key or made of candidate keys. BCNF form is not normally used in database development.

There are also fourth normal, fifth normal, sixth normal, and domain/key normal forms. For more information about these, you can consult either a good database design book or look on the Web.

Basic MySQL Reference

In this section, you'll take a very brief glance at the Structured Query Language (SQL), as well as some basic functions you can use with MySQL to make development a lot easier. See the MySQL manual at http://www.mysql.com/ for a comprehensive list of MySQL functions and language elements, or for a good introduction to using MySQL, pick up my book *Teach Yourself MySQL in 24 Hours*.

PLACEHOLDERS

Throughout this appendix, anything inside brackets should be considered placeholder text. For example, you would replace `[yourDBName]` with your actual database name in the command.

In the sections addressing MySQL-related functions, realize these are specific to MySQL and are not available in other databases such as Oracle, Microsoft SQL Servers, or even SQLite (which you'll learn about in Appendix F). However, the basic elements of SQL are common to such SQL-aware databases.

Creating or Dropping a Database

Starting with something simple, you can use the SQL CREATE command to create a new database. The syntax is this:

```
CREATE DATABASE [yourDBName];
```

When you create a database with this command, you're really just creating a directory to hold the files that make up the tables in the database.

To delete an entire database from the system, use the DROP command:

```
DROP DATABASE [yourDBName];
```

Be extremely careful when using the DROP command, because once you delete the database, all of the tables are removed as well!

Creating or Dropping a Table

You can also use the SQL CREATE command to create a table within the current database. The syntax is this:

```
CREATE TABLE [yourTableName] ([fieldName1] [type],
[fieldName2] [type], ...) [options]
```

To delete a table from the current database, use the DROP command:

```
DROP TABLE [yourTableName];
```

Be extremely careful when using the DROP command, because once you drop the tables, they're gone!

Altering a Table

The SQL ALTER command gives you the opportunity to modify elements of a particular table, such as renaming columns, changing the type of a column, adding columns, deleting columns, and so on. Following are some common uses:

- To add a column to a table, use this:

  ```
  ALTER TABLE [yourTableName] ADD [newColumn] [fieldDefinition];
  ```

- To delete a column from a table, use this:

  ```
  ALTER TABLE [yourTableName] DROP [columnName];
  ```

- To change a column from one type to another, use this:

  ```
  ALTER TABLE [yourTableName] CHANGE [columnName] [newfieldDefinition];
  ```

- To make a unique column in your table, use this:

  ```
  ALTER TABLE [yourTableName] ADD UNIQUE [columnName] ([columnName]);
  ```

- To index a column in your table, use this:

  ```
  ALTER TABLE [yourTableName] ADD INDEX [columnName] ([columnName]);
  ```

Using the ALTER command alleviates the need to delete an entire table and re-create it just because you spelled a field name incorrectly or made other minor mistakes.

Inserting, Updating, or Replacing Within a Table

The SQL INSERT and REPLACE commands populate your tables one record at a time. The syntax of INSERT is this:

```
INSERT INTO [yourTableName] ([fieldName1], [fieldName2], ...)
    VALUES ('[value of fieldName1]', '[value of fieldName2]'...);
```

When inserting records, be sure to separate your strings with single quotes or double quotes. If you use single quotes around your strings and the data you are adding contains apostrophes, avoid errors by escaping the apostrophe (\') within the INSERT statement. Similarly, if you use double quotes around your strings and you want to include double quotes as part of the data, escape them (\") within your INSERT statement.

Here is an example of a string where escaping is necessary:

```
O'Grady said "Wow"
```

If you enclose your strings in double quotes, the INSERT statement would look like this:

```
INSERT INTO table_name (column_name) VALUES ("O'Grady said \"Wow\"");
```

If you enclose your strings in single quotes instead, the INSERT statement would look like this:

```
INSERT INTO table_name (column_name) VALUES ('O\'Grady said "Wow"');
```

The REPLACE statement has the same syntax and requirements as the INSERT statement. The only difference is that you use REPLACE to overwrite a record in a table when the replacement is based on a unique value:

```
REPLACE INTO [yourTableName] ([fieldName1], [fieldName2], ...)
    VALUES ('[value of fieldName1]', '[value of fieldName2]'...);
```

The UPDATE command modifies parts of a record without replacing the entire record. To update an entire column in a table with the same new value, use this:

```
UPDATE [yourTableName] SET [fieldName] = '[new value]';
```

If you want to update only specific rows, use a WHERE clause:

```
UPDATE [yourTableName] SET [fieldName] = '[new value]' WHERE [some
expression];
```

UPDATE can be a very powerful SQL command. For example, you can perform string functions and mathematical functions on existing records and use the UPDATE command to modify their values.

Deleting from a Table

Like the SQL DROP command, using DELETE without paying attention to what you're doing can have horrible consequences in a production environment. Once you drop a table or delete a record, it's gone forever. Don't be afraid—just be careful. To delete all the contents of a table, use the following:

```
DELETE FROM [yourTableName];
```

If you want to delete only specific rows, use a WHERE clause:

```
DELETE FROM [yourTableName] WHERE [some expression];
```

If you're going to start deleting records, be sure you have a backup, just in case something goes wrong. Everyone screws up once—and hopefully never again.

Selecting from a Table

When creating database-driven Web sites, the SQL SELECT command will likely be the most often-used command in your arsenal. The SELECT command causes certain records in your table to be chosen, based on criteria that you define. Here is the basic syntax of SELECT:

```
SELECT [field names] FROM [table name]
      WHERE [some expression]
      ORDER BY [field names];
```

To select all the records in a table, use this:

```
SELECT * FROM [yourTableName];
```

To select just the entries in a given column of a table, use this:

```
SELECT [columnName] FROM [yourTableName];
```

To select all the records in a table and have them returned in a particular order, use an expression for ORDER BY. For example, if you have a date field for record entries and you want to see all the record entries ordered by newest to oldest, use this:

```
SELECT * FROM [yourTableName] ORDER BY [dateField] DESC;
```

DESC stands for "descending." To view from oldest to newest, use ASC for "ascending." ASC is the default order.

You can also perform mathematical and string functions within SQL statements (specific to your database), thereby using SELECT to do more than just echo existing data. Some examples follow.

A Few MySQL-Specific String Functions

This list contains only a few of the many string-related functions listed in the MySQL manual. Visit http://www.mysql.com/doc/ and check out the entire manual for more information.

- You can concatenate values using the CONCAT() function. The syntax is this:

  ```
  SELECT CONCAT([field1],[field2],...) AS [newName] FROM [yourTableName];
  ```

- Convert your results to lowercase using the LOWER() function. The syntax is this:

  ```
  SELECT LOWER([field1],[field2],...) FROM [yourTableName];
  ```

- Convert your results to uppercase using the UPPER() function. The syntax is this:

  ```
  SELECT UPPER([field1],[field2],...) FROM [yourTableName];
  ```

A Few MySQL-Specific Date and Time Functions

This list contains only a few of the many date- and time-related functions listed in the MySQL manual. Visit http://www.mysql.com/doc/ and check out the entire manual for more information.

- Get the day of the week (1 = Sunday, 2 = Monday, ...) from a date field using the DAYOFWEEK() function. The syntax is this:

  ```
  SELECT DAYOFWEEK([date]) FROM [yourTableName];
  ```

- Get the weekday (0 = Monday, 1 = Tuesday, ...) from a date field using the WEEKDAY() function. The syntax is this:

  ```
  SELECT WEEKDAY([date]) FROM [yourTableName];
  ```

DAYS OF THE WEEK

The difference between the DAYOFWEEK() and WEEKDAY() functions is the starting point of the week. When getting the day of the week, the week starts at Day 1, which is Sunday. When getting the week day (or "work week"), the week starts at Day 0, which is Monday.

- Get the day of the month (1 through 31) from a date field using the DAYOFMONTH() function. The syntax is this:

```
SELECT DAYOFMONTH([date]) FROM [yourTableName];
```

- Get the day of the year (1 through 366) from a date field using the DAYOFYEAR() function. The syntax is this:

```
SELECT DAYOFYEAR([date]) FROM [yourTableName];
```

- Get the month (1 through 12) from a date field using the MONTH() function. The syntax is this:

```
SELECT MONTH([date]) FROM [yourTableName];
```

- Get the month name (January, February, ...) from a date field using the MONTHNAME() function. The syntax is this:

```
SELECT MONTHNAME([date]) FROM [yourTableName];
```

- Get the day name (Monday, Tuesday, ...) from a date field using the DAYNAME() function. The syntax is this:

```
SELECT DAYNAME([date]) FROM [yourTableName];
```

- Get the week (0 through 53) from a date field using the WEEK() function. Start the week with Sunday (0) or Monday (1). The syntax is this:

```
SELECT WEEK([date], [0 or 1]) FROM [yourTableName];
```

- Get the year (1000 through 9999) from a date field using the YEAR() function. The syntax is this:

```
SELECT YEAR([date]) FROM [yourTableName];
```

Grouping, Ordering, and Selecting Unique Values

You can group the data you get back from a SELECT statement using the GROUP BY syntax:

```
SELECT FIELD1, FIELD2, FIELD3
FROM Table
GROUP BY GroupField
```

When you use the GROUP BY command, all records that match a given key value (in our case, the GroupField value) will be grouped together. You would normally use some sort of a calculation field, such as AVG (average) with a grouping command to determine average data for a given group. For example, if you had a list of salespeople and their commissions in a table called Sales, you could get back an average commission for each of them over the year by using:

```
SELECT SalesName, AVG(Commission)
FROM Sales
GROUP BY SalesName
```

This statement would return one record for each salesperson, along with the average of all of their commissions over the period of time stored in the table.

Likewise, you can order data in a selection statement using the ORDER BY clause of the SELECT SQL function:

```
SELECT * from Sales
ORDER BY SalesName
```

In this example, we get back all of the salespeople from the sales table, sorting them by the name of the salesperson.

Finally, you can select only unique values within a table in the database using the DISTINCT statement. Imagine, for example, that you want to know the names of all of the salespeople in the Sales table, but you want their names only once. You could use the following statement:

```
SELECT DISTINCT SalesName
FROM Sales
```

This would return a unique list of salespeople names, with no duplicates, regardless of how many commission entries they might have.

Using the SHOW Command

There are several types of SHOW commands that will produce output to help you administer your MySQL database. The usual method for executing these commands is through the MySQL Monitor, the command-line interface to MySQL, which you used in Chapter 1, "Installing and Configuring MySQL."

The basic SHOW commands are SHOW DATABASES and SHOW TABLES, which simply display the names of the databases and tables on your server. If you use the SHOW CREATE TABLE command, it shows you the exact SQL statement used to create the specified table.

If you need to know the structure of the table but don't necessarily need the SQL command to create it, you can use the SHOW COLUMNS command (see Figure E.1):

```
mysql> SHOW COLUMNS FROM [testTable];
```

Figure E.1 The SHOW COLUMNS command.

For administrative purposes, the SHOW STATUS and SHOW VARIABLES commands quickly provide important information about your database server. For more information on the numerous rows of output from these commands, please read the relevant sections of the MySQL manual, found at http://www.mysql.com/doc/.

F

Using SQLite

In Appendix E, "Database Normalization and SQL Reference," you learned about the importance of a normalized database and potential problems with the flat file. However, there are many instances in which your PHP applications might need only a single database table, and there's nothing wrong with that. For instance, suppose that you're just archiving the content of simple contact forms sent through your Web site, as a backup in case the e-mailed version never arrives. This simple table might have fields for name, e-mail address, comments, and date sent—no real need to normalize that!

If you find yourself in a development situation without a database and some mandate that you must not install one, PHP 6 contains another option—the capability to utilize SQLite, which is a flat file database with a SQL-based interface.

VERSION CHANGE!

SQLite is enabled by default in PHP 6. For detailed information beyond what's covered in this appendix, please visit the SQLite Web site at http://www.sqlite.org/ or search the PHP manual section for SQLite at http://www.php.net/sqlite/.

To use SQLite, you must still have a fundamental understanding of how databases, tables, and fields all work together and SQL syntax itself. Everything you have learned in this book is still viable with regards to the process of connecting to a database, issuing queries, and obtaining results—except that you learned to use the MySQL-specific functions for sending the commands to the MySQL server. SQLite has its own set of functions that you use to perform the same types of tasks.

Examples of SQLite in Action

This section steps through some of the basic tasks in working with databases, using the SQLite version of things. Before doing anything, you must create a database:

1. Open a new file in your text editor and start a PHP block:

```
<?php
```

2. Use the PDO() function to open a database called `test.db` one level up from the document root—do not worry that it has not been created yet, because this function will create the file if it does not already exist.

```
$dbh = new @PDO('sqlite:foo.db');
```

USING USERNAMES AND PASSWORDS

You might notice that no username or password is used to create or open a SQLite database. This is true because the SQLite database is technically just a plain file, with no requirements for access other than the capability to read and write to the directory in which you are placing the file.

---

3. Close the PHP block.

```
?>
```

Save this file as `sqlite1.php` and place it in the document root of your Web browser. Access the script at http://127.0.0.1/sqlite1.php to create the database.

NO MESSAGES?

There will be no output if this script is successful. You will see a message only if the script fails to perform.

Now that you have a working SQLite database, you can move on to creating tables and issuing queries.

Creating a Table and Storing Data with SQLite

When you created tables using MySQL, and in fact when you create a table in any relational database system, you specifically defined the field types and field lengths. For example, you might have had a field called `name` that was a 25-character `varchar` field, or a field called `start_date` that was a `datetime` field. SQLite is *loosely typed*, meaning the contents of all fields, regardless of what type they actually are, are stored as strings. Thus, SQLite does not require you to define your fields when you create a table, and if you do, they will be ignored.

In the next example, you will create a table that just holds first names, last names, and e-mail addresses and populate the table with a few records:

1. Open a new file in your text editor and start a PHP block:

```
<?
```

2. Use the `sqlite_open()` function to open the database previously created:

```
$db = sqlite_open("../test.db") or die(sql_error_string());
```

3. Use the `sqlite_query()` function to issue a table-creation command:

```
sqlite_query($db, "CREATE TABLE my_friends (first_name, last_name,
email)");
```

4. Use the `sqlite_query()` function to add a few entries using the SQL `INSERT` command:

```
sqlite_query($db, "INSERT INTO my_friends
    VALUES ('John', 'Smith', 'john@smith.com')");
sqlite_query($db, "INSERT INTO my_friends
    VALUES ('Jane', 'Doe', 'jane@doe.com')");
sqlite_query($db, "INSERT INTO my_friends
    VALUES ('Julie', 'Meloni', 'julie@thickbook.com')");
```

5. Close the PHP block:

```
?>
```

The complete script should look like this:

```
<?
$db = sqlite_open("../test.db") or die(sql_error_string());
sqlite_query($db, "CREATE TABLE my_friends (first_name, last_name, email)");
sqlite_query($db, "INSERT INTO my_friends
    VALUES ('John', 'Smith', 'john@smith.com')");
sqlite_query($db, "INSERT INTO my_friends
    VALUES ('Jane', 'Doe', 'jane@doe.com')");
sqlite_query($db, "INSERT INTO my_friends
    VALUES ('Julie', 'Meloni', 'julie@thickbook.com')");
?>
```

Save this file as `sqlite2.php` and place it in the document root of your Web browser. Access the script at http://127.0.0.1/sqlite2.php to issue these SQLite commands. Again, there will be no output if this script is successful. You will see a message only if the script fails to perform one or more of the commands.

In the next section, you will retrieve items from your table.

Retrieving Items with SQLite

Now that you have records in your SQLite table, you can retrieve them. Again, the process is quite similar to retrieving data from a MySQL table.

1. Open a new file in your text editor and start a PHP block:

```
<?
```

2. Use the `sqlite_open()` function to open the database previously created:

```
$dbh = new PDO('sqlite:foo.db');
```

3. Use `query()` function to issue a SELECT command, intended to retrieve records in ascending order by last name:

```
foreach ($dbh->query
    ('
        SELECT * FROM my_friends ORDER BY last_name ASC
    ',
      PDO::FETCH_ASSOC) as $row)
    {
        echo $row[first_name];
        echo " ";
        echo $row[last_name];
        echo "<BR>";
    }
```

4. Close the PHP code block:

```
?>
```

Your entire code should look like this:

```
<?php
$dbh = new PDO('sqlite:foo.db');
foreach ($dbh->query
    ('
        SELECT * FROM my_friends ORDER BY last_name ASC
    ',
      PDO::FETCH_ASSOC) as $row)
    {
        echo $row[first_name];
        echo " ";
        echo $row[last_name];
        echo "<BR>";
    }
?>
```

Figure F.1 SQLite script in action.

Save this file as `sqlite3.php` and place it in the document root of your Web browser. Access the script at http://127.0.0.1/sqlite3.php to issue these SQLite commands and display the output (see Figure F.1).

Now that you've seen that the process for working with SQLite is procedurally similar to working with other databases, you can glance through the next section to pick up some other tidbits of information.

Performing Other Tasks with SQLite

In the previous sections, you've seen how to create SQLite databases and tables and insert and select elements into these tables. It's safe to make the leap that you can issue DELETE and DROP commands similarly to remove records and tables, and you can also use UPDATE to change fields within a record—all of these actions are simply variations on the SQL query that is issued using the `sqlite_query()` function.

As to the tasks you can perform with SQLite, they're the same tasks that you can perform with MySQL; all of the MySQL-based code in this book can be rewritten to use SQLite. However, there are two things the code relied on when using MySQL that haven't been covered in this appendix: auto-incrementing fields and date-stamping.

To implement the use of auto-incrementing fields, you simply have to make some changes to the `sqlite2.php` script:

1. Open `sqlite2.php` in your text editor.

2. Change the table-creation command to:

```
$dbh = new PDO('sqlite:foo.db');
$dbh->exec
("
CREATE TABLE my_friends2 (id INTEGER
    PRIMARY KEY, first_name, last_name, email)
");
```

3. Change the record-insertion commands to:

```
$dbh->exec
("
INSERT INTO my_friends2
    VALUES (0, 'John', 'Smith', 'john@smith.com');
");
$dbh->exec
("
INSERT INTO my_friends2
    VALUES (1, 'Jane', 'Doe', 'jane@doe.com');
");
$dbh->exec
("
INSERT INTO my_friends2
    VALUES (2, 'Julie', 'Meloni', 'julie@thickbook.com');
");
```

Save this file as `sqlite4.php` and place it in the document root of your Web browser. Access the script at http://127.0.0.1/sqlite4.php to issue these SQLite commands. Again, there will be no output if this script is successful. You will see a message only if the script fails to perform one or more of the commands.

To see if this script did the trick, modify the `sqlite3.php` script to retrieve and print the ID field:

1. Open `sqlite3.php` in your text editor.

2. Change the name of the table in the loop and query:

```
foreach ($dbh->query
    ('
        SELECT * FROM my_friends2 ORDER BY last_name ASC
    ',
      PDO::FETCH_ASSOC) as $row)
{
    echo $row[id];
    echo " ";
    echo $row[first_name];
    echo " ";
    echo $row[last_name];
    echo "<BR>";
}
```

Figure F.2 Fetching rows in SQLite.

Save this file as `sqlite5.php` and place it in the document root of your Web browser. Access the script at http://127.0.0.1/sqlite5.php to issue these SQLite commands and display the output, as shown in Figure F.2.

Just like in MySQL, the ID fields automatically incremented upon record insertion.

Next, let's take a look at how to handle date-stamping of records, because there's no `now()` function as there is in MySQL, nor are there particular methods for formatting date-related fields. The solution is simply to store an integer, the output of the PHP `time()` function. You can then format this stored value any way you want using PHP when you retrieve it for display.

The next steps will work again with the same tables and records used in this appendix, just building on the previous steps.

1. Open `sqlite4.php` in your text editor.

2. Change the table-creation command to:

```
sqlite_query($db, "CREATE TABLE my_friends3
    (id INTEGER PRIMARY KEY, first_name, last_name, email,
    date_added)");
```

3. Change the record-insertion commands to:

```
sqlite_query($db, "INSERT INTO my_friends3
    (first_name, last_name, email, date_added) VALUES
    ('John', 'Smith', 'john@smith.com', '".time()."')");
sqlite_query($db, "INSERT INTO my_friends3
    (first_name, last_name, email, date_added) VALUES
    ('Jane', 'Doe', 'jane@doe.com', '".time()."')");
sqlite_query($db, "INSERT INTO my_friends3
    (first_name, last_name, email, date_added) VALUES
    ('Julie', 'Meloni', 'julie@thickbook.com', '".time()."')");
```

Save this file as `sqlite6.php` and place it in the document root of your Web browser. Access the script at http://127.0.0.1/sqlite6.php to issue these SQLite commands. Again, there will be no output if this script is successful. You will see a message only if the script fails to perform one or more of the commands.

DATES AND SQLITE

In this example, the `date()` function formats the value of the data stored in the `date_added` field. You can learn more about the numerous formatting options for the `date()` function in Appendix B, "Basic PHP Language Reference," and in the PHP manual at http://www.php.net/date.

To see if this script did the trick, modify the `sqlite5.php` script to retrieve, format, and print the values in the `date_added` field:

1. Open `sqlite5.php` in your text editor.

2. Change the name of the table in the query and order the records by ID:

```
$r = sqlite_query($db, "SELECT * FROM my_friends3 ORDER BY id ASC");
```

3. Add the following inside the `while` loop after the line that defines the value of `$email`:

```
$date_added = date("l, M d Y, h:i:s A", $record[date_added]);
```

4. Change the `echo` statement inside the `while` loop to:

```
echo "record ID# $id: $last_name, $first_name ($email)
added on $date_added<br>";
```

The complete code should look something like this:

```
<?php
$dbh = new PDO('sqlite:foo.db');
foreach ($dbh->query
    ('
        SELECT * FROM my_friends2 ORDER BY last_name ASC
    ',
      PDO::FETCH_ASSOC) as $row)
    {
        $date_added = @date("l, M d Y, h:i:s A", $r[date_added]);
        echo "ID# ";
        echo $row[id];
        echo ": ";
```

```
            echo $row[first_name];
            echo " ";
            echo $row[last_name];
            echo "($row[email])";
            echo "added on: ";
            echo $date_added;
            echo "<BR>";
        }
    ?>
```

Figure F.3 The output of the date script.

Save this file as `sqlite7.php` and place it in the document root of your Web browser. Access the script at http://127.0.0.1/sqlite7.php to issue these SQLite commands and display the output. You should see something like Figure F.3, including the formatted version of the date-stamp stored in the SQLite table.

As you can see, virtually anything you can do with MySQL, you can do (with a little elbow grease in some instances) with SQLite. Should you find yourself without a database server, nothing should keep you from utilizing this new feature of PHP 6.

G

Getting Help

One of the greatest aspects of the open source community is that people are eager to help you learn as much as you can, so that you can become an advocate as well. However, you probably should attempt to find answers to your questions before posing them to the community at large. Doing so includes reading available manuals and FAQs, searching through mailing list archives, and visiting Web sites. Chances are good that someone else has had the same question you have.

The source code for this book can be found at **www.courseptr.com/downloads**.

PHP Resources

PHP-related Web sites, newsgroups, and mailing lists are abundant, and the ones listed here are just a smattering of what's available.

Web Sites

The majority of these sites are maintained by normal people on their own time, so if you use any of their resources, try to give back to the community by helping others with their questions when you can, contributing code snippets to code repositories, and so forth.

www.php.net

The home of PHP is http://www.php.net. The annotated online manual is here, as well as the PHP FAQs, bug reports, links to ISPs that offer access to PHP, news articles, and much more.

snaps.php.net

The newest releases of PHP can be found at snaps.php.net. This site has the developer snapshots of the current builds of the software. This is not production code, but it can be useful if you want to see what is coming out next.

www.zend.com

Zend Technologies, the folks behind the Zend engine of PHP, have created a portal site for PHP developers. This personalized site not only showcases how you can build a high-traffic, dynamic site using PHP, but it also provides pointers, resources, and lessons on how to maximize the potential of PHP in all your online applications.

DevShed (www.devshed.com)

This site contains many user-submitted tutorials, news articles, interviews, and competitive analyses of server-side programming languages. It covers PHP as well as many other topics of interest to developers, such as servers and databases.

PHPBuilder (www.phpbuilder.com)

This is a very good tutorial site for intermediate and advanced PHP developers. It contains How To columns for real-world applications, such as "Building Dynamic Pages with Search Engines in Mind," "Generating Pronounceable Passwords," and tons more. Recommended!

WeberDev (www.weberdev.com)

A longtime favorite of PHP developers, this site contains development tricks and tips for many programming languages (just to be fair), as well as a content-management system for people to add their own code snippets, tutorials, and more. It has a great weekly newsletter and high traffic. Go contribute!

px.sklar.com

This is a bare-bones code repository, but who needs graphics when all you're looking for is code snippets? Borrowing from the "take a penny, leave a penny" mentality, you grab a code snippet to start with and then add your own when you feel confident in sharing.

Webmonkey (hotwired.lycos.com/webmonkey/)

The company that brings us *Wired* magazine also brings us HotWired, which spawned Webmonkey, a developer's resource site with a section devoted to PHP. Don't limit yourself to the PHP section of Webmonkey, for there's much information to be had in other sections as well.

PHP KnowledgeBase (php.faqts.com)

The PHP KnowledgeBase contains questions and answers posed on PHP mailing lists. Anyone can answer questions at the Web site or ask new ones.

Mailing Lists

Several high-traffic mailing lists are available for PHP discussion in English as well as other languages. Please remember your netiquette when asking a question: Be polite, offer as many examples as you can (if you're describing a problem), provide your system information (if looking for a solution), and did I mention to say please and thank you?

You can find mailing list subscription information at http://www.php.net/mailing-lists.php. The English PHP mailing lists are archived and available for searching at http://marc.theaimsgroup.com/. Just look for the PHP-related lists under the www heading.

User Groups

Sometimes, knowing other developers in real life can prove helpful. You can find a list of PHP user groups at http://www.phpusergroups.org/.

MySQL Resources

Many of the PHP-related Web sites listed earlier also contain information on development with MySQL, but the MySQL Web site at http://www.mysql.com/ is the place to start for comprehensive MySQL information.

The online MySQL manual is immense, but it's so well written and useful that its size should not scare you. You can find the manual at http://www.mysql.com/doc/. If you're looking for a quick introduction to MySQL, I've (Julie Meloni) written a book called *Teach Yourself MySQL in 24 Hours*, available in bookstores worldwide. Other recommended books on MySQL include anything written by Paul DuBois (and in fact, he is responsible for a majority of the MySQL manual itself!).

As with PHP, several high-traffic mailing lists are available for MySQL discussion, in English as well as other languages. You can find mailing list subscription information at http://www.mysql.com/documentation/lists.html, and the MySQL mailing lists are archived and available for searching at http://marc.theaimsgroup.com/ as well.

Apache Resources

Start at the Apache Foundation Web site, http://www.apache.org/, for server documentation and a list of FAQs. Many of the developer-oriented Web sites listed above, such as DevShed, offer Apache-specific tutorials—you just have to hunt them down.

The ApacheWeek Web site (http://www.apacheweek.com/) is full of Apache-related tips, articles, reviews, and much more. Content is published weekly (hence the name), and an archive of past issues is available.

Index